THE JEWISH LAW ANNUAL

VOLUME TWENTY ONE

Volume 21 of the *Jewish Law Annual* features articles on philosophical aspects of coercion, on procedural aspects of legal decision-making involving assessment, and on legal sub-cultures confronting the challenges of the universalism/particularism dilemma. One of the articles on coercion presents a taxonomy of the talmudic discourse on free will and coercion; the second offers a critical analysis of R. Joseph Albo's account of the distinction between free and coerced acts, and the related connection between regret and repentance. The articles on decision-making consider two different contexts where the court has recourse to assessment. One article invokes statistical theories to analyze the talmudic *sugyot* on how courts aggregate divergent values quoted by appraisers; the other analyzes three situations where restitution must be made for a broken object (theft, robbery, and damage not involving misappropriation), parsing the differences between them. Both articles on specific legal sub-cultures break new ground in contextualizing halakhic jurisprudence. One explores the impact of Sasanian culture on the Babylonian Talmud's tolerant attitude to Noahide incestuous unions, showing how it contributed to the disparity between the Palestinian Rabbinic outlook, which sought to universalize the levitical sexual prohibitions, and the Babylonian, which did not. The second compares the Maimonidean realist–rationalist stance on the 'presumption of honesty' to the idealistic approach favored by the German Pietists, which mandated repudiation of suspicion, but only within Pietist circles. Rounding out the volume is a review of a recent book on the interpretive methodology of R. Meir Simha of Dvinsk.

The Institute for Research in Jewish Law
Faculty of Law, The Hebrew University of Jerusalem

THE JEWISH LAW ANNUAL

VOLUME TWENTY ONE

THE INSTITUTE FOR RESEARCH IN JEWISH LAW
FACULTY OF LAW
THE HEBREW UNIVERSITY OF JERUSALEM

Routledge
Taylor & Francis Group
LONDON AND NEW YORK

First published 2015 by Routledge

2 Park Square, Milton Park, Abingdon, Oxfordshire OX14 4RN
52 Vanderbilt Avenue, New York, NY 10017

Routledge is an imprint of the Taylor & Francis Group, an informa business

First issued in paperback 2020

British Library Cataloguing in Publication Data
A catalogue record for this book is available from the British Library

Library of Congress Cataloging-in-Publication Data
A catalog record for this book has been requested

ISSN 0169-8354
ISBN13: 978-0-415-74269-6 (hbk)
ISBN13: 978-0-367-59730-6 (pbk)

Typeset in Palatino
by Apex CoVantage, LLC

Editorial communications should be addressed to Dr. Benjamin Porat, Institute for Research in Jewish Law, Faculty of Law, Hebrew University of Jerusalem, at jewishlaw@savion.huji.ac.il. Contributors should consult the style sheet that appears at the end of the volume; it is also available from the editor upon request. Submissions are welcome from all. Neither the editor nor members of the Board of Editors are to be associated with the views expressed by contributors.

This book is part of a series. The publisher will accept continuation orders, which may be cancelled at any time, and which provide for automatic billing and shipping of each title in the series upon publication. Please contact jewishlaw@savion.huji.ac.il for details.

CONTENTS

FROM THE EDITOR

The *Jewish Law Annual* has now been published for close to four decades. On the occasion of the publication of this volume, volume 21, I would like to express my heartfelt gratitude to Professor Berachyahu Lifshitz, who served as Editor of the eight preceding volumes.

Professor Lifshitz's contribution, not only to the actual selection and editing of the articles, but also to the advancement of research into Jewish law more generally, is familiar to everyone working in the field of halakhic research. Under his editorship, the *Jewish Law Annual* solidified its status as one of the discipline's central forums for publishing pivotal studies by leading scholars.

This is not an occasion for seeking to summarize and evaluate Professor Lifshitz's own scholarly contributions, which are equally well known. Indeed, his research is ongoing with characteristic intensity, and he has several new research projects planned. But it is certainly an appropriate time to pay tribute to his longstanding devoted editorship of the *Jewish Law Annual*, and his profound contribution to the publication of the volumes that appeared under his tutelage. To express to Professor Lifshitz the *Jewish Law Annual* community's deep appreciation for all he has done, let me paraphrase the dictum of Simon the Imsonite in bBaba Kama 41b: Just as you have been rewarded upon stepping down (*perisha* from your editorial duties), so may you be rewarded for your continuing research into, and future expositions of, Torah and Jewish law (*derisha*).

Benjamin Porat
Institute for Research in Jewish Law
Faculty of Law
The Hebrew University of Jerusalem

The Jewish Law Annual, Vol. XXI

Free Will and Coercion in the Talmud: A Preliminary Taxonomy

Hanina Ben-Menahem*

* Faculty of Law, Hebrew University of Jerusalem

16. transgressing under duress
17. harm caused under duress
    1. directly-caused harm
    2. indirectly-caused harm
    3. actively-caused harm
    4. passively-caused harm
    5. harm caused to avoid a greater harm (to oneself)

C. Nature of the coercion exerted

- I. External coercion – duress by threat
  1. threat to one's life
  2. threat of bodily harm
  3. threat of monetary loss
  4. threat to one's reputation
  5. threat to a relative
  6. verbal pressure (כפיה בדיבורים)
  7. force majeure
- II. Internal coercion – duress by circumstances
  1. self-imposed obligation (religious, moral, or other)
  2. financial constraints
  3. error
  4. irresistible desire
- III. The paradox of coercion

D. Criteria for ascribing consent in cases of coercion

- I. Verbal declaration of assent
  1. extracted by the court re a religious obligation
  2. extracted by an individual
- II. Alleged benefit accruing to the coercee
  1. atonement, as when one is coerced to bring a sin-offering
  2. compliance with dictates of the Sages, as when one is coerced by the court to divorce his wife
  3. financial consideration, as when one is coerced to sell her land
     - partial consideration
     - full consideration
  4. bodily pleasure, as when one is coerced to consume matza during Passover

E. Policy considerations and epistemic considerations

A. Introduction

In the Talmud, the question of freedom usually arises in the legal context rather than the metaphysical context familiar to us from general philosophy. In the philosophical context, the primary concern is that the concept of human freedom might clash with either metaphysical theories premised on predestination or determinism, or with scientific theories deemed to have deterministic implications. This putative conflict between the freedom we all seem to know from personal experience, and the determinism posited by theorists, is indeed addressed in the writings of the medieval Jewish philosophers, notably Maimonides, Crescas, and Albo.[1]

But in the Talmud, as I said, the main point of concern is not the aforementioned dissonance, but rather, situations where there is apprehension that agents, in taking legal actions or carrying out religious precepts, do so not of their own volition, but under duress. The Talmud seems to assume that free action is not only metaphysically possible, but routinely manifested in ordinary – that is, non-'pathological' – actions and omissions. The cases we will be focusing on in this article are those that can be considered 'pathological' – namely, cases where force is exerted to bring about a non-voluntary action. Nevertheless, we must not lose sight of the apparent premise, implicit though it is, that free action is possible.

But even if no such assumption is being made, the talmudic legal discourse is undeniably framed in terms of the distinction between freely-willed acts and coerced acts. To be sure, the Talmud does not put forward a direct characterization of free will. The talmudic discussion is conducted using the idiom of absence or presence of coercion, rather than that of freedom, but we can safely infer that on the talmudic understanding, a free act is an act that accords with the agent's will. (Note that this is precisely the compatibilist definition of freedom – the ability to act in accordance with our desires – and on this understanding, actions can be free even in a deterministic world.) As we will see, however, the Talmud contemplates the possibility that though an action might reflect one's will, what is being willed may nonetheless be the result of coercion or manipulation.

1 See Warren Zev Harvey, "Albo on Repentance and Coercion," pp. 47–57 in this volume.

Before setting out to ascertain and analyze the talmudic understanding of coercion, it is helpful to consider the connection between coercion and slavery. To what extent is the talmudic attitude to coercion informed by the idea that the Israelites are slaves of the Almighty? A feeling of being enslaved to God could generate two opposed tendencies: on the one hand, the sense that the exercise of coercion is the prerogative of God alone, and all other forms of coercion are unacceptable. This line of thought is expressed in the talmudic dictum: "'For they are My servants' (Lev. 25:42) – they are My servants, but not servants of servants" (bBaba Metzia 10a; bBaba Kama 116b). On the other hand, it might trivialize the notion of coercion: if we are all slaves in any event, coercion should evoke no particular interest, let alone indignation. These responses, or variants thereof, and the tension between them, I contend, appear to underlie talmudic discussions of human coercion.

A central question here, as is often the case in philosophical investigations of this kind, is whether the Talmud's account is consistent and comprehensive, or ad hoc, context-specific, and partial. We will see that the concepts invoked by the Talmud in discussing the disparate cases involving the exercise of coercion are never unified into a single theory. Consider the following questions:

- In observing a precept, must one intend to observe the precept, or is the mere performance of the act in question sufficient?
- Whose merit is greater: those enjoined to observe the precepts, or those who observe the precepts without being so enjoined, but purely of their own free will?
- If a side to a legal transaction has unvoiced reservations about the deal, is this of any legal consequence?
- Can an anticipated coerced transaction be preemptively nullified by issuing a declaration to that effect?
- What is the basis for the ascription of legal responsibility? Is legal responsibility ascribed solely on the strength of external behavior, or is the actor's mental disposition to be taken into account as well?
- How is one to conduct oneself if forced to break the law?
- What is the relation between the talmudic principle that a mortal threat supersedes all the prohibitions but three – idolatry, incest and bloodshed – and the principle that no punishment can be inflicted if the agent was coerced? To put it differently, there are acts which, though prohibited, are not punishable. What is the relation between prohibition and punishment?

- What is the status of an act that was entered into under duress, but during which the coercee came around, so to speak, and consented to what he was doing?

All these questions would have to be addressed by a comprehensive account of coercion, and while the Talmud does indeed address them, it does so on a case-by-case basis. Moreover, the various talmudic *sugyot* in which these questions are tackled appear to reach conclusions that are of limited scope, and sometimes inconsistent with each other. As is the case with regard to numerous other concepts, the Talmud's apparent aversion to grand theories is in evidence here too. The implicit message, I would argue – vis-à-vis coercion and in general – is that a full-blown theory is an impediment rather than a desideratum, since individual cases are held hostage to the theory.

Nozick's seminal article on coercion is presented as an "explanatory study," and Nozick reminds us that "in philosophy questions and problems often outlive specific proposed answers and solutions."[2] This may well be true of the talmudic analysis as well, inasmuch as the Talmud's specific answers and solutions to these perennial questions do not purport to be universal. The Talmud, however, sensitive to the complexity of human nature and human drives, does provide us with the relevant concepts for thinking about individual cases. The concepts of coercion (*kofin, onsin*), verbal pressure (*kofin bemilei*), intention (*kavana*), will (*rotze ani*), seduction (*pitui*), consent (*beliba niha lei*), mental reservation (*dvarim shebalev*), resolve (*gmirat daat*), error (*libekha anasakha*), and irresistible desire (*yetzer albesh, yitzro mitgaber alav*), all figure in the talmudic discussions of coercion.

Speaking of talmudic terminology, let me point out that words with the same lexical root – אנס (*a-n-s*) – are repeatedly used to denote the status of those subjected to coercion, though given the significant disparities between the different types of coercion involved, one might have expected the contexts in question to be distinguished. The root *a-n-s* is used by the Talmud in connection with a wide range of contexts that have little in common with the paradigmatic cases of coercion (the ruffian who confronts an innocent citizen, forcing him at knife-point to commit an offense, and so on): one is described as coerced – *anus/anusa* – when forced by someone else to act in a certain way, or prevented from acting in

2 R. Nozick, "Coercion," in S. Morgenbesser et al. (eds.), *Philosophy, Science and Method: Essays in Honor of Ernest Nagel* (NY: 1968), 441.

a certain way due to force majeure, and so too when raped, but also when one errs, falls asleep, or cannot resist temptation. (Use of the root *a-n-s* in seemingly disparate contexts predates the talmudic literature, being evident even in Ben Sira, a Palestinian Hebrew document from early in the second century BCE. Ben Sira uses words with the root *a-n-s* to refer to rape, irresistible desire for certain foods, and the exercise of force in legal transactions.[3])

Dissimilar though they may be, the common denominator these diverse contexts do share, namely, lack of freedom, is – on the talmudic understanding – decisive. It is seen as overriding the features that might appear to differentiate between the said contexts (for instance, between being 'forced' to miss an event because one is sleeping, and being hijacked at knifepoint). Any lack of freedom is such a cardinal feature of a situation that it renders all other elements of the situation secondary. And it is this existential importance that underlies use of the same term in the disparate contexts.

Many of the ancillary issues that arise in the course of considering the problem of free will are not taken up in the Talmud itself, but introduced by the post-talmudic commentators. My focus here, however, will not be the historical evolution of the legal material, and I will approach the issues in question from the jurisprudential perspective. The subject matter can be further delineated by noting that the mundane coercion that is involved whenever the law is enforced will not be of concern here, except when exercised in cases where the agent is explicitly required to act of her own volition. Throughout, my focus will be the coercee's perspective rather than the coercer's.

Let me now present a tentative taxonomy of coercion as reflected in the talmudic sources.[4]

B. Deontic status of the coerced act

Cases of coercion can be divided into two categories: those in which coercion is exerted prior to, or simultaneously with, the act in question, and those in which coercion is exerted after the fact, preventing one from achieving that which one undertook to do, as for instance, when coercion is exerted to nullify an act carried out in order to keep

3 BS 20:3; 31:37.

4 *Responsa Rashbash*, #339 also offers an elemental taxonomy of coercion.

a promise. In cases falling into the first category, the act itself is carried out under duress; it is these cases that will interest us.

The cases in which coercion is exerted prior to, or simultaneously with, the act in question, can in turn be classified into three sub-categories on the basis of the deontic status of the coerced act: cases in which the coerced act is forbidden; cases in which the coerced act is legally obligatory; and cases in which the coerced act is optional. I will survey these cases in reverse order.

The cases in question are all discussed in the talmudic literature, which adduces them at two different levels: some at the level of theoretical analysis, and others, at the level of concrete judicial decision-making. As is often the case, examination of the relation between the two treatments may prove instructive: it may give us an idea of the extent to which concrete cases were decided on the basis of the theoretical analysis, and the extent to which they were decided on an ad hoc basis.

I. Cases in which the coerced act is optional

1. sale under duress
2. undertaking an obligation under duress
3. gift under duress
4. betrothal under duress
   a. a man coerced into betrothing
   b. a woman coerced into being betrothed
5. vows made under duress

II. Cases in which the coerced act is legally obligatory

6. divorce under duress
7. betrothal imposed by the court on one who divorces a wife he raped before marrying
8. observance of a precept under duress
9. offering a sacrifice under duress
10. immersion in a ritual bath under duress
11. levirate marriage
12. levirate repudiation
13. sanctification of the New Moon under duress

The last-mentioned case is the only one in which a court is coerced; all the others are cases in which one individual coerces another, or an individual is coerced by the court.

With regard to cases 4, 6, 8 and 9, the validity of the act in question is explicitly conditional on its being carried out willingly; as to the others, with the exception of cases 7, 11 and 13, this requirement is not explicit, but logic dictates that in these cases too, the agent must act of his own volition. With regard to case 11, it is explicitly specified that there is no need for consent on either side, hence coerced levirate marriage is always valid. Why this case is exceptional is an open question that merits discussion.

Regarding observance of a precept under duress, the Talmud uses two different formulations: one is coerced to perform the precept "until his soul departs" (bKetubot 86b) or "until he says, I want to do it" (mArakhin 5:6). Is this terminological variance simply stylistic, or does it have legal significance? Does it reflect different types of coercees? Or does it, perhaps, have something to do with the distinction between consequence-oriented and motivation-oriented precepts? Precepts are consequence-oriented if their objective is to achieve a particular outcome; motivation-oriented if their objective is to foster specific values. With respect to the former (giving charity, for example), the mental disposition of the agent is of no significance, but with respect to the latter (blowing the shofar, for example), it is critical.

Let me suggest a more plausible explanation of the terminological distinction. I would argue that it corresponds to different approaches to the problem of whether or not precept-observance requires intention (*kavana*). On the view, held by some of the talmudic Sages, that precept-observance requires intention, coerced observance of a precept is meaningless – that is, of no legal effect – unless the coercee ultimately agrees to carry out the prescribed act, hence "until he says, I want to do it." But if intention is not crucial, as maintained by other Sages, it is **consent** that is immaterial, and a transgressor can be coerced "until his soul departs." In other words, if intention is vital, consent is imperative, but if intention is not vital, consent can be dispensed with. This may be an illustration of my earlier claim that the Talmud does not always expressly articulate the connections between different talmudic concepts.

Rounding out this deontic survey, the cases in which the coerced act is forbidden are the following:

III. Cases in which the coerced act is forbidden

14. false testimony under duress
15. idol worship under duress
16. transgressing under duress
17. harm caused under duress
    1. directly-caused harm
    2. indirectly-caused harm

3. actively-caused harm
4. passively-caused harm
5. harm caused to avoid a greater harm (to oneself)

How is one to act when forced to carry out a forbidden act, for instance, to give false testimony: ought one surrender to the threat in order to save his life, or should he refuse to carry out the act, regardless of the threatened consequences? The well-known legal principle that a mortal threat supersedes all but three prohibitions – idolatry, incest, and bloodshed (bKetubot 19a) – is not exhaustive (it doesn't cover all the cases in which one should suffer rather than commit the sin) even apart from the premise that it does not address situations involving non-mortal threats. For it is not clear whether the principle applies only to prohibited acts that are 'between man and God,' or also to prohibited acts 'between man and his fellow.'

The questions associated with this type of coercion are familiar to anyone acquainted with the criminal law, and I will not elaborate on them here.

Having mapped out the question of the deontic status of the coerced act, let me now move on to another rubric central to the proposed taxonomy, namely, the nature of the coercion exerted.

C. Nature of the coercion exerted

The cases that will interest us most are those in which the coercion is brought to bear on the **will** of the coercee, who chooses to submit to the coercion in preference to the alternative, as opposed to cases in which the coercee is physically compelled to act in a certain way. A talmudic example of the latter scenario is the case of one who is physically compelled to worship an animal: he is forced – bodily – to bow down to it (bAvoda Zara 54a). Coercion of this type not only exonerates the coercee, but the transgression is in no way associated with him. That is, it legally 'undoes' the act, rather than merely rendering the agent non-blameworthy. Although an animal that has been worshipped – even if the worship was (non-physically) coerced – is deemed unfit to be brought as a Temple offering, no legal consequences ensue if the coercion was physical. Such an animal is fit to be brought as an offering. As I said, we will not be discussing cases involving this sort of direct bodily coercion.

Let me now present a brief survey of the types of coercion that can be exerted on the coercee's will.

The cases of duress discussed in the Talmud can almost always be classified as instances of either external coercion or internal coercion, a distinction akin to, but not quite overlapping, that between duress by threat and duress by circumstances.

I. External coercion – duress by threat
1. threat to one's life (bBaba Batra 47b)
2. threat of bodily harm (bBaba Batra 47b)
3. threat of monetary loss (bBaba Batra 40b)
4. threat to one's reputation
5. threat to a relative (anyone unfit to testify on one's behalf because he is related, or for whom one is obligated to observe a period of mourning) (mNedarim 3:3)[5]

The threat itself suffices to constitute duress, and actual coercion need not take place. The threat must, however, be both real and imminent.

But other types of external coercion are less manifestly malevolent. Consider the following categories:

6. verbal pressure[6] (כפיה בדיבורים) (bKetubot 52a)
7. force majeure (mNedarim 3:3)

II. Internal coercion – duress by circumstances
1. self-imposed obligation (religious, moral, or other)[7]
2. financial constraints (bBaba Batra 47b)
3. error (bShevuot 26a)
4. irresistible desire (bKetubot 51b; bRosh Hashana 28a)

Coercion becomes an issue in the case of self-obligation when, for example, one commits oneself, by taking an oath, to divorce his wife. Is the divorce that follows fully volitional, or was it granted under duress, and hence void? With regard to financial constraints due to poverty and debt, the talmudic worldview casts doubt on the very possibility of free will. Consider, for instance, one who is induced to sell her property due to penury. Though this is undoubtedly a rational decision, she is regarded as having been coerced into selling. The Talmud even compares sale due to financial constraints to sale by "one who was struck a hundred blows with a hammer" (bKetubot 53b). This insightful

5 See too *Responsa Rashba attributed to Nahmanides*, #273.

6 E.g., being asked to do something by a respected mentor; being told to do something by someone of higher status or authority.

7 *New Responsa Maharik*, #29.

observation, however, does not mean that the Talmud rules that such a sale is flawed: it is, indeed, regarded as valid.

Coercion by irresistible desire is often regarded as a mitigating consideration vis-à-vis holding one responsible for his actions. Of all the rubrics invoked in the Talmud's various discussions of coercion, the notion of internal coercion is, perhaps, the most astonishing; its like is not found – at any rate, not to a comparable degree – in Western legal systems. To my mind, it is astounding that a legal system which makes great demands on the individual in terms of his conduct in virtually every realm of daily life, at the same time makes allowances for 'carnal incontinence,' regarding it as a form of duress, with the attendant legal consequences.

III. The paradox of coercion

The notion of coercion presents an intriguing epistemic puzzle: is an act carried out under duress but nonetheless chosen in preference to the alternative – namely, the threatened harm – freely willed, or not? If we decide that such an act, since chosen, constitutes exercise of free will, how do we distinguish it from a non-voluntary coerced act? Or is it the case that **any** act done under duress in preference to the alternative is freely willed? This question emerges from the talmudic *sugyot*, though it is not expressly stated, let alone formulated in precisely these terms. It is, however, explicitly treated by R. Joseph Albo, a late medieval philosopher, in his *Book of Principles* (IV, 27). Albo's treatment more or less follows Aristotle's account in the *Nicomachean Ethics*.[8]

Addressing this issue, Albo invokes a normative criterion: he suggests that whether or not an act is to be considered coerced is determined on the basis of how one ought to behave in the case under consideration. Albo asserts: "we see that there must be certain acts, rather than do which, one ought endure any pain in the world. Such acts, when done, must be classified as voluntary rather than compulsory." And conversely, when one is threatened with infliction of pain unless one performs an act which is such that one ought not suffer for complying with the demand, he is **coerced**.

Nozick, in a slightly different context, makes a similar argument, which I will discuss below.

8 See Harvey, n. 1 above, esp. 49, 55.

But this conflates the normative with the descriptive, or as philosophers say, the 'ought' with the 'is.' The conflation is due, apparently, to Albo's belief that once we decide that an agent has been coerced, we must exonerate him. On closer analysis, however, it can be seen that how an act is described, and the moral/legal status we choose to associate with a given description, are two separate issues. In the Talmud, determination of the nature of an act (coerced or voluntary) does not rest on any moral evaluation, but is based on external signs indicating the agent's state of mind. Admittedly, the talmudic approach, though couched in purely descriptive terms, does involve a certain element of fiction.

Two criteria for acts that, though carried out under duress, the coercee is deemed to have ultimately consented to, are invoked in the talmudic sources: verbal declaration of assent by the coercee, and alleged benefit accruing to the coercee. As is to be expected, the Talmud does not discuss the relationship between these two criteria, but they do not seem to be jointly necessary: the presence of either one suffices to establish that the act was, ultimately, voluntary. The remainder of my remarks will explore these criteria, an exploration that will provide insight into the fictitious element just alluded to.

D. Criteria for ascribing consent in cases of coercion

I. Verbal declaration of assent

In some cases, the Talmud distinguishes between coerced acts to which verbal consent was given, and coerced acts to which no verbal consent was given. Inasmuch as it is clear that the verbal consent was, under the circumstances, coerced, it can hardly be taken to attest to voluntary consent, raising the question of what contribution is made by extracting verbal assent by force. Is not the very notion of 'assent extracted by force' an oxymoron? If the verbal consent is forcibly extracted by a court of law, one could perhaps adduce an inner self that ultimately aspires to comply with the dictates of the Sages. I will return to this notion of such an inner self below. But this does nothing to explain what contribution might be made by an 'extracted' declaration in civil cases, where the coercion is exercised by individuals, not by the court.

We might try to argue that 'verbal assent' is a metaphor for a genuine change of heart, providing a way for the other party to gain assurance that the coercee now truly desires to perform the act in question.

The problem with this explanation is that generally there is no objective sign for a change of mind apart from the assertion, and the assertion, in and of itself, is no indication that a genuine change of heart has actually taken place, since there is no reason to suppose that the coercee's motive for making the assertion is anything other than desire to bring about an abatement of the coercion.

Might it be the case that verbal consent – even if coerced – is required because there is some almost-mystical element in the articulation of consent that renders the coerced act voluntary? Might it be, to use philosophical parlance, a performative utterance?

This calls to mind the midrashic exegesis that the Torah is binding because it was 'willingly' accepted by the Israelites:

> "And they stood at the nether part of the mount" (Exod. 19:17). R. Abdimi b. Hama b. Hasa said: This teaches that the Holy One, blessed be He, overturned the mountain upon them like a cask, and said to them, If ye accept the Torah, 'tis well; if not, there shall be your burial.[9]

Two points are noteworthy: first, use of the verb *kafa* (כפה), which, though generally encountered, in the Tannaitic sources, in the sense of 'overturn,' certainly alludes to *kafa* in the mishnaic sense of coercion, as in the idiom, "*kofin oto ad sheyomar rotze ani*" (he is forced until he says, 'I want to do it').[10] More importantly, the dictum emphasizes that the coercion is meant to ensure not mere obedience, but acceptance. The Talmud construes the coerced declaration of acceptance as constituting the legal basis for regarding the Israelites as having taken upon themselves the obligation to obey the law.

I would like to suggest that this undertaking at Sinai in some way informs the talmudic attitude, imparting profound legal significance to coerced utterance of the formula, 'I want to do it.' There is, I am suggesting, a dialectical relationship of mutual influence. The mishnaic notion that one can be 'forced' into voluntary acceptance inspired the midrashic exegesis, which in turn enhanced the philosophical import of the notion.

But recognition of such declarations of assent in civil cases could generate a serious problem. Why would the coercer insist on extracting such a statement and not be satisfied simply with commission of

9 bShabat 88a.

10 mArakhin 5:6; bRosh Hashana 6a; bJebamot 106a; bKidushin 50a; bBaba Batra 48a; bArakhin 21a.

the act? Presumably, the coercer seeks to preserve the appearance of an act that was carried out willingly. The doctrine that such a coerced verbal declaration indeed constitutes a sign of consent might encourage would-be extortionists to extract such a declaration and thereby 'legitimize' the transaction.

II. Alleged benefit accruing to the coercee

In general, the Talmud's attitude is that if the coerced individual derives any benefit, the assumption is that ultimately, there was consent to the act, and the element of coercion is canceled out. In terms of Nozick's analysis, we can say that if some benefit accrues to the coercee, the situation changes from a threat to an offer, and the coercee is regarded as having accepted an offer made him by the coercer. Thus the test that distinguishes non-voluntary coerced acts from seemingly-coerced (but actually voluntary) acts is whether or not the coercee derived any benefit from being coerced.

Among the personal benefits alleged to accrue from coercion and deemed indicative of either 'true' consent or a posteriori consent are the following:

1. atonement, as when one is coerced to bring a sin-offering
2. compliance with dictates of the Sages, as when one is coerced by the court to divorce his wife
3. financial consideration, as when one is coerced to sell her land
    - partial consideration
    - full consideration
4. bodily pleasure, as when one is coerced to consume matza during Passover

The first two kinds of benefit – atonement and compliance with the dictates of the Sages – assume that there is an inner self that may not be fully in sync with the external self. This inner self may be at odds with the self inferable from one's external behavior. Coercion serves to bring this inner self to the fore, and to enable one's external comportment to reflect the inner self – which is the true self – and its true will.

The talmudic discussion thus presupposes that, in the final analysis, one is eager to conduct his life according to the dictates of the Sages. In the present-day halakhic literature, however, much discussion is devoted to cases in which the agent is wont to ignore rabbinical directives. With respect to such cases, coercion cannot be said to bring out the coercee's true wishes, and hence the above analysis is inapplicable.

The last two kinds of benefit are carnal in nature. Here, the role of coercion is not to bring to the fore some postulated inner self, or remove obstacles to the expression of some inner reality, but rather, to ensure consent: the benefits serve to neutralize the negative aspects of coercion, and, as it were, 'bribe' the individual into giving his or her after-the-fact consent to the act.

Now the benefit that is supposed to neutralize the element of coercion is a forced benefit, and the coercee might still prefer not to enjoy it. This generates a new dilemma: is the test for determining whether or not the coercee benefited from the coercion objective or subjective? That is, what counts – the 'objective' benefit that was forced on the coercee, or her subjective preference?

The Talmud (bPesahim 25b) considers the question of a prohibited benefit that one is forced to experience. Is one permitted to enjoy a forbidden benefit one is being forced to experience? The Talmud concludes that if the coercee's preference is that he not be subjected to the benefit forced upon him, he may enjoy it. (Obviously, the Talmud is assuming, here, that we can control what we enjoy.) In this context, the test is clearly the coercee's subjective preference, but this test is not applied by the Talmud in all contexts where a coerced benefit comes into play, and in some contexts, is manifestly rejected. In the case of a coerced sale, for example, the payment, though not desired by the vendor at the outset, is perceived as an unequivocal benefit, rendering the sale final.

Thus far, the benefit in these examples is a function of the specifics of the act in question – in the forced sale, for instance, the benefit is the money paid to the vendor; in the case of coerced precept-observance, it is divine approbation, and so on. The benefit would accrue even were the act voluntary, and no coercion exerted. But the Talmud also contemplates the possibility of benefit that is not related to the coerced act, but solely a function of the coercion exerted: namely, when the benefit is simply termination of the coercion.

Consider the following scenario. A woman is being chased by a vicious dog. A suitor who happens to be nearby offers her – on condition she consents to marry him – a piece of meat to throw to the dog and thereby escape (bKidushin 8b). The Talmud ponders: does her consent under these circumstances constitute freely-given consent, consent given in preference to the alternative? Or is it the case that, since anyone who witnesses her peril, the suitor included, is obligated to save her, the rescue cannot be regarded as consideration for her consent to marry him? If so, she did not agree to become betrothed in exchange for something, but was coerced, plain and simple.

This scenario is similar to an example discussed by Nozick:

> Q is in the water far from shore, nearing the end of his energy, and P comes close by in his boat. Both know there is no other hope of Q's rescue around . . . P says to Q, "I will take you in my boat if and only if you promise to pay me $10,000 within three days of reaching the shore with my aid." Is P offering to take Q to shore if he makes the promise, or is he threatening to let Q drown if Q does not make the promise?[11]

Nozick's analysis of the case, however, differs from the talmudic analysis. According to Nozick, the answer to the question "depends upon what the normal or expected course of events is." If it is clear that P is morally expected to save Q, then his exchange with Q constitutes a threat and not an offer. (Here again, we see the conflation of the normative and the descriptive that I pointed out earlier apropos Albo). For the Talmud, on the other hand, even though all are legally and morally obligated, and fully expected, to rescue someone in danger, it may nonetheless be the case that fulfilling this obligation can be regarded as a benefit bestowed on the rescued party, in return for which he consented to the offer.

Prima facie, there is a difference between a case in which someone causes a threat and conditions its removal on performance of a certain action, and a case in which the threat originates independently of the one who can remove it, but conditions her intervention on performance of a certain act. And indeed, according to Nozick's account, the two cases are not analogous: if one does not have an obligation to intervene on behalf of someone in peril, Nozick regards the proffered conditional help as an offer. But Nozick would certainly regard the first scenario as a threat, and the imperiled person as coerced into accepting it.

For the Talmud however, the two cases are on a par, since there is always an obligation not to threaten one's fellow, and to come to his aid if he is imperiled.

Unable to reach a conclusion, the Talmud leaves the question undecided. To the extent that removal of a threat is recognized as a benefit enjoyed by the coercee in return for which he consents to carry out the act in question, any submission to a threat of force constitutes

11 Nozick, n. 2 above, 449.

valid consent. If this is indeed the case, it follows that all coerced acts are voluntary, and the distinction we are trying to elucidate, namely, that between non-voluntary coerced acts and seemingly-coerced (but actually voluntary) acts, collapses, a position that is counterintuitive, though it may, perhaps, merit consideration.

E. Policy considerations and epistemic considerations

As I have sought to show, the Talmud identifies those instances where seemingly-coerced acts are regarded as voluntary, not by invoking moral norms, but in terms of the descriptive facts of the matter, or – yet again in philosophical parlance – by applying empirical, testable criteria. An agent acts of his own volition either because he uttered the 'I want to do it' formula, or because he benefited from the coercion and in return can be deemed to have given his consent. Yet, might not the Talmud's presenting its rulings in this manner, I want to conjecture, be simply a rhetorical justification for a policy consideration? Might not the underlying motivation be a desire to minimize the number of acts for which an agent does not bear responsibility? Allowing claims of coercion, and thereby negating the validity of putatively legal transactions, could interfere with the smooth operation of the legal order, though as I speculated above, upholding the validity of coerced assent – i.e., denying claims of coercion – might encourage would-be extortionists to engage in strong-arm tactics.

That the Talmud is not deterred by the latter possibility suggests that what I started out by describing as 'pathological' cases, cases involving the use of force to bring about non-voluntary actions, are indeed infrequent.[12]

12 This article is based on a talk delivered at a conference on 'Free Will, Responsibility and Coercion in the Talmud,' which took place at Harvard Law School, May 18-20, 2008.

The Jewish Law Annual, Vol. XXI

On Suspicion: Justice, Ethics, and Society – between Rationalism and Pietism

Itzhak Brand*

I. The legal context: presumption of innocence

The problem of average citizens coming under the suspicion of national authorities and society at large is generally discussed in the legal context of the presumption of innocence – a person is presumed to be innocent until proven guilty. What is the nature of this presumption? This question was debated in Christian Europe in the twelfth and thirteenth centuries. Two main positions can be distinguished. The realist–rationalist position bases the presumption on social reality: the vast majority of citizens are upstanding, and innocent of criminal acts. The realism underlying this position gives rise to a qualification of the presumption, making it contingent on prior conditions: suspects enjoy the presumption of innocence only if their social status

* Jewish Law, Faculty of Law, Bar Ilan University

or previous behavior attests to honesty and integrity. In other words, the qualified presumption is that an upright and honest person does not turn to crime readily. Hence if such an individual is suspected of a crime, there is a reasonable doubt of her guilt, and she should not be convicted.[1]

On the other hand, thirteenth-century canon law presented the presumption of innocence as reflecting a moral status applicable to all. On this approach, there is no need for prior information about a person's decency and uprightness. The assumption is that human beings are created in the divine image and are honest by nature.[2] Therefore, absent any clear-cut evidence of culpability, everyone is considered to be upright and innocent.[3]

The medieval legal debates about the presumption of innocence were paralleled by another social–ethical debate, this one about suspicion. In the Jewish world, it took place between two schools of thought: the rationalist–realist school exemplified by Maimonides, and the normative–idealist school that emerged among the disciples of R. Judah

1 Joseph C. Cascarelli, "Presumption of innocence and natural law: Machiavelli and Aquinas," 41 *American Journal of Jurisprudence* (1996): 234-68; Rolf-Jürgen Köster, *Die Rechtsvermutung der Unschuld: historische und dogmatische Grundlagen* (PhD dissertation, Rheinische Friedrich-Wilhelms-Universität, 1979), 8-19.

2 Köster, ibid., 9, 23-6. During the Middle Ages, secular jurisprudence, under the influence of Greek philosophy, also upheld this position. See Burr W. Jones and Spencer A. Gard, *Jones on Evidence: Civil and Criminal* (Rochester NY: 1972), 1:152.

3 Beginning with the modern period, the 'normative moral status' reading of the presumption of innocence has adduced sociopolitical ethics as its ground. This liberal rationale views the presumption of innocence as protecting the individual from the tyranny of the authorities, since it keeps the sovereign power from using punishment to force its will and beliefs on the ordinary citizen. See Rinat Kitai-Sangero, *Pre-trial Detention: Deprivation of Liberty Before Conviction* (Hebrew), (Jerusalem: 2011), 63-64. Another rationale, the communitarian rationale, takes the presumption of innocence to be a means of limiting conflictual relationships between the individual, the state, and society. See Köster, n. 1 above, 162-64. On this view, the presumption helps strengthen ties between the individual and the group, particularly during criminal proceedings. See C.J.A. Mittermaier, *Theorie des Beweises im peinlichen Prozesse* (Mannheim: 1809), 31-32, accessible at: http://reader.digitale-sammlungen.de/en/fs1/object/display/bsb10395061_00003.html

the Pious of Regensburg. This article will explore the various aspects of this debate.

II. The halakhic context: presumption of honesty

Alongside the aforementioned debates over the **presumption of innocence**, a similar debate over the **presumption of honesty** took place in the Jewish world. Those who subscribe to this presumption contend that if there is doubt as to the nature of a given Jew's conduct, one should assume that the individual in question is upstanding and decent. Two understandings of this presumption are found in the medieval halakhic discourse. One view, which can be described as rationalist–realist, maintains that most people are not criminals or sinners, hence ordinary actions should be assumed to be appropriate and proper. This is the position taken by R. Hayim, the son of R. Isaac of Vienna, author of *Or Zarua*,[4] regarding an argument between his father and his father's teacher, R. Simha of Speyer.[5]

The disagreement arose from an incident where a betrothal was carried out by an agent (*shaliah*) at the wrong address. The incident unfolded as follows. An agent was sent to betroth a woman, with whom a match had been arranged, using a ring and gifts. The intended recipient refused to accept the goods she was offered, and even went so far as to cover her face so as not to see them. At the same time, another woman, who was standing next to the intended bride, agreed to accept the gifts and become betrothed to the party who had sent the agent to carry out the betrothal. R. Simha of Speyer maintained that the betrothal was invalid because the betrothal money was accepted improperly. R. Isaac of Vienna disagreed, contending that the betrothal was valid. The latter's son, R. Hayim, gave the following explanation for his father's position. One must assume that the woman who accepted the ring and gifts did so for the purpose of becoming betrothed, and not for her own personal needs or in order to steal them. This assumption rests on a more general presumption that the said woman is a decent person, not a thief.[6] This presumption, in turn,

4 Germany, thirteenth century.

5 Germany, twelfth-thirteenth centuries. On R. Simha and his responsa, see Simcha Emanuel, *Fragments of the Tablets: Lost Books of the Tosaphists* (Hebrew), (Jerusalem: 2007), 154-57.

6 R. Hayim refers to this presumption as the "presumption of the righteous woman" (*hezkat tzadeket*); this is also the term used by the Tosafists and

> is based on the majority of cases, for most people are not thieves. . . . Therefore, because it is known that the young man sent this ring for the purpose of betrothal, and that when the ring was conveyed from the agent [to the second woman], it was for the purpose of betrothal, and the woman now has it in her possession, and says it is hers, and everyone sees that she now has it in her possession and says that it is hers; she certainly took the ring to be betrothed and, in taking it, was indeed betrothed.[7]

An alternative view formulates the presumption of honesty in normative–idealist terms. This view was espoused by R. Samuel di Medina (the Maharashdam) in sixteenth-century Salonika:

> It is well-known that all Jews are presumed to be upright (*ksherim*). . . . God made every Jew honest (*yashar*) from the moment he was created **and he is still presumed to be honest** (*kasher*) until such time as it becomes clear to you that he is seeking stratagems and roundabout ways to depart from the path of truth and rectitude (*yosher*).[8]

The two views resonate in the background of several disputes about the bounds of the presumption of honesty. In these disputes we can discern both the realistic outlook, which limits the presumption to plausible circumstances, and the idealistic, which expands the presumption even to cases where honesty is unlikely.

i. One dispute concerned the legitimacy of a child born after his putative parents, who were married, had lived apart for over a year. R. Shimon Kaiara (*Behag*), author of the *Halakhot Gedolot*, asserts that such a child is legitimate, that is, not deemed to have been born to a married woman from someone other than her husband (i.e., not a *mamzer*). Because of the presumption of honesty, the mother is presumed

those who followed in their wake; see *Tosafot*, bHulin 11b s.v. *kegon*; *Tosafot Rosh*, bGitin 17a. s.v. *mishum bat*; *Rosh*, bKetubot, 1:18; *Responsa Rosh*, 20:17.

7 *Responsa Or Zarua*, #26 (Monzon edition, 9a-10b, on 10a).

8 *Responsa Maharashdam*, HM, #310. As pointed out above, this position was widespread in medieval jurisprudence, where it is expressed in language very similar to that used by di Medina. See also Aryeh Leib Hakohen, *Avnei Miluim* 127:2 (and see Haim Pinhas Sheinberg, *Miluei Even*, *Avnei Miluim* ad loc., 10-11); Jacob Joshua Falk, *Pnei Yehoshua*, on *Tosafot*, bGitin 17a s.v. *mishum bat ahoto*. See also Joseph Dov Soloveitchik, *Responsa Beit Halevi* 2, §4, "Every Jew, so long as we do not suspect him [of wrongdoing], is presumed to be honest, definitely and without doubt, and it is **not merely on the basis of the majority of cases** that we presume everyone to be honest" (emphasis added).

not to have engaged in forbidden relations.[9] Maimonides disputes this conclusion. He maintains that it is unlikely a pregnancy could last longer than a year, hence the newborn cannot be considered the child of his mother's husband.[10] According to Maimonides, the presumption of honesty is not absolute, but is to be applied only within the sphere of the plausible.

ii. Another dispute concerns the link between the presumption of honesty and the reliability of vendors of kosher foods. According to Maimonides, one may purchase food only from someone known to be honest (*shehuhzak bekashrut*).[11] It is thus forbidden to purchase food from an uneducated person. Apparently, Maimonides believes that in such a situation it is unreasonable to simply assume that the seller is honest, hence the presumption of honesty does not apply. R. Abraham b. David of Posquières (Raavad) disputes this claim. He takes the presumption of honesty to be a normative determination that all Jews are honest, and states that "it does not matter [whether a vendor can be presumed to be knowledgeable about the laws of kashrut], since an uneducated [vendor] is not suspected of substituting [unkosher for kosher] foods or selling something forbidden, unless there is reason to suspect him."

The Raavad also disputed Maimonides' ruling regarding another form of the honesty presumption. The ruling in question, based on

9 "One is not concerned that a girl is deemed to have been born to a married woman from someone other than her husband (*mamzeret*). What sort of case does this apply to? E.g., where people say, Her husband traveled abroad, and she had relations and bore a daughter. We are not concerned [that the daughter is a *mamzeret*], for we say, Perhaps her husband came secretly in the night and had relations with her" (*Halakhot Gedolot*, Laws of Divorce [Hildesheimer edition], 2:183-84). R. Elijah of Vilna asserts that the reason for this law is that we "rely on a presumption of honesty" (*Biur Hagra*, EH 4:33); see too *Talmudic Encyclopedia* (Hebrew), "Presumption of fitness," 14:29 n. 29.

10 "When a married woman is pregnant and says, This fetus is not my husband's, she is not deemed reliable with regard to rendering the child illegitimate. [Instead,] we assume that the child is fit [i.e., legitimate]. . . . If the father says that it is not his child or he was overseas, we assume that the child is illegitimate (*mamzer*). . . . A fetus will not remain in its mother's womb for more than twelve months" (*Code*, Laws concerning Forbidden Intercourse 15:19).

11 *Code*, Laws concerning Forbidden Foods 11:25.

Geonic precedents,[12] asserts that "A man does not engage in intercourse with promiscuous intent."[13] According to "some Geonim," sexual relations that take place in the presence of witnesses, but were not explicitly stated to be for the purpose of contracting a marriage, nevertheless give rise to the requirement that the man give the woman a bill of divorce (*get*). This ruling is based on the presumption that the relations were not, in fact, promiscuous, but rather were engaged in for the purpose of consummating a marriage.

Similarly, the Geonim ruled that if a man has a child from relations with his slave, one should assume that this child was the result of permitted relations between them; in other words, that the master had manumitted the woman before having intercourse with her.[14] This, too, is based on the presumption that one who engages in sexual relations does not do so with promiscuous intent.

Maimonides criticizes both rulings harshly:

> And in my eyes, these various rulings are very far from the paths of Torah judgment, and it is not appropriate to rely on them. For our Sages only set down this presumption with regard to a wife whom one had divorced, or in the case of someone who betrothed a woman conditionally and then

12 *Otzar Hageonim*, bJebamot 23a, 7:39-42 (responsa).

13 Maimonides, *Code*, Laws concerning Divorce 10:19. See *Mishne Lamelekh*, quoting R. David Solomon ibn Zimra (Radbaz) on *Code*, Laws concerning Divorce 10:18; Masoud Hai Rokeiah, *Maase Rokeiah*, *Code*, Laws concerning Marriage 7:23; *Responsa Sheagat Arye*, quoted in E.Z. Margolioth, *Responsa Beit Efraim*, *SA*, EH #42; Isaac Elhanan Spector, *Responsa Beer Yitzhak* on *SA*, EH #3 §5; Haim Eleazar Shapira, *Responsa Minhat Eleazar*, 1, #61.

However, according to R. Meir Simha of Dvinsk, *Or Sameiah*, *Code*, Laws concerning Divorce 10:19 (Warsaw 1902 edition, 2:87), this presumption is a statistical rule to be used in cases of doubt (e.g., in the case of one who was alone with a woman after divorcing her, a woman who was betrothed conditionally, etc.). See also *Talmudic Encyclopedia* (Hebrew), "A man does not engage in intercourse with promiscuous intent," 1:553.

14 The ramifications of this law are that the child is not considered to be the child of a slave, but rather a Jew in every respect. Hence if the master dies with no other children, his wife is exempt from the requirement of levirate marriage. It should be noted that the mishnaic law, in mJebamot 2:5, is different: "If a man has any kind of child, such a child renders his father's wife exempt from [being required to enter into a] levirate marriage . . . and he counts as his child in every respect, unless he is the child of a bondwoman or a Gentile woman." See Maimonides, *Code*, Laws concerning Levirate Marriage and Halitzah 1:4.

> had sexual relations without clarifying his intent. For in these instances the woman is the man's wife, and with regard to a man's wife, we presume that he does not engage in intercourse with promiscuous intent. . . .
>
> With regard to other women, however, whenever [a man has relations with] a harlot, we assume that his intent is promiscuous, unless he explains that he intends to betroth her. Needless to say, this applies with regard to a bondwoman [viz., a slave] or to a Gentile woman, to whom our marriage laws do not apply, and we have no concerns at all [that a valid marriage has been contracted] with them. A child born from these relations is presumed to be a Gentile or a slave until it can be definitively determined that his mother was manumitted or converted.[15]

According to Maimonides, the 'no promiscuous intent' presumption renders sexual relations lawful only when the parties involved are man and his former or conditionally betrothed wife. The presumption does not legitimize relations that are fundamentally improper – between a master and his bondwoman or between a man and woman whose intercourse is not undertaken for the purpose of consummating a marriage. Consequently, a child born of intercourse between a master and his slave is likewise a slave.

The Raavad disputes Maimonides' decision and justifies the Geonic ruling:

> With regard to his bondwoman, whom he has the power to manumit, the Geonic statement is true, because "he would not leave what is permitted and eat what is forbidden,"[16] unless the said individual was already presumed to be sexually dissolute. The same is true in the case of a Jewish woman who has relations in the presence of witnesses. If [the individuals] were not already suspected of being sexually dissolute, we should apply the [operative] presumption regarding Jewish men and women, and they are presumed to be upright (*behezkat kashrut*), and not to engage in dissolute promiscuity in the presence of witnesses – and the ruling of the Geonim, of blessed memory, is valid.[17]

In this dispute, as in the previous ones, Maimonides takes the presumption of honesty, and the associated presumptions, as realistic evidentiary principles to be applied within the sphere of the plausible. If a master has relations with his slave, or a man has relations with a woman outside of a marital relationship, they are transgressing, and there is no plausible justification for invoking the presumption that they

15 *Code*, Laws concerning Divorce 10:19.
16 bHulin 4a-b, bAvoda Zara 39b, bGitin 37b.
17 *Hasagot Haraavad*, *Code* ad loc.

are acting properly. The Raavad, upholding Geonic opinions, views the presumptions as normative in nature, as reflecting the moral premise that people, by their very nature, are honest, a premise that can be set aside only if there is clear evidence to that effect.

III. The social and ethical context: suspicion

The relation between the presumption of honesty and the boundaries of legitimate suspicion is reciprocal.[18] On the one hand, since honesty is the default assumption, unwarranted suspicion is prohibited. In other words, it is forbidden to suspect honest people of wrongdoing. On the other hand, when there is plausible suspicion about someone, the presumption of honesty may be void.[19] In this article, my primary focus will not be the formal legal boundaries of warranted suspicion, but rather the substantive social and ethical aspects of suspicion. With respect to these aspects of suspicion, too, two opposed approaches are manifest. The first is Maimonidean in spirit: we saw the legal side of this outlook in the previous section, on the presumption of honesty, and we will see its ethical side in the next section, which discusses the rationalist–realist attitude to suspicion.[20] This approach was rejected by R. Judah the Pious of Regensburg (Speyer 1150–Regensburg 1217) and his followers, referred to as the German Pietists (*hasidei ashkenaz*), who instead espoused a normative–idealist approach. Before turning to the debate between these opposed approaches, let me first offer a general characterization of the two schools of thought they represent.

Proponents of the rationalist–realist school, chief among them Maimonides, maintain that one's actions should, for better or for worse, be judged by one's typical patterns of conduct. Under certain circumstances, suspicion may be legitimate and perhaps even required. The opposed view is championed by the Pietist–idealist school of thought,

18 This is made explicit by R. Isaac b. Sheshet (Ribash): "We never ascribe [a woman's pregnancy] to extramarital relations so long as it can be ascribed to her husband, even if that possibility appears unlikely, for we do not suspect honest women [of wrongdoing]" (*Responsa Ribash*, #447).

19 See Raavad, Laws concerning Forbidden Foods 11:25, quoted above at n. 11. See also *Talmudic Encyclopedia* (Hebrew), "Presumption of fitness," 14:33.

20 My analysis of Maimonides' attitude to suspicion is based primarily on texts from his ethical writings and from those of his legal writings that address ethical issues.

which arose within the circle of students and followers of R. Judah the Pious. Its reference group is not Jewish society as a whole, but rather a closed elitist group – the Pietists – within which suspicion is deemed to be entirely unacceptable.[21]

IV. The rationalist position: suspicion is legitimate

1. "When you judge any person, incline the balance[22] in his favor"

As a rule, rationalist positions tend to evaluate the world in general, and human behavior in particular, just as they are, without idealized reshaping or romantic whitewashing. Maimonides took such a position in his commentary on the mishnaic dictum, "When you judge any person, incline the balance in his favor" (mAvot 1:6):

> This means that if it is someone unknown to you, and you do not know whether he is righteous or evil, and you saw that he did something or said something such that, if interpreted in one way, it is good, and if interpreted in another way, it is evil – adjudge it to be good, and do not think evil of him.
>
> But if this person is known to be righteous and renowned for his good deeds, and you see him commit an act that all indications suggest is evil, and it is impossible to decide conclusively that it is a good act without very forced explanations involving remote possibilities – it is required that it be interpreted as good, because there is some possibility that it might be good. And you are forbidden to suspect him [of wrongdoing]; and about such a case it is said, "One who is suspicious of the upright (*hahoshed bikhsherim*) will suffer bodily affliction" (bShabat 97a).
>
> Similarly, if someone is evil, and his [mis]deeds are notorious, and one sees him commit an act that all indications suggest is good, but there is some remote possibility that it is evil – it is required that one be wary of him

21 It must be kept in mind that the *Book of the Pious* addresses a closed circle, whereas Maimonides' work is addressed to society at large. On the surface, R. Judah the Pious does not disagree with Maimonides with respect to the latter; both maintain that suspicion may sometimes be legitimate in the context of society at large, as opposed to the circumscribed circles of the pious. Nevertheless, both schools are presenting their respective models of desirable ethical standards for how the individual should relate to his fellows. Maimonides' realistic model condones warranted suspicion, whereas the Pietists' idealistic model has reservations even about warranted suspicion.

22 Of the scales of justice. Another translation of the dictum is: Incline [the scales] toward merit. The scales of justice have two pans, one for considerations indicative of merit/innocence, one for those indicative of guilt.

> and not believe that the deed is good, because there is a possibility that it is evil, as it is said, "Though he be fair-spoken, do not trust him, for seven abominations are in his mind" (Prov. 26:25).
>
> And if someone is unknown, and his act is inconclusive as to which side it falls within [i.e., good or evil], **the path of piety requires** (*hova baderekh hahasidut*) that we incline the balance in his favor, to one of the two sides.[23]

Maimonides believes that the dictum mandating that the balance be tilted in favor of one whose deed is being weighed applies only to those whose moral character is a matter of doubt: "if someone is unknown, and his act is inconclusive as to which side it falls within." In such a case, when it is unclear who the individual is and what type of act he committed, the act should be interpreted in a favorable light. The dictum that the balance should be inclined in a person's favor is a requirement of "the path of piety"; that is, a lofty ethical standard – sometimes referred to as an equitable norm or a supererogatory norm, in contrast to an ordinary legal norm – that the "pious" individual seeks to uphold. This need not necessarily be the path of the "wise" individual, who is bound only by the ordinary ethical norms.[24]

In the case of a righteous or wicked person, there is no doubt about how one should judge and interpret their actions. Hence there is no need for a directive to tilt the balance toward innocence: the scale is not balanced, but is clearly inclined toward the 'good' side (for the righteous) or the side of 'evil' (for the wicked). If someone is presumed to be righteous, any action she takes should be interpreted as a good deed,

23 Maimonides, *Commentary on the Mishnah*, mAvot 1:6 (Kafih edition, 270) (emphasis added).

24 See Maimonides' own definition of "pious" and "wise" in his *Commentary on the Mishnah*, mAvot 5:7. "A pious person (*hasid*) is someone wise who increases his virtues, that is to say, increases his moral virtues, until he inclines slightly to one pole . . . and when his actions exceed his wisdom, on this account he can be called pious, on account of his added virtue." Similarly, in *Code*, Laws concerning Ethics 1:4-5: "Anyone whose dispositions (*deiot*) are all moderate and temperate is called 'wise.' One who takes it upon himself to be exceedingly meticulous, and departs somewhat from moderate dispositions, to one extreme or the other, is called 'pious.'" See also *Code*, Laws concerning Neighbors 14:5: "For the Sages did not command these priorities [but merely recommended them], for it is the way of the pious and of those of good spirit to act in this manner." See Aaron Kirschenbaum, "Supererogation" (Hebrew), *Da'at* 44 (2000): 5-57, esp. 22, 26-38; "Equity," in H. Ben-Menahem et al., *Windows onto Jewish Legal Culture: Fourteen Exploratory Essays* (Oxford and New York: Routledge, 2010), 2:3-42.

and neither she nor her actions should be suspected of being evil. On the other hand, if someone is presumed to be wicked, she is not to be trusted, and one should be wary of her.

Maimonides' stance on suspicion thus takes into account an individual's moral character. One may not suspect the upright; hence the Sages said, "One who is suspicious of the upright will suffer bodily affliction"[25]: the dictum specifically mentions "the upright," and does not mandate categorical desistance from suspicion. Indeed, the wicked should be deemed suspect, and avoided. Though a generally suspicious attitude is not recommended, suspicion is not necessarily bad. The legitimacy of warranted suspicion is derived from rational evaluation of human conduct: individuals should be judged on the basis of their usual behavior.

Maimonides demarcates the boundaries of warranted suspicion very flexibly. As his rulings attest, he understands the obligation to incline the balance in someone's favor as a 'soft' norm, required by "the path of piety."[26] But he also maintains that suspicion is sometimes legitimate, namely, when rational evaluation shows that it is warranted. As to the former aspect of his approach, Maimonides states that the obligation to incline the balance in someone's favor is an elitist norm that applies solely to scholars:

> Just as the wise man is recognized through his wisdom and his character traits, and by these is differentiated from the rest of the people, so too he should be recognized through his actions – his eating, drinking, sexual intercourse, hygiene, his speech, and his comportment, mode of dressing, household management, and business dealings. All these actions should be exceedingly becoming and proper. . . . A Torah sage, when speaking, should not shout or shriek like a wild animal or beast, and should not raise his voice excessively. Rather, he should speak softly to everyone . . . and he should greet every person promptly, so that they will be pleased with

25 bShabat 97a; bYoma 19b.

26 Cf. the formulation in the *Book of Precepts*, Affirmative Precept 177: "Judges are commanded to treat litigants equally . . . as He stated: 'Judge your kinsman fairly' (Lev. 19:15). Furthermore, every individual is commanded to judge according to the laws of the Torah when he knows them, and when [doing so] will end the quarrel between litigants. . . . This precept also includes [the guideline] that it is fitting to incline the balance in one's fellow's favor . . . and not to interpret his actions and words any way other than as good and kind deeds." The first two laws are "commandments" ("Judges are commanded," "Every individual is commanded"), whereas "incline the balance in one's fellow's favor" is a guideline for recommended conduct ("It is fitting to. . .").

> him. And in judging any person, he should incline the balance in his favor, speak positively of his fellow and say nothing negative about him at all, love peace, and pursue it.[27]

The sage's great wisdom demands of him conduct that is "exceedingly becoming and proper," and this includes the obligation to "incline the balance" in someone's favor. It should be noted that this obligation, which we can also formulate in contemporary language as 'give people the benefit of the doubt,' does not apply to everyone; it is incumbent only on scholars, in accordance with the above characterization of the duty as one that is required by "the path of pity."[28]

Maimonides also presents the 'do not suspect' injunction as a somewhat tenuous norm that most people do not consider binding. Among the twenty-four impediments to repentance, Maimonides includes five sins for which it is difficult to repent, because "Most people regard these matters lightly. Hence [when committing such a sin] one sins without realizing that he has done so."[29] The fifth sin on this list is:

> One who suspects upright people (*ksherim*). He will [also] say to himself, I have not sinned, for he will say [to himself], 'What have I done to him? All I did was raise a doubt as to whether he committed the deed or did not

27 *Code*, Laws concerning Ethics 5:1, 7.

28 Here, the obligation to give people the benefit of the doubt is described as addressed to the "wise" individual. Above, by contrast, it is addressed to the "pious" individual, as distinct from the "wise" one (see n. 24 above). This seeming contradiction is due to the polysemy of the Hebrew term "wise man" (*hakham*) in *Code*, Laws concerning Ethics. In chapter 1 it has an ethical sense, referring to one "whose dispositions are all moderate and temperate." In chapter 5, it denotes the "Torah sage." On this ambiguity, see *Guide for the Perplexed* 3:54.

29 *Code*, Laws concerning Repentance 4:4. See also Adiel Kadari, *Studies in Repentance: Law, Philosophy, and Educational Thought in Maimonides' Hilkhot Teshuva* (Hebrew), (Beer Sheva: 2010), 151-52. Kadari argues that Maimonides is speaking of unvoiced, internal suspicion, not suspicion that has been verbalized, which explains the relative lightness with which it is viewed. Kadari contends that this claim is difficult to sustain in light of the classic biblical prooftexts and textual sources, because Moses and the court elders do voice their suspicions; see bShabat 97a, cited in n. 25 above. Moreover, this claim has no support in Maimonides' formulation, since Maimonides explicitly states that he is speaking of someone who not only suspects his fellow, but also excuses that suspicion with the claim, 'All I did was raise a doubt as to whether he committed the deed or did not commit the deed' (*Code*, Laws concerning Repentance 4:4).

> commit the deed.' He does not recognize that it is a sin to deem someone of upright character to be a transgressor.[30]

Maimonides is saying that most people regard suspicion, even of honest people, as legitimate; the fact that the 'incline the balance' rule is to be applied with flexibility, taking into account the empirical facts, rather than rigidly, makes it seem permissible to set it aside altogether.

2. Legitimate suspicion

As we saw, in his *Commentary on the Mishnah*, Maimonides does not require that one completely forgo suspicion: what is prohibited is suspicion of the upright, those who are virtuous and deserving of the public's trust. One may not suspect them of wrongdoing. Because of this 'immunity,' they are permitted to carry out actions that would raise suspicions if undertaken by ordinary people.[31] By contrast, the wicked are not deserving of trust, nor are litigants in the courtroom. According to a law stated in the Mishnah, a judge must view the litigants who

30 *Code*, ibid.

31 According to Maimonides, a sage may not receive compensation for examining a firstborn male animal for blemishes (which would permit its slaughter); there is a suspicion that receiving compensation would affect the decision and incline the sage toward permitting the slaughter: "when someone is paid for inspecting firstborn animals for blemishes, the animal may not be slaughtered on the basis of his rulings. . . . He should not take payment for [inspecting] any given animal more than once . . . so that no suspicions will be aroused." On the other hand, if he is "a great expert and the sages know that there is no one [whose expertise is] comparable," he may be "allotted a fee for the visit and the inspection, whether a blemish is found or [the animal] is found to be unblemished" (*Code*, Laws concerning Firstlings 3:7). The immunity from suspicion that Maimonides grants the expert is criticized by Nahmanides: "When it comes to suspicion, we do not differentiate between a scholar and anyone else, regardless of the [specifics of the] case" (*Nahmanides*, bBekhorot 29b s.v. *gemara* [Hershler edition, col. 64]). According to Nahmanides, the prohibition against receiving compensation stems not from suspicion that a paid inspector would not be objective, but from the general prohibition against taking a fee for observing a precept. This second prohibition is qualified in nature; in the case of an acknowledged expert, who may receive a fee for the time he spends examining firstborns, "They permitted him to receive compensation, because everyone brings [his firstborn] to him, and he must examine them at all hours . . . and utterly neglects his work. [Therefore] the Sages instituted an average wage as his payment."

appear before him with suspicion: "And when the litigants stand before you, let them be like the wicked in your eyes."[32] Maimonides interprets this injunction as follows:

> Always view the litigants as if they are wicked, and operate under the presumption that both of them are lying. Adjudicate according to your perception of the situation. And when they have finished appearing before you, having accepted the judgment, let them be like the righteous in your eyes; and in judging each of them, incline the balance in their favor.[33]

A judge must strive to be totally fair. Full trust in the litigants could limit the judge's efforts to reach the truth, hence he must relate to the litigants as liars and as wicked throughout the proceedings in his courtroom.[34] Only after the case has ended can the litigants be considered like everyone else, that is, as individuals in whose favor the balance should be inclined.[35]

In another context, Maimonides instructs the court on how to relate to a guardian handling orphans' assets if there are rumors that the guardian's personal or professional (i.e., as guardian) conduct has been improper:

> If the court appointed a guardian and afterwards heard that he was eating, drinking, and making other expenditures beyond what would have been expected of him, they should be apprehensive that he is using the orphans'

32 mAvot 1:7, according to MS Kaufmann (in other versions of mAvot, 1:8).

33 *Code*, Laws concerning the Sanhedrin 23:10. See also Maimonides, *Commentary on the Mishnah*, mAvot 1:7, and see ad loc.: *Rashi*; *Rabbenu Jonah [Gerondi]'s Commentary on mAvot*; R. Shimon b. Tzemah Duran, *Magen Avot*; Maharam Joseph Alashkar, *Mirkevet Hamishne*. See also *Responsa Ritba*, #202.

34 This law appears in a collection of statutes, Laws concerning the Sanhedrin 23, whose goal is to ensure that honest judgments are rendered. Among these statutes are the prohibition against taking bribes (1-3); the prohibition against judging a relative, friend, or enemy (6-7); and the mandate to issue honest judgments: "He should know whom he is judging, before Whom he is judging, and Who will ultimately exact retribution from him if he deviates from the path of truth. . . . Whenever a judge does not render a genuinely true judgment, he causes the divine presence to depart from Israel" (8-9).

35 While there may seem to be a patent contradiction between the mandate to incline the balance in someone's favor, that is, to give the benefit of the doubt, and the mandate that it is imperative for judges to be suspicious of litigants during legal proceedings, Maimonides directs the judge to act in accordance with the former mandate once the legal proceedings have ended.

> resources. They should remove him from his position and appoint someone else. . . .
>
> Similarly, if a guardian was appointed by the orphans' father, and had a praiseworthy reputation, was known to be honest and to observe the precepts with alacrity, and he became a glutton and a drunkard and began conducting himself in suspect ways, or became reckless with regard to vows and [engaged in] acts that smacked of stealing (*avak gezel*), the court must remove him from his position and require him to take an oath. It must then appoint an appropriate guardian.
>
> And regarding all these matters, the judge must do as he sees fit. For each and every court is tantamount to the father of orphans.[36]

In executing his duties, a guardian owes a duty of fidelity both to the wards under his care and to the court. Hence if his behavior is questionable, and he displays ethical and religious failings, he is no longer presumed to be faithful to the orphans' best interests. In these circumstances, the court must remove him and appoint a more appropriate guardian in his stead. This case, too, illustrates that the balance between trust and suspicion is not invariant, but depends on the context and circumstances.

3. Suspicion – the ethical justification

Maimonides' rationalist approach to the evaluation of action recognizes the ethical and halakhic legitimacy of warranted suspicion. More generally, Maimonides sees human conduct as, in part, the result of inborn predilections, but mainly a matter of traits that are acquired through habit:

> It is impossible for one to have, by nature, from his earliest existence, a virtue or shortcoming, just as one cannot have, by nature, mastery of a practical craft. But it is possible for one to be naturally inclined to a virtue or deficiency, by the fact that actions of one type are easier for him than those of another type.[37]
>
> And know that the virtues and shortcomings in one's dispositions are indeed acquired, and settle in the soul, through repetition, many times over

36 Maimonides, *Code*, Laws concerning Inheritance 10:7; see *Or Sameiah* ad loc.

37 *Introduction to Tractate Avot* (also known as *Eight Chapters*), ch. 8 (Shilat edition, 248). According to Aristotle, moral traits are not inborn, but rather acquired by being put into practice, then ingrained through repetition, just as one learns the construction trade by building houses; see *Nicomachean Ethics*, II 1-2.

> a long period, of the actions to which this disposition gives rise, and we become used to them.[38]

That is, the 'righteous' and the 'wicked' are those who have become habituated to doing what is just and proper, or alternatively, what is unjust and evil. Hence it makes sense to interpret their actions in light of how they ordinarily behave.

When someone's traits or habits are unknown to us, we are to look at her basic character. Here Maimonides seems to reject the naïve, romantic view that human beings are essentially good. In his discussion of the existence of evil in the world, Maimonides lays the blame for much of this evil on humankind's repugnant traits:

> The evils of the third kind are those that are inflicted upon any individual among us by his own action; this is what happens in the majority of cases. . . . All men lament over evils of this kind; and it is only seldom that you find one who is not guilty of having brought them upon himself. . . . Solomon has said about evils of this kind: "The foolishness of man perverts his way. . ." (Prov. 19:3). He also has explained with reference to evils of this kind that they are done by man to himself; his dictum being: "Behold, this only have I found, that God hath made man upright, but they have sought out many thoughts" (Eccles. 7:29), these thoughts are those that bring these evils upon him. About this kind it has also been said: "For affliction comes not forth from the dust, neither does trouble spring out of the ground" (Job 5:6). Immediately afterward it is explained that this sort of evil is brought into existence by man, for it is said: "For man is born to trouble" (Job 5:7). This kind is drawn toward all the vices, I mean concupiscence for eating, drinking and copulation, and doing these things with excess in regard to quantity, or irregularly, or when the quality of the foodstuffs is bad.[39]

Adam was created upright, and initially, conducted himself on the basis of his intellect. But in the wake of his sin, he rendered himself aware of, and in the thrall of, his impulses and appetites. In his folly, Adam led himself astray, indeed, sinned against himself; this same folly afflicts most people, save but a few ("it is only seldom that you find one who is not guilty of having brought them upon himself").[40]

38 Ibid., ch. 4 (Shilat edition, 236).

39 Maimonides, *Guide for the Perplexed* 3:12 (Pines translation, 445, with minor adjustments).

40 Earlier in the *Guide*, Maimonides similarly states:

> For the intellect that God made overflow unto man and that is the latter's ultimate perfection, was that which *Adam* had been provided with before he disobeyed. It was because of this that it was said of him that he was created *in the image of God and in His likeness*. . . . However, when he disobeyed and inclined toward his desires of the imagination

The rules Maimonides sets down for evaluating and judging human conduct are thus derived from his understanding of human nature. An individual's actions should be interpreted on the basis of what she usually does: a righteous person's actions should be interpreted favorably, and a wicked person's, unfavorably. An average person's actions should be related to impartially, and not necessarily be presumed good. Hence the mandate to interpret actions favorably, that is, to incline the balance in such a person's favor, is incumbent only on those who seek to follow "the path of piety." On the other hand, suspicion of such an average individual is not unavoidable. Maimonides emphasizes that those who suspect "the upright" – which excludes those not actually known to be upright – will suffer bodily affliction.[41]

V. The Pietists' position: rejection of suspicion on moral grounds

Let us now turn to the second attitude to suspicion in medieval Jewish thought, namely, that espoused by the German Pietists (*hasidei ashkenaz*).

1. Preventive measures

The *Book of the Pious* (*Sefer Hasidim*), written in Germany at the turn of the thirteenth century, reflects the social and religious views of the German Pietists.[42] Over twenty-five sections, distributed throughout the book, address the issue of suspicion.[43] The dominant attitude to sus-

---

> and the pleasures of his corporeal senses . . . he was punished by being deprived of that intellectual apprehension. (ibid., 1:2 [Pines 24-25])

See also Sara Klein-Braslavy, *Maimonides' Interpretation of the Adam Stories in Genesis* (Hebrew), (Jerusalem: 1986), 157 n. 24.

41 See the passage from Maimonides, *Commentary on the Mishnah*, mAvot 1:6, quoted above at n. 23.

42 Isaac Baer, "The religious-social tendency of 'Sepher Hassidim'" (Hebrew), *Zion* 3 (1937), 1-50. Reprinted in I.G. Marcus (ed.), *The Religious and Social Ideas of the Jewish Pietists in Medieval Germany* (Hebrew), 2nd edition (Jerusalem: 1999), 81-131. For an overview of the extensive literature on the Pietists, see Marcus's introduction, 14-22. See too Marcus's *Piety and Society: The Jewish Pietists of Medieval Germany* (Leiden: 1991). All quotes from *Sefer Hasidim* in this article are from *Sefer Hasidim*, ed. J. Wistinetzki (Berlin: 1891; Frankfurt: 1924 [2nd edition]).

43 The prolific literature on the *Book of the Pious* barely mentions this subject. An exception is Y.N. Simhoni, "Medieval German Pietism" in Marcus 1999, ibid., 47-81 (originally published in *Ha-Zefirah*, 1916/17, issues 12-32). Simhoni states, e.g., "We hear several times in the *Book of the Pious* about suspicion of the pious person, and such comments appear to have a basis in real-life experience in Germany, because on occasion, the [Jewish] multi-

picion voiced in the *Book of the Pious* is utter rejection: the individual is enjoined to do everything in his power to avoid suspicion, both of himself and of others.[44] Suspecting someone else is deemed a "grave iniquity"[45] with serious consequences: "One who is suspicious of the upright will suffer bodily affliction."[46] As a corollary, one wrongfully suspected of misconduct is obligated to do everything in his power to dispel this suspicion; if he does not do so, the suspected party bears the culpability for the suspicion and any ensuing punishment he incurs.[47] So too, a thief is obligated to admit his sin in public, "so that others not be suspected [of wrongdoing] when he is guilty."[48] And more generally,

> One who has transgressed, but others are suspected [of having committed the transgression], must say, 'I am the one who sinned,' so that people do not suspect the upright.[49]

---

tude would mock and curse the Pietists, not understanding their conduct" (65). On the historiographical importance of Simhoni's article, see Marcus's introduction, 15-16.

44 However, one who seeks to dispel suspicion of his own actions should do so cautiously; it is preferable that he do so indirectly, i.e., by intimation, and without casting aspersions on the other party's good name; see *Sefer Hasidim*, §82 (based on an episode recounted in bShabat 51b-52a). "One should not dispel suspicion of his own actions in a way that will embarrass his fellow" (§83). Another section, addressing the case of a charity warden who is suspected of improper disbursement of donated monies and must reveal the identities of the needy individuals who received support from the charity, asserts: "It is better that he should be embarrassed, and not the recipient, for if the warden mentions the needy person, he will embarrass him" (§908).

45 "And the fact that they would have suspected you [i.e., your intentions] would have been deemed their grave iniquity" (§77).

46 Ibid., §1260. This is said, in particular, with regard to one whose actions lead him to be suspected, by someone who is dying, of trying to harm him. See too §1885: "One must be very careful not to be suspected by someone who is ill. Even though after the sick person dies, he [i.e., the deceased] will realize that no harm was meant, one must be careful, for when sick people die in pain . . . they will seek revenge even in death . . . and he [i.e., the individual who is suspected] will be punished."

47 "One should not act in a manner that raises suspicion, for if he does so but did not, in fact, sin, others will be punished [for suspecting him, though he did not commit the suspected sin] on his account" (§78). The one who acted suspiciously thus bears responsibility both for causing others to wrongly suspect him, and for any punishment they incur as a result.

48 §74.

49 See too §89.

By the same token, if one is able to incline the balance in his fellow's favor, he must do so. Hence in the case of a dispute between two people, if one of the parties can be led to change his mind about the other, and see him in a positive light, one may, to bring about this end, listen to that party's hurtful statements about the other party, in order to defend the latter, and thereby preemptively lessen the injury that might be caused him.[50]

The injunction to avoid suspicion is also expressed in another way: one must take special precautions when carrying out actions that could arouse suspicion:

> One should always weigh his silver or count his coins before giving them to someone else or upon receiving them from someone else, even if the other person is trustworthy, lest the amount be short, though he does not know this, or the other person takes them, and as he has not counted [the coins] or weighed the silver, [upon discovering the shortfall], suspects his fellow or his fellow suspects him.[51]

On the other hand, excessive punctiliousness and extreme caution for the purpose of preempting suspicion could lead to strange and improper conduct. For example, someone asked to give advice regarding a matter in which he had an interest might, rather than be suspected of having an interest in the matter and giving biased advice for personal gain, prefer to give bad advice that could harm the inquirer and others.[52]

50 One should so act where possible: "If you can tip the scales [vis-à-vis] your friend, so that he will be viewed favorably, and you can also say, 'Your fellow loves you,' [do so]. If he accepts [what you say], all is well; if not, listen to him, but do not believe him or tell others what he says about your fellow. For if you do not accept what he says, he will go and tell others; he will create a scandal and others will believe him or tell his fellow, who will quarrel with him" (§1335).

51 §1259.

52 The *Book of the Pious* denounces such behavior and stipulates that this is an "unpardonable sin." In the words of the party harmed by the improper advice, "It is inconceivable that in order to dispel suspicion of yourself, you gave [harmful] advice that cannot be undone. . . . And the fact that they would have suspected you [i.e., your intentions] would have been deemed their grave iniquity, and you would have received a great reward for bearing the pain of the suspicion. [And in acting as you did,] you have transgressed [the precept] "thou shalt not put a stumbling-block before the blind" (Lev. 19:14)" (§77). Consequently, the binding norm is: "If they ask him for advice, and he knows that if he provides correct advice, they will

2. Suspicion, society, and religion

The *Book of the Pious* offers several justifications for its unyielding policy vis-à-vis suspicion. These justifications reflect the social and religious values espoused by the German Pietists, and the group's unique interests.

a. *Separatism*

Extreme caution about suspicion serves the Pietists' ideal of separatism.[53] The Pietist must separate himself from the company of questionable individuals, so that he will not be suspected of acting as they do. Eschewing suspicion is invoked as a rationale for separating and distancing the community of Pietists from the sinful multitude, as evidenced by the following recommendation:

> Take care not to reside near someone from whom you will not learn good deeds. Moreover, you will cause others to suspect you of evil, for they will say, It is not for nothing that you joined with him, and they will impute his evil actions to you.[54]

b. *Trust and social cohesiveness*

The social ideal espoused by the *Book of the Pious* is an egalitarian society with complete social cohesiveness and cooperation.[55] Such a social

---

suspect him, [but] if he remains quiet, they will act improperly – it is better for him to provide the advice even though they will suspect him."

53 "[It so happened that] in one locale, there lived only good people, and they had good leaders. One elder told them, 'What good does it do us if we marry others [i.e., people from other locales] and others marry us, and we find our children taking after their bad ways? Rather, let us institute a ban, so that no man will give his daughter in marriage to a man who is not of this city, so that he can join us, lest he taint us.' . . . People who search the land for a place to live should examine the ways of those who live in a [given] city, and whether the Gentiles there are licentious . . . for in most places, Jews conduct themselves like their Gentile neighbors" (§1301). On the value the Pietists attached to self-segregation, see Joseph Dan, *Rabbi Judah He-Hasid* (Hebrew), (Jerusalem: 2006), 53-61; I.G. Marcus, "The politics and ethics of Pietism in Judaism: the *hasidim* of medieval Germany," *Journal of Religious Ethics* 8 (1980), 227-58.

54 §78.

55 Baer 1937, n. 42 above, 21. The Pietists, Baer notes, maintained that the world was created equal in social terms so that "everyone would live

framework requires trust among members of the community. Indeed, the *Book of the Pious* recommends that trust be a test for solidarity.

> If you wish to go into partnership with someone, first study well whether he has been a companion and partner to someone else. . . . If you see that when he is angry he admits the truth, and when he is experiencing loss and could force you to take an oath so as to transfer the burden of the oath and loss onto your shoulders, but nevertheless, does not suspect you – choose him as your companion.[56]

Trust, especially under problematic circumstances, is the acid test of a strong social bond and partnership. In a similar vein, the individual is urged to be forgiving of his fellow even if he suspects him of wrongdoing.

> [Regarding the case of] Reuben, who told Shimon, 'Look at how Levi embarrasses you! When you come to him, he shuts his [money] chest, for he is afraid you will steal [from him]': [Reuben] should not suspect [Levi] . . . "One who is suspicious of the upright will suffer bodily affliction." One must be amiable to his fellow: "As face answers to face in water, so does one person's heart [answer] to another's" (Prov. 27:19).[57]

Averting suspicion is presented as reinforcing an important Pietist value, namely, fostering strong bonds of interpersonal trust and amity.

Indeed, minimizing suspicion is a constitutive aspect of consolidating any group founded on the values of trust, amity, and partnership.[58] Many sections of the *Book of the Pious* imply that the repudiation of suspicion is directed, not outwardly, toward the world

peaceably with others." The social directives in *Sefer Hasidim* were "meant to guide the entire community on a path of unity, amity, and mutual religious responsibility" (41). See also idem, "The theory of the natural equality of early man according to Ashkenazi Hasidim" (Hebrew), *Zion* 32 (1967), 129-36; Gershom Scholem, "Hasidism in medieval Germany," *Major Trends in Jewish Mysticism* (NY: 1941), 80-118, 369-77.

56 *Book of the Pious*, §1253.

57 §1260. For more on the Pietists' teachings regarding relations between partners, see Baer 1937, n. 42 above, 32-33.

58 On the sociological aspects of the Pietist outlook on suspicion, see Morton Deutsch, "Trust and suspicion," *Journal of Conflict Resolution* 2 (1958): 265-79; Herbert W. Kee and Robert E. Knox, "Conceptual and methodological considerations in the study of trust and suspicion," *Journal of Conflict Resolution* 14 (1970): 357-66.

at large, but inwardly, toward the Pietist community.[59] The obligation to incline the balance in favor of one's fellow is limited to "one who associates with good people."[60] But there is no such obligation regarding "evildoers":

> One who speaks poorly of others – do not judge him favorably. . . . And you should know that anyone who speaks poorly of others may be suspected of the same bad deeds he alleges were carried out by others, for, as the Sages said, "One who disqualifies others does so on the basis of his own blemish" (bKidushin 70b). . . . For one who discredits others cannot invent his fellow's blemish, but rather, he tells others about his own blemishes.[61]

Maligning others is indicative of an inner flaw, and one who speaks poorly of others is himself flawed; hence, "do not judge him favorably." Moreover, the stringent prohibition against suspecting others applies only to the "upright":

> The Sages said, "One who is suspicious of the upright will suffer bodily affliction"; but they also said, "View every man as a bandit." [The first statement applies to] suspicion voiced aloud; but one may surely be wary of someone else. Moreover, if you already know this person, you should not be wary, for R. Jose and R. [Judah] [sent] two students to [the son of] R. Hanina b. [Antigonus], who assigned a youth to watch over the pure foods. R. Jose was angry that he [R. Hanina's son] did not trust them.[62]

59 This tendency is typical of the German Pietists' general outlook. Simhoni notes that: "[Pietism] was not intended for the general population, and therefore did not have to concede the radical consequences of its major ideas" (n. 43 above, 46).

60 *Book of the Pious*, §108. Similarly, one should also favor Pietists over others when it comes to charity and doing good deeds; see Marcus 1980, n. 53 above, 276-77.

61 §92. The "evildoers" are those who are not Pietists. See Marcus, ibid., 262.

62 §1260. I have modified the text slightly, on the basis of the talmudic passage that recounts the incident, bBekhorot 30b (according to MS Florence II.I.7):

> R. Judah and R. Jose were in doubt concerning a matter of ritual purity. They sent a pair of scholars to the son of R. Hanina b. Antigonus. They went and asked him to inquire into the matter. They found him watching over ritually pure food. He seated some of his own scholars with them, while he rose to [go] examine the question. They came and informed R. Judah and R. Jose [of his conduct toward them]. R. Judah said to them: His father held scholars in contempt, and he also holds

One who is known to be blameless ("you already know this person") should not be the object of caution and suspicion.[63] One should, however, be wary of someone unknown, suspicion of whom is justified.[64]

Similarly, the obligation to refrain from actions that arouse suspicion, so that others will not suspect you, is limited to contexts involving "those who trust," and does not apply to everyone:

> The verse states, "You shall be clear before the Lord and before Israel" (Num. 32:22) – and not before all of Israel. One must clear himself for those who trust, and not for those who do not trust. For if someone does not trust you [even when] you clear yourself before him, what benefit have you gained by clearing yourself, inasmuch as he does not trust you?[65]

The rule applicable in the specific case of the charity warden, referred to above, can be inferred from this general principle: a charity warden suspected of improperly disbursing funds must respond only to suspicions raised by the virtuous, and should ignore criticism and suspicion voiced by the malicious.[66]

---

scholars in contempt. R. Jose replied to him: Let the dignity of the elder remain undisturbed.

63 This conclusion is drawn from the contradiction between the two dictums ("One who is suspicious of the upright will suffer bodily affliction"; "View every man as a bandit"). The latter dictum is found in Kallah Rabbati 8:1, MS Parma 2785/18 (de Rossi 327/15); see Yachin Epstein, Studies in Tractate Kallah Rabbati: Text, Redaction, and Period (Hebrew), (PhD dissertation, Hebrew University of Jerusalem, 2009), 237, 406; accessible at https://sites.google.com/site/yachinepstein/Home/kallarabati

64 Therefore, a fortiori one should suspect those who are evil of wrongdoing, as illustrated by the following case:

> Some students were staying in a house whose landlord was a Pietist. One of the students was stealing the landlord's wine. His fellow students said to him, Why are you stealing the wine? He will suspect us, and you will bear the sin! He said to them, I have been told that he declared his wine ownerless, so if we steal it, it is not a sin. He [further] said, Anyone who reveals to him what I have done will be put under a ban. They said to him, We will pay no heed to your words, and they went and told the landlord, Do not suspect us; but be wary of so-and-so. (*Book of the Pious*, §1416).

65 Ibid., §84. See also ibid., §1975: "When must one clear himself before someone who suspects him? When the person who suspects him is righteous."

66 See n. 44 above, and §909-910 as well. "A charity warden whom scoundrels suspect of stealing, or of giving [charity fund monies] to those he favors, should not take [their comments] to heart or halt his work on their account,

3. Conduct in off-limits situations

The Pietists' ethical code required the pious individual to conceal his own good deeds as much as possible.[67] Moreover, it was deemed a religious duty for the pious person to confront his desires and passions, a confrontation that might sometimes call for deliberate exposure to sins and sinners.[68] There might thus be situations where the pious individual is in a sinful environment amidst circumstances in which his actions appear to be evil. In these precarious situations, the pious individual must take steps to clarify matters so that bystanders interpret his actions in a positive light. But this raises a problem: the obligation to be modest, and not to flaunt one's good deeds, precludes someone in the said situation from making the necessary clarifications. The pious person is thus caught in a bind between the imperatives of the manifest situation (religious propriety) and those of the hidden situation (ethical propriety).

The Pietists' solution to this quandary is to mandate extreme meticulousness with regard to suspicion. Pietists are enjoined not to suspect that apparently-transgressive actions of a pious person, actions that take place in off-limits circumstances, are indeed sins. They must interpret the deeds of fellow members of the community as good – even if they appear to be sinful. A notable expression of the quandary and its

---

for even Moses himself was the subject of suspicion" (§910). The same principle is operative regarding a different type of case: a judge whom "one of the litigants suspects and seeks to have recused from a case because he studies the case deeply and is an expert on the litigants' tricks, and [the litigant] fears that if [the judge] tries the case he will be found guilty, because [the judge] is well-versed in the law and knows it well – should not refrain from trying this case" (§1379, and see a parallel in §1975).

67 Baer 1937, n. 42 above, 9-10; Dan 2006, n. 53 above, 13-14.

68 The Pietists' maintained that man's greatest virtue was his struggle with the evil inclination (*yetzer hara*), and his ability to overcome it: "'Let us make man' (Gen. 1:26): that he shall have a heavenly heart – the good inclination (*yetzer hatov*) – and a terrestrial heart [the evil inclination]. If the heavenly heart, i.e., the good inclination, prevails over the terrestrial heart, i.e., the evil inclination, he is more praiseworthy than the heavenly beings" (§1957). See Simhoni, n. 43 above, 71-72 (overcoming one's evil inclination is a test of one's fear of God); Joseph Dan, "The problem of martyrdom in the theoretical doctrine of the German Pietist movement," in Marcus 1999, n. 42 above, 214 ("Man came into this world to face a test. The world was created . . . to make it difficult for man to attain all his objectives."). And see Dan 2006, n. 53 above, 74-76, 84-85, 98, 145.

solution is found in two sections of the *Book of the Pious*. The first section weighs the desideratum of modesty against the desideratum of issuing a clarification that explains the propriety of a seemingly off-limits action.

> [Consider the case of a] window or opening [from a room] onto the public domain [i.e. a street], and there are stores of silver and gold in that room. And someone [on the street], wishing to give charity, turns to take [money] from his purse, but the people around him believe he is taking silver [from the storeroom] through the window, and now he realizes that they suspect him. May he say, I have just given charity, to dispel suspicion of his action; or is it forbidden for him to do so, inasmuch as he would thereby appear to be commending himself for giving charity, and it would be better to let others suspect him?[69]

The next section, which presents the "story of a pious man," serves to resolve the dilemma.[70] The protagonist is a pious man who, in a dream, inquires into who will be seated next to him in Paradise; in a nighttime vision, he is told that his neighbor will be "a young man [who lives] in a faraway place . . . an utter wastrel." Despite his disappointment, the pious man insists on meeting his future neighbor, and journeys to the latter's house. There, from an adjacent chamber, the pious man observes the young man's conduct. At night, the youth assembles all the town's prostitutes in one room and plies them with wine until, intoxicated, they fall asleep. He then leaves the room. When the pious man beholds this scene, he weeps, astounded by the sad fate Heaven has ordained for him, that he should have such an evil neighbor in Paradise. To relieve his perplexity, the pious man asks the young man to explain his actions, which he does, as follows:

> All that you saw was done with good intentions. I make myself out to be a libertine, and all the dissolute fellows tell me which prostitute they have hired. Then I go in secret and pay them a higher fee to come to me, and they believe that I had relations with them, because they were intoxicated throughout the night. I also told my mother to come and drag me outside by my hair, so if [the prostitutes] ask me on the morrow, Why didn't you have relations with us? I can answer, You know that my mother beat me.

69 *Book of the Pious*, §79.

70 §79 ends with the words, "[The quandary] can be resolved on the basis of the [following] case," referring to §80. The incident recounted in §80 is thus explicitly presented as a source for resolving the dilemma in the previous section. Modern scholars are divided regarding the hagiographic nature of incidents reported in the *Book of the Pious*. Simhoni, n. 43 above, asserts that the "'story of a pious man' . . . is not fictional, but rather, a tradition" (53).

> In the meantime, I prevent the dissolute fellows from sinning. I do not care if they suspect me [of sinning], and I forgive them.[71]

The lesson is clear. The fact that one who endeavors to be pious must live a religiously-observant life on the borders of desire and sin, and the concomitant obligation not to publicize one's success in coping with the challenge, places a demand on onlookers, particularly if they, too, aspire to piety: the conduct of others should not be judged critically, with suspicion, but positively; and "one who thinks ill of the good is a sinner."[72]

4. Supererogatory conduct as an obligation

We should also consider one last Pietist justification for eschewing suspicion, a justification that is somewhat peripheral. On the rationalist–realist approach, the obligation to avoid suspicion and to view the actions of others in a positive light is required by those who wish to take "the path of piety" and to behave fittingly, but it is not mandated by a religious precept.[73] So conceived, this obligation is incumbent only on the few, not on everyone. The Pietists, however, were unwilling to let that conception suffice. One of the most salient aspects of Pietism is meticulous observance of the precepts at a higher and stricter level than required by the law.[74] Hence norms that, on the rationalist–realist approach, are construed as supererogatory, are taken by the Pietists to be absolute

71 §80.

72 §81. The utter rejection of suspicion is based on the words of the woman of Tekoa to David after Absalom had Amnon slain: "And the woman said, 'Why then have you planned such a thing against God's people? In making this pronouncement, Your Majesty condemns himself'" (2 Sam. 14:13). Earlier, the woman had come to him with a made-up tale, saying that one of her sons had killed his brother in the heat of an argument, and now her family wanted to avenge the blood of the slain brother by killing the murderer. After David believes her, she rebukes him for even considering that God's people could kill someone without a proper trial (see *Rashi*, *Metzudat David*, and *Malbim* ad loc.). According to the woman, the king's suspicion is improper, and in voicing it, he "condemns himself." Thus, "one who thinks ill of the good is a sinner."

73 See discussion above, at nn 23-27.

74 Simhoni, n. 43 above, 68; Baer 1937, n. 42 above, 12; Dan 2006, n. 53 above, 18-20. This is especially true regarding injunctions governing interpersonal relations; see Simhoni, 48; Scholem, n. 55 above, 143.

obligations.[75] Pietism demands of every individual that he avoid suspicion and view others in a favorable light. For the Pietists, this is a commandment mandated by the Torah.[76]

VI. Afterword

The rabbinical discussion of suspicion took place in parallel with the legal debate over the presumption of innocence in Christian Europe during the twelfth and thirteenth centuries. Yet these discourses occupy two entirely different spheres: whereas the rabbinical discussion addresses ethical and social issues, the debate over the presumption of innocence is conducted on the legal plane. The differences between

75 Scholem, ibid., 144, states that R. Eleazar of Worms attempted to articulate a binding halakhic definition of the Pietistic ideal, seeking to expand the halakha's reach beyond its traditional scope.

76 "And if he is an average person . . . you must incline [the balance away from] the uncertainty [as to his conduct] and judge him favorably. . . . **And this is an affirmative precept (*mitzvat ase*) of the Torah**, as it is written, 'Judge your kinsman fairly' (Lev. 19:15)" (R. Jonah Gerondi, *Shaarei Teshuva*, gate 3, §218 [Dessler edition, 206-207], emphasis added). Gerondi, though a Spaniard, was greatly influenced by the German Pietists as a result of his studies at the yeshiva in Évreux, and practiced Pietism. See Israel M. Ta-Shma, "Ashkenazi Hasidism in Spain: R. Jonah Gerondi, the man and his work" (Hebrew), in *Studies in Medieval Rabbinic Literature* (Hebrew), vol. 2, *Spain* (Jerusalem: 2004), 109-48, esp. 112-17. In another context, R. Jonah asserts that one who conducts himself in accordance with the "piety criterion" (*midat hahasidut*) must not suspect even an evildoer: "And when they have finished appearing before you, having accepted the judgment, let them be like the righteous in your eyes – this is [conduct that accords with] the **piety criterion**, for [although] **you know that one [of them] has made a false claim**, you should (never) consider him to be a liar and an exasperating litigant; you should not suspect him, for he has accepted the judgment . . . and you should consider him to have repented" (*Rabbenu Jonah's Commentary on mAvot*, 1:8, emphasis added).

R. Jonah, like the *Book of the Pious*, not only eschews suspicion of others, but also requires the party suspected of misconduct to do whatever he can *ab initio* to avert suspicion, and, after his guiltlessness comes to light, to forgive those who suspected him: "Do not suspect your fellow . . . and do not bring yourself to the point of suspicion . . . lest people sin on your account by suspecting you [of wrongdoing]. Forgive all who suspect you" (*Sefer Hayira* (Book of Awe), in *Shaarei Teshuva*, §66 [Dessler edition, 300]). On the connection between this work and German Pietism's influence on R. Jonah, see Ta-Shma, 114-15.

these domains impact the reasoning and arguments employed in the respective debates. In the legal realm, the discussion focuses on the individual qua monad, and seeks to determine her fundamental essence. In the ethical–social realm, by contrast, the focus is on the individual qua social being. In this context, suspicion is considered primarily in terms of one's relationship to other individuals, or to the society in which she lives. There is a feature of the realist position that is common to both spheres. Realism does not, as a default position, make the presumption that individuals are inclined to act properly. Rather, it assesses specific acts on the part of an individual against the background of that individual's usual conduct – for better or for worse.

Albo on Repentance and Coercion

Warren Zev Harvey*

In his classic study of Philo of Alexandria, Harry Austryn Wolfson expounded on the clear difference between the Jewish concept of repentance (*teshuva*), and the analogous Greek philosophical concepts of *metameleia* and *metanoia*. "In Greek philosophy," states Wolfson, "repentance is never held up as a virtue." For Aristotle, he explains, the penitent is always a "bad" person since the good person has no reason to repent. Wolfson contrasts this Greek view with the Jewish one: "In Judaism . . . repentance . . . came to be regarded as a Mosaic commandment" binding on everyone, including the good and the wise, "which in the language of Philo means that it is a practical virtue."[1] Wolfson's description of this fundamental difference between the Greek and Jewish notions of repentance is instructive and undoubtedly correct. It is therefore curious that R. Joseph Albo (c. 1380-1444), in his *Book of Principles*, IV, 27,[2] defined the Jewish concept of repentance (*teshuva*) in terms of Aristotle's concepts of *metameleia* and *metanoia*.[3] Albo's recourse to Aristotle's notion of regret involves him in consideration of the distinction between voluntary and compulsory acts.

The "great difficulty"

Albo discusses the concept of repentance (*teshuva*) in *Principles*, IV, 25-28.[4] At the beginning of IV, 27, he remarks on a "great difficulty" (*safek gadol*) concerning this notion. Since the transgression was a deed,

* The Hebrew University of Jerusalem

1 Wolfson, *Philo: Foundations of Religious Philosophy in Judaism, Christianity, and Islam* (Cambridge MA: 1968 [1947]), 2:252-59).

2 Albo, *Book of Principles*, ed. and trans. Isaac Husik (Philadelphia: 1946), 4:257-64 (henceforth, *Principles*). Quotations will sometimes be modified.

3 *Nicomachean Ethics*, III, 1-2, 1109b-1112a.

4 *Principles*, 4:220-72; see also IV, 18 (4:164). Historian Marc Saperstein notes that "One of the most interesting and important [disputed questions in fifteenth-century Spanish Jewish homiletic literature] is on the efficacy

how can it be overturned by mere words? If one has taken a life or profaned the Sabbath, does the utterance of "confession and regret" (*vidui veharata*) revive the murdered individual or transform that profaned Sabbath into an observed one? "It is like a person throwing down a house and then rebuilding it with his mouth."[5] Albo does not distinguish here between transgressions against human beings and those against God, and couples together murder and profanation of the Sabbath. One might have expected him to distinguish between transgressions against human beings, which often involve material damage, and transgressions against God, which often do not involve such damage.[6] Beyond this, it is surprising that Albo refers to both "confession and regret" as "mere words," since in previous chapters he explained that "the matter of repentance depends on the confession of the mouth and the regret of the heart."[7] More precisely, it involves three things, "thought, speech, and act," where "thought" refers to regret.[8] Thus according to Albo's explicit statements in previous chapters, regret does not consist of "mere words."

Having voiced his "great difficulty," Albo proceeds to raise the question of which human acts are deserving of praise or blame. Such acts, he argues, have three characteristics: (1) they are voluntary, i.e., acts of the will (*ratzon*); (2) they are the result of choice (*behira*), i.e., the preference of one thing over another; and (3) they are done knowingly (*haose otan yodeia . . . shehu ose hapeula hahi*) or consciously. Thus, drunkards excuse themselves for acts committed when drunk, claiming they did not know what they were doing, even though their acts exhibited will and choice. Similarly, one is not praised or blamed for acts committed involuntarily (*meihekhrah haones*), even though by choice and knowingly; for example, an act done in order to avoid punishment.[9] Albo

---

of *teshuvah*. . . . This question appears in several different sermons of the period. The sermons show that the doctrine of repentance was under philosophical attack at the time, and the preachers felt the need to . . . defend it philosophically" (M. Saperstein, *Your Voice Like a Ram's Horn: Themes and Texts in Traditional Jewish Preaching* [Cincinnati: 1996], 85, 289-99).

5 *Principles*, 4:257.

6 Cf., e.g., mYoma 8:9: "the Day of Atonement atones" for transgressions against God, but not for those against human beings "until one appeases one's fellow."

7 *Principles*, IV, 25 (4:222); but cf. 223 (on Hosea 14:3).

8 Ibid., IV, 26 (4:235); cf. 253.

9 See H. Ben-Menahem, "Free will and coercion in the Talmud: a preliminary taxonomy," pp. 1–17 in this volume.

does not mention the possibility of an act done voluntarily and knowingly but without choice. He concludes: "Acts to which praise or blame do not apply at all are those of absolute compulsion (*haones hagamur*), which are acts that the agent does not know of, does not want, and does not prefer to other acts." An example of such "absolute compulsion," according to Albo, is a purely accidental homicide, such as "when a person throws a stone and another puts out his head, is struck, and dies." He notes that biblical law distinguishes between purely accidental homicide, which does not require the killer's exile, and negligent homicide, which does require it (Num. 35:11-34; Deut. 19:1-10).[10] The example of the stone-thrower who kills unintentionally is found in Numbers 35:22-25.[11] Albo's dictum that acts deserving praise or blame are those that are (1) voluntary, (2) chosen, and (3) done knowingly, is an accurate condensation of Aristotle's comments in *Nicomachean Ethics*, III, 1-2, 1109b-1112a; the example of the unknowing drunkard is adduced by Aristotle at 1110b25-27.

Albo then turns to the complex cases of acts that are part compulsory and part voluntary. For example, someone does something bad out of fear of being punished by ruffians. Is the act compulsory or voluntary? Albo answers that such an act is usually considered compulsory, since one did it against one's will. However, he continues, if the evil of the act was of a high order, e.g., striking one's parent, rebelling against one's king, or rebelling against God, then it is considered voluntary, since one is expected to endure great pain rather than do such things.[12] Aristotle addresses the subject of "mixed" acts that are part voluntary and part compulsory in *Nicomachean Ethics*, III, 1, 1110a-1110b2, where he gives the example of one who is coerced by a tyrant "to do something shameful." Aristotle also asserts there that there are certain evil acts that "one cannot be compelled to do," and one is expected to choose to undergo great pain or death rather than do them. He calls Alcmaeon "ridiculous" for murdering his mother out of fear of threats. Aristotle and Albo are thus saying that one can be coerced by armed thugs to give them a few coins, but cannot be coerced by armed thugs to murder one's parents. In other words, even when one is coerced, one **chooses** to be coerced.

10 *Principles*, IV, 27 (4:258-59).

11 Cf. Aristotle's example of the stone mistaken for pumice in *Nicomachean Ethics*, III, 1, 1111a12.

12 *Principles*, IV, 27 (4:259-60); see too Ben-Menahem, n. 9 above, 11.

Next Albo discusses the paradigmatic case of seafarers discarding their cargo during a great storm. "Nobody throws one's goods overboard voluntarily and the act would seem compulsory," writes Albo. "Nonetheless," he continues, "since one chooses to do so in order to avoid pain and danger, it is properly considered voluntary." Albo adds a further observation: the act was clearly voluntary, since after the passengers have safely reached shore, they remain pleased with their decision "because they owe to it their survival." This further observation is important to Albo. He holds that one's subsequent attitude toward a conflicted decision is a test of whether it was voluntary or compulsory. "Anything that was done voluntarily at the time" but which afterwards the agent disavows and "desires had not been done" should be considered either compulsory or a mistake; similarly, an act that was originally carried out under some sort of coercion, but which the agent afterwards welcomes and affirms, should be considered voluntary.[13] Aristotle discusses the case of the seafarers discarding their cargo during a great storm in *Nicomachean Ethics*, III, 1, 1110a8-20. He states that the terms "voluntary" and "compulsory" should be used with reference to "the time of action," i.e., to the time of the storm, when the seafarers chose to save their lives at the expense of their property. Although Aristotle emphasizes that the evaluation of whether the seafarers' act was voluntary or compulsory depends on "the time of action," he does not mention the test required by Albo, namely, whether the act was subsequently reaffirmed or disavowed.

A reference to this test of voluntariness or compulsion is found by Albo in a talmudic rule concerning the laws of vows (bNedarim 22b). According to this rule, regret (*harata*) is a justified reason for annulment of a vow. In trying to ascertain whether one regrets having vowed, the Rabbis allowed leading questions to be asked, such as, "Are you still of the same mind?" and "Do you feel remorse?" (21b).[14] Albo infers from such questions that "everything depends on the continuance of

13 Ibid., 260-61.

14 Ibid., 261. Just as a "mixed" act, according to Aristotle, is judged to have been voluntary or not with regard to "the time of action," so too, according to Rabbinic law, a vow is judged to have been valid or not with regard to the time of the vowing (*meiikara*). Had the vower, at the time of the vowing, been clearheaded and knowledgeable, would he or she have made the vow? See R. Nissim b. Reuben Girondi (Ran) (d. 1376), bNedarim 21b s.v. *amar lei lo* and *kedu teheit*. See also R. Joseph Habiba, *Nimukei Yosef*, bNedarim 22b s.v. *amar raba amar rav nahman*. The Ran was the teacher of

the will" (*kiyum haratzon*): if it is unchanged (*kayam*), the vow remains valid; if it has changed, the vow is considered a mistake and annulled.[15] Repentance, argues Albo, is similar, for the penitent regrets his transgression, wishes it had never been committed, and undertakes not to do it again, all of which shows that his transgression was committed "by mistake" and "without knowledge or understanding." This conclusion, Albo declares, is consonant with Aristotle's opinion in the *Nicomachean Ethics*, "acts of reason (*sekhel*) are not subject to regret."[16] By drastically reducing the province of repentance to acts done "by mistake" or "without knowledge or understanding," Albo overtly, but questionably, applies to it the criterion of regret operative with regard to the annulment of vows or oaths. However, the analogy between repentance and the annulment of vows or oaths is limited and problematic. For example, penitents often repent of deeds done intentionally and knowledegably, but according to Jewish law, vows or oaths made intentionally and knowledegably are generally not annullable. As for Albo's concept of the "continuance of the will," it may be indebted to a discussion of vows by his older colleague, R. Zerahiah Halevi Saladin. Zerahiah's discussion was in turn indebted to Thomas Aquinas.[17]

Albo's notion of an intentional or voluntary act was recently summed up as follows: "On Albo's view, an identifying feature of an intentional

---

R. Hasdai Crescas (c. 1340-1410/11), Albo's teacher; and Habiba, Albo's older contemporary, was a student of the Ran and Crescas.

15 *Principles*, IV, 27 (4:261-62).

16 Ibid., 262. The statement attributed to the *Nicomachean Ethics* is not found there verbatim; but cf. IX, 4, 1166a29: the virtuous individual, whose true self is *nous*, "has no regret." R. Meir Alguades' 1305 Hebrew translation reads: "he does not repent of his deeds, for they [were carried out] with reason (*besekhel*) and are worthy to remain" (Aristotle, *Sefer Hamidot* [Berlin: 1790], 2:126b). Alguades translated from Robert Grosseteste's Latin translation (revised by William of Moerbeke). Cf. *Sententia Libri Ethicorum*, Aquinas' commentary on Aristotle's *Nicomachean Ethics*, IX, *lectio* 4: "since he always acts according to reason (*secundum rationem*), he does not easily have regret."

17 In his Sermon on Vows, Zerahiah expounded on the importance of the continuance of the will (*ratzon kayam*), arguing, like Aquinas, that a good reason for making a vow is that it causes the will to remain unchanged. See Zerahiah Halevi Saladin, *Derashot*, ed. Ari Ackerman (Beersheba: 2012), 131-32. Cf. Aquinas, *Summa Theologiae*, II-II, q. 88, a. 4. See Ackerman, "Zerahia Halevi Saladin and Thomas Aquinas on vows," *Journal of Jewish Thought and Philosophy* 19 (2011), 47-71. Zerahiah, like Albo and Joseph Habiba, was a student of Hasdai Crescas. Albo and Zerahiah both participated in the Disputation of Tortosa (1413-1414).

or voluntary act is that the agent, in performing it, wants it to remain in his or her biography."[18] Though this summation is basically correct, it would be more precise if rewritten as follows: On Albo's view, an identifying feature of an intentional or voluntary act is that the agent, in performing it **or in retrospect**, wants it to remain in his or her biography.

To conclude his Aristotelian discussion of repentance, Albo cites two talmudic passages to illustrate his views.

The first passage he quotes is from bYoma 86b. The text reads: "When is one a penitent (*baal teshuva*)? An illicit sexual encounter comes his way twice and the second time he escapes it. R. Judah says: 'at the same season, the same place, and with the same woman.'" Albo explains that the repetition of the same precise conditions that obtained at the time of the sin proves that the penitent truly regrets his sin, and sinned "by mistake" and "without knowledge or understanding."[19] Albo ignores the possibility that the penitent sinned intentionally, but subsequently had a change of heart. Indeed, Albo sums up his discussion of the talmudic passage by repeating his general rule: "One should not be punished for a transgression [that one regrets], as one should not be blamed for an act done by mistake and in ignorance."[20]

The second passage Albo quotes is from bKidushin 40b. The passage is an exegesis of Ezekiel 18:24; 33:13: "When the righteous one turns away from his righteousness and commits iniquity . . . ; for his trespass that he trespassed . . . he shall die." The Rabbis ask: why should this ex-righteous sinner not be treated as half meritorious and half guilty? The answer given is: the Prophet refers to someone "who regrets the former deeds." From this passage Albo learns that if one regrets doing a good act, it is "not deserving of praise or reward."[21]

Concluding the chapter, Albo comments: "Repentance (*teshuva*) benefits the sinner" by canceling his sin, "rendering it as if it had been done in error or unknowingly," and "by divine grace (*hesed*) turning it into a merit."[22] This final brief remark about divine grace is the chapter's sole departure from its Aristotelian framework. The comment, however, connects with a statement made by Albo in a previous chapter, according to which repentance is not based on reason (*sekhel*), but on "divine grace."[23]

18 Peter A. French, *War and Moral Dissonance* (Cambridge: 2011), 110.
19 *Principles*, IV, 27 (4:262-63).
20 Ibid.
21 Ibid., 263.
22 Ibid., 264.
23 Ibid., IV, 25 (4:222-23).

In the course of his attempt to resolve his "great difficulty," Albo in effect interprets the Hebrew concept of *teshuva* in light of the Greek notions of *metameleia* and *metanoia*, on the one hand, and in light of the talmudic laws of vows and oaths, on the other. Three times in the chapter Albo affirmed that *teshuva* pertains to transgressions committed "by mistake" and "in ignorance," that is, involuntarily. One might wonder how a learned sage like Albo could think of interpreting the Hebrew concept of *teshuva* in light of Aristotle's concept of regret, but one must admire his originality and resourcefulness in trying to do so. As for the "great difficulty," namely, how "mere words" can alter reality, this could be characterized as a philosophical problem borrowed from discussions of the efficacy of vows and oaths and imported into the discussion of repentance. Repentance, however, does not deal primarily with "words," but with a change of heart.

Assigning praise or blame

Aristotle observes that the ability to distinguish between voluntary and compulsory acts is important not only for philosophers, but also for legislators who must assign honors and punishments, for one is justly praised or blamed only for acts done voluntarily.[24] Albo, as we have seen, follows Aristotle's analysis closely. Like Aristotle, he holds that a voluntary act is characterized by will, choice, and knowledge; and like him, he holds that what is crucial is the individual's state of mind at "the time of action." However, as we also saw, Albo added the "continuance" test for deciding whether an act was voluntary or not: a past voluntary act can be considered voluntary in the present only if the agent continues to affirm it.

Albo's stipulation is a strange one. Counterexamples easily come to mind. A ruffian accosts a coward and demands her money; she complies. She then sees a therapist, and is cured of her cowardice. If stopped by a ruffian tomorrow, she will resist. She now disavows her past cowardice, but cannot deny that it was voluntary. Would Albo deny it? Another example. A man indulges in an illicit sexual encounter, which he enjoys immensely. He then hears Albo give a sermon, repents of his lascivious ways, and becomes pious. When he runs into the same woman in the same place and at the same season, he rejects her advances. He regrets his previous encounter with her, but cannot deny that it was voluntary. Would Albo? A third example. A woman

24 *Nicomachean Ethics*, III, 1, 1109b30-35.

gives money to beggars and is lauded for her generosity. She then reads some works on economics, becomes an avid capitalist, and stops giving charity. She regrets her previous generosity as foolish, but cannot deny that it was voluntary. Would Albo? A fourth example. The ruffian who robbed the cowardly woman is nabbed and brought before a judge. He argues for his acquittal, claiming that his act was involuntary. As proof, he swears that he no longer approves of robbery and regrets having robbed the woman. Were Albo the judge, would he acquit the ruffian?

Albo clearly thought his unusual test for deciding whether an act was voluntary or coerced was Aristotelian. We saw that he supports the test by invoking Aristotle, paraphrasing his stance as "acts of reason are not subject to regret." What Aristotle in fact argued, however, is that the virtuous individual, who is also the rational individual, does not regret his or her **rational** acts. As long as this individual remains rational, he or she should have no regrets about past rational behavior.[25] Yet even if Aristotle supposed that virtuous individuals are constant and unchanging, he did not hold this about unvirtuous individuals. He states that unvirtuous people have "strife in their soul," one part of their soul being pained by abstinence from bad deeds, and the other part pleased by it.[26] The behavior of such unvirtuous individuals is fickle and full of regret: a person might one day follow the pained part of his or her soul and another day follow the pleased part. A rational individual will regret an irrational act, but since the rational individual, qua rational individual, could not have carried out such an act voluntarily, it must be assumed that it was committed under coercion. Thus in a rational individual, regret is indeed a sign that the act in question was committed under duress, whereas in an ordinary individual, regret has no such significance.

In addition, Albo's test works reasonably well for acts that are involuntary due to ignorance (e.g., acts carried out on the basis of erroneous information) or coercion (e.g., acts carried out for fear of punishment). In such cases, one acted involuntarily at the time and the act presumably remains contrary to one's will. However, the test is not adequate for distinguishing voluntary from compulsory acts, since it does not take into consideration voluntary acts followed by a change of heart. But often, it is precisely such acts that are the focus of repentance.

25 Ibid., IX, 4, 1166a.
26 Ibid., IX, 9, 1166b20.

Mixed acts: voluntary or compulsory?

The two examples given by Aristotle and Albo of acts that are part voluntary and part compulsory, namely, one who does something base for fear of punishment by a tyrant, and sailors who throw their goods overboard in a threatening storm, clearly differ: one involves coercion by human agency and the other, compulsion caused by nature. However, with regard to the distinction between voluntary and involuntary, there does not seem to be a clear difference between the two examples for either Aristotle or Albo. In both examples, one acts involuntarily, doing something one would not ordinarily want to do, but at the same time, voluntarily, choosing to do the deed in order to avoid a greater evil. Both Aristotle and Albo consider such "mixed" acts to be primarily voluntary.

Both examples take on an additional dimension when a third party is involved. Thus, the tyrant may say, 'Rob X or I will punish you' or 'Kill X or I will punish you'; and the sailors may be forced to throw goods belonging to other passengers overboard, or may even be forced to throw other passengers overboard. Both Aristotle and Albo hold that individuals are responsible for their actions, and demand that one suffer pain or death rather than commit a heinous crime, such as killing X to appease a tyrant or throwing other passengers overboard, in order to save one's own life. Though coerced, these heinous crimes are, on their view, voluntary. Thus, in Aristotle's example, Alcmaeon is to be condemned for **voluntarily** murdering his mother.

Conversos

Albo was a young boy during the 1391 riots in which thousands of Spanish Jews were murdered by Christian mobs and about 150,000 were forcibly converted to Christianity. Reading Albo's comments on coerced acts, one wonders if he had in mind the **conversos**, who, in order to save their lives, outwardly converted to Christianity, though often secretly continued to observe Jewish rites. Albo, it will be recalled, sets down two propositions that are manifestly relevant to the conversos' situation. First, he argues that one is not blamed for acts committed involuntarily (*meihekhrah haones*), even though by choice and knowingly; for example, an act done in order to avoid punishment.[27] Second,

27 See above at n. 9.

he asserts that higher-order evil acts, for example, striking one's parent, rebelling against one's king, or rebelling against God, are considered voluntary, even if done for fear of threats, since one is expected to endure great pain rather than commit such acts.[28] The first proposition might be taken to indicate that Albo's attitude to the conversos was lenient or forgiving. The second proposition might be taken to indicate that his attitude to the conversos was harsh. In Hebrew, the common term for the conversos is "coerced ones" (*anusim*), from the term "*ones*," meaning coercion, the same term used in Albo's expression "*meihekhrah haones*," translated above as "involuntarily," but literally meaning "out of the necessity of coercion."[29] The distinguished decisor R. Isaac b. Sheshet Perfet (Ribash), (1326-1408), who himself became a converso in 1391 in Valencia, but escaped to Muslim Algiers where he resumed his Jewish identity and his rabbinical activity, ruled unequivocally: "One who converted out of coercion (*mitokh haones*) is still an Israelite, even if he worshipped idols and desecrated Sabbaths in public, for he did not do so except out of coercion"; and "the court does not punish him, for 'the Merciful One exempts the coerced' [bNedarim 27a]."[30]

The Jew threatened by Christian mobs would seem to be in the situation of the individual threatened by a tyrant or ruffian: in some cases one might be excused for converting under duress, but in others one might be required to choose death. Like the individual threatened by a tyrant or ruffian, the threatened Jew would presumably be expected to assess the situation, try to gauge the repercussions of conversion, and act accordingly.[31]

Postscript

Albo's discussion of repentance ranges over four chapters in part IV of the *Book of Principles*, namely, chapters 25-28. It is only in chapter 27 that he interprets the concept of repentance (*teshuva*) in terms of the

28 See above at n. 12.

29 On the lexical root *a-n-s*, see Ben-Menahem, n. 9 above, 5-6.

30 *Responsa Ribash*, #11; cf. #4.

31 Maimonides distinguishes, e.g., between a private situation, in which one may violate the law, and a public situation, in which one may not. See *Code*, Laws concerning the Fundamental Principles of the Torah 5:1-4. It has been argued that Albo's rejection of determinism (see *Principles*, IV, 5 [4:41-42]) was in part intended to reprove those conversos who saw their situation as fated or coerced. See Shira Weiss, Joseph Albo's Concept of Free Choice in his Philosophic Exegesis (PhD dissertation, Yeshiva University, 2013), 179-83.

Aristotelian notion of regret. In chapters 25, 26, and 28 (cf. also ch. 18), he presents the concept of repentance in a manner consonant with the rabbinical literature. He argues in those three chapters that repentance is a commandment "of great rank"; it is the only commandment that by itself allows one to achieve the true purpose of the Law, which is love of God and eternal life; it transforms sins into merits[32]; it cannot be explained by logic or justice, but only by divine grace and charity; it is necessary for all human beings, since no one is free of sin; and it was created before the creation of the world,[33] for without it the human race could not attain its purpose.[34]

Years ago I wrote an essay on Albo's theory of time. I found that his revolutionary concept of time as an "imagined flow" (*hameshekh hamedume*) was developed in a single well-crafted chapter (*Principles*, II, 18), but not mentioned elsewhere in the book, and, moreover, not supported by the book's occasional discussions of physics.[35] In another essay I wrote on Albo, this one on his theory of passionate love, I found that his brilliant definition of the Hebrew term "*heshek*" as reasonless love was developed in a single well-crafted chapter (*Principles*, III, 37), but not mentioned elsewhere in the book, and, moreover, not supported by his discussions of love in other chapters.[36] A similar phenomenon is manifest in the present discussion of Albo's concept of repentance. His uncommon Aristotelian interpretation of *teshuva* is presented in a single well-crafted chapter (*Principles*, IV, 27), but not mentioned elsewhere in the book, and, moreover, not supported by the other three chapters on the concept of repentance. Albo was an extraordinary philosophic homilist, not a systematic thinker.[37]

32 See bYoma 86b.

33 bPesahim 54a.

34 *Principles*, IV, 25 (4:220-26, 231-34); IV, 28 (4:267, 272). And see David Shatz, "Freedom, repentance and hardening of the hearts: Albo vs. Maimonides," *Faith and Philosophy* 14 (1997), 478-509.

35 "Albo's discussion of time," *JQR* 70 (1980), 210-38.

36 "Albo on the reasonlessness of true love," *Iyyun* 49 (2000), 83-86.

37 Dror Ehrlich makes an interesting attempt to argue that the contradictions in Albo's *Principles* are intentional and reflect his exoteric and esoteric doctrines. See Ehrlich, *The Thought of R. Joseph Albo: Esoteric Writing in the Late Middle Ages* (Hebrew), (Ramat-Gan: 2009), esp. 327 s.v. *teshuva*.

The Jewish Law Annual, Vol. XXI

Noahide Law and the Inclusiveness of Sexual Ethics: Between Roman Palestine and Sasanian Babylonia

Yishai Kiel*

1. **Introduction**
2. **Noahide Law: natural or positive?**
3. **Biblical foundations**
4. **The Sinaitic and Noahide codes of sexual conduct**
5. **The *sugya* in the Palestinian Talmud**
6. **The *sugya* in the Babylonian Talmud**
7. **The Zoroastrian doctrine of *xwēdōdah***
8. **Explaining the differences**
9. **Incest riddles**
10. **Zoroastrian connections**

1. Introduction

This article explores the talmudic treatment of the Noahide laws[1] of prohibited sexual partnerships – that is, the sexual prohibitions which the Rabbis deemed applicable to the conduct of non-Jews – and more broadly, Rabbinic stances on the question of the universality of sexual norms. The sexual prohibitions, which were part of the broader system of Noahide law, were set down by the Rabbis against the backdrop of

* Yishai Kiel is a lecturer and postdoctoral associate at Yale University's Program in Judaic Studies.

1 On Noahide law, see tAvoda Zara 9:4; bSanhedrin 56a-60a; Genesis Rabbah 16:6 (Theodor-Albeck edition, 149-51), and parallels. The secondary literature on the subject is vast, see, e.g., D. Novak, *The Image of the Non-Jew in Judaism: An Historical and Constructive Study of the Noahide Laws* (NY and Toronto: 1983); S.L. Stone, "Sinaitic and Noahide law: legal pluralism in Jewish law," 12 *Cardozo Law Review* (1991), 1157-214; N. Rakover, *Law and the Noahides: Law as a Universal Value* (Jerusalem: 1998); D. Steinmetz, *Punishment and Freedom: The Rabbinic Construction of Criminal Law* (Philadelphia: 2008), 20-39.

the Sinaitic laws of prohibited sexual partnerships that governed the conduct of Jews. Whereas the Sinaitic laws of prohibited sexual partnerships were deduced primarily from the prohibitions in Leviticus 18 and 20, the Noahide laws were either extrapolated from the levitical list or derived independently from pre-Mosaic legislation and narrative.

As I will show, comparing the Babylonian Talmud's discussion of Noahide sexual prohibitions to parallel accounts in Palestinian Rabbinic works reveals a profound and systematic difference (though not a dichotomy) between the Palestinian and Babylonian approaches to the inclusion of non-Jews in the levitical system of sexual ethics. The Palestinian sources tend to extend the levitical laws of prohibited sexual partnerships to non-Jews, thereby applying a nearly-universal (there are a few exceptions) standard of sexual morality; the Babylonian Talmud takes a particularistic approach, differentiating between Jews and non-Jews vis-à-vis accountability for sexual misconduct. On the Babylonian Rabbinic approach, the levitical sexual prohibitions apply only to Jews, whereas the sexual prohibitions governing non-Jews are derived from pre-Mosaic legislation and narrative. Consequently, the legal standards that apply to non-Jews are considerably more lenient, as non-Jews are essentially permitted to engage in a number of sexual partnerships that are prohibited to Jews.

It will further be shown that the divergent positions manifested in the Babylonian and Palestinian Rabbinic works reflect a fundamental difference in outlook between the two Rabbinic centers with respect to the status of non-Jews and the existence of universal standards of sexual ethics independent of positive law. Palestinian Rabbinic discourse is characterized by inclusive rhetoric, according to which the non-Jewish other is called to partake, in one form or another, in a shared space of holiness realized through sexual norms, whereas Babylonian Rabbinic discourse reflects a particularistic and exclusive rhetoric, which safeguards the boundaries of Israel as a sacred community vis-à-vis the levitical sexual norms, denying the non-Jewish other access to this sacred space. This differentiation largely supports recent studies on the image of the non-Jew in Palestinian and Babylonian representations of Rabbinic culture.[2]

2 See, e.g., J. Labendz, *Socratic Torah: Non-Jews in Rabbinic Intellectual Culture* (Oxford: 2013), 191-211; V. Noam, "Another look at the Rabbinic conception of Gentiles from the perspective of impurity laws," in B. Isaac and Y. Shahar (eds.), *Judaea-Palaestina, Babylon and Rome: Jews in Antiquity*, TSAJ 147

Alongside this legal–theoretical interpretation of the differences between the two Rabbinic centers in terms of natural and positive law, the study puts forward a contextual–cultural reading of the data. This reading situates the Palestinian Rabbinic approach in the context of Greco-Roman and Christian rhetoric, and the Babylonian Rabbinic approach in the context of the ambient Iranian culture. In particular, it focuses on the significance of Pahlavi (Middle Persian) literature for a more nuanced and contextual understanding of Babylonian Rabbinic discourse, by examining the Babylonian Talmud's treatment of the sexual prohibitions in light of the well-attested Zoroastrian doctrine of *xwēdōdah* (Av. *x^{v}aētuuadaθa*).[3] Although the original Avestan meaning of this term is somewhat unclear,[4] in the Pahlavi sources *xwēdōdah* is said

(Tübingen: 2012), 89-11; M. Lavee, "No boundaries to the demarcation of boundaries: the Babylonian Talmud's emphasis on demarcation of identity," in R. Nikolsky and T. Ilan (eds.), *Rabbinic Traditions between Palestine and Babylonia* (Leiden: 2014), 84-116.

3 On this Zoroastrian doctrine, see, e.g., J.S. Slotkin, "On a possible lack of incest regulations in Old Iran," *American Anthropologist* 49 (1947), 612-17; O. Bucci, "Il matrimonio fra consanguinei (Khvêtûkdâs) nella tradizione giuridica delle genti Iraniche," *Apollinaris* 51 (1978), 291-319; R.N. Frye, "Zoroastrian incest," in G. Gnoli and L. Lanciotti (eds.), *Orientalia Iosephi Tucci Memoriae Dicata*, Serie orientale Roma 56, 1 (Rome: 1985), 445-55; C. Herrenschmidt, "Le *xwētōdas* ou mariage 'incestueux' en Iran ancient," in P. Bonte (ed.), *Épouser au plus proche: inceste, prohibitions et stratégies matrimoniales autour de la Méditerranée*, Civilisations et Sociétés 89 (Paris: 1994), 113-25; M. Macuch, "Inzest im vorislamischen Iran," *Archaeologische Mitteilungen aus Iran* 24 (1991), 141-54; B. d'Arx, "Mystère du choix de la deuxième vertu: courte réflexion sur l'inceste à l'Iranienne," *Barbares et civilisés dans l'antiquité*, Cahiers Kubaba 7 (Paris: 2005), 248-65; A.V. Williams, *The Pahlavi Rivāyat accompanying the Dādestān ī Dēnīg*, Royal Danish Academy of Sciences and Letters: Historisk-filosofiske Meddelelser 60, 1-2 (Copenhagen: 1990), 2:126-32.

4 The Avesta does not provide explicit details about the meaning and semantic range of the term *x^{v}aētuuadaθa*, and the Avestan passages that mention the term are, for the most part, ambiguous and enigmatic. The term's meaning in the Old and Young Avestan texts is discussed in Prods Oktor Skjærvø, "Next-of-kin marriages in Zoroastrianism," *Encyclopaedia Iranica*, online edition, 2013, available at http://www.iranicaonline.org/articles/marriage-next-of-kin. At least as far as the Young Avestan texts are concerned, important information can be gleaned from juxtaposing the Zoroastrian material with Greco-Roman reports of next-of-kin marriages among the Persians, which go back to the fifth century BCE. See W.S. Fox and R.E.K. Pemberton, *Passages in Greek and Latin Literature relating to Zoroaster and Zoroastrianism* (Bombay: 1929), 1-145; Frye, n. 3 above, 447-49;

to refer to endogamous marital unions, especially between father and daughter, mother and son, and brother and sister, and is considered one of the most pious and laudable deeds in the Zoroastrian tradition.[5]

Adducing the Greco-Roman and Christian writings on incest, which generally promote universal standards of sexual conduct[6] and explicitly condemn Iranian deviation from these norms, as we will see below, sheds light on the Palestinian Rabbinic advocacy of inclusive standards of sexual ethics. On the other hand, we can shed light on the Babylonian Talmud's espousal of exclusive, particularistic sexual norms, and relatively tolerant approach to non-Jewish incest, by adducing the Zoroastrian practice of *xwēdōdah* and the related doctrine of moral relativism expressed in the Pahlavi literature. I will argue that the Babylonian Rabbinic discussion of Noahide sexual prohibitions invokes certain legal and theological considerations found in the Pahlavi discourse.

While it is likely that the Babylonian Rabbis witnessed the practice of next-of-kin marriages, and that this in turn influenced their approach to doctrinal issues pertaining to incestuous unions, the Babylonian Talmud does not simply respond to the practice of next-of-kin marriages during the Sasanian period.[7] I contend, rather, that the Babylonian Talmud actually engages with important strands of contemporary

---

A. de Jong, *Traditions of the Magi: Zoroastrianism in Greek and Latin Literature*, Religions in the Greco-Roman World 133 (Leiden: 1997), 424-32; P. Vasunia, *Zarathushtra and the Religion of Ancient Iran: The Greek and Latin Sources in Translation* (Mumbai: 2008), 173-78. Skjærvø notes that among the "earliest Greek references to non-royal incest are [remarks] made by Xanthus of Lydia in his *Magica*, quoted by Clement of Alexandria, that the Magi have sex (*coire*) with their mothers, daughters, and sisters (*Stromata* 3.2.11.1; Fox and Pemberton, 2)... and [by] Ctesias of Cnidus about a brother–sister marriage (... Fox and Pemberton, 124)."

5 The Pahlavi sources on *xwēdōdah* will be cited below.

6 On Christian and Islamic interpretations of incest regulations (in Leviticus, the Quran and Canon law) as universally binding, see E. Archibald, *Incest and the Medieval Imagination* (Oxford: 2001), 9-52; G.J. van Gelder, *Close Relationships: Incest and Inbreeding in Classical Arabic Literature* (London: 2005), 78-121. In Roman law, incest regulations are similarly referred to either in terms of *ius gentium* or in terms of natural law. See, e.g., S. Treggiari, *Roman Marriage: Iusti Coniuges from the Time of Cicero to the Time of Ulpian* (Oxford: 1991), 39; M. Satlow, *Tasting the Dish: Rabbinic Rhetorics of Sexuality*, Brown Judaic Studies 303 (Atlanta: 1995), 51-52.

7 On the extent of the actual practice of next-of-kin marriages before and during the Sasanian period, see M. Mitterauer, "The customs of the Magians: the problem of incest in historical societies," in R. Porter and M. Teich

Zoroastrian discourse on *xwēdōdah*, discourse preserved in the Pahlavi corpus.

To be sure, the Babylonian Rabbis had no wish, nor were they in a position, to challenge the sexual restrictions listed in Leviticus 18 and 20 (which strictly forbid intercourse between first-degree relatives) insofar as Jewish norms were concerned.[8] The prohibitions against incest and certain other sexual unions were widely accepted by the post-biblical traditions, Rabbinic and non-Rabbinic alike, and could hardly have been challenged by the Babylonian Rabbis. Nevertheless, I will demonstrate that alongside the prohibitions that are applied to Jews, the Babylonian Talmud voices novel, often subversive stances on incestuous relations among non-Jews, tolerating such relations to varying degrees. Unlike other non-Zoroastrian discussions of incest, which, for the most part, are polemical and critical, the Babylonian Talmud's approach to next-of-kin partnerships is nuanced and complex. Although occasionally polemical,[9] the discussion in the Babylonian Talmud is far less critical of the practice of incestuous unions among non-Jews, and even seems to engage with certain key rhetorical and doctrinal arguments made in the Pahlavi writings.

2. Noahide Law: natural or positive?

Scholars have long debated whether, and to what extent, the Rabbis presuppose natural law, that is, the existence of moral truths grounded in nature – either in the natural world or in human nature – that are rationally accessible and universally binding.[10] The answer to this question is often sought in the realm of Rabbinic speculation about legal arenas distinct from the Mosaic law, and specifically, the realms of pre-Sinaitic

(eds.), *Sexual Knowledge, Sexual Science: The History of Attitudes to Sexuality* (Cambridge: 1994), 235-36.

8 Mother–son and brother–sister sexual relations are clearly forbidden in the levitical verses, while the prohibition against father–daughter relations is either taken for granted, or implicit in the verses. See J. Milgrom, *Leviticus 17-22: A New Translation with Introduction and Commentary*, Anchor Bible 3A (NY: 2000), 1527-30; B.J. Schwartz, *The Holiness Legislation: Studies in the Priestly Code* (Hebrew), (Jerusalem: 1999), 137-44.

9 See Y. Kiel, "Confessing incest to a rabbi: a talmudic story in its Zoroastrian context," *Harvard Theological Review* 107 (2014), 401-24.

10 The literature on the subject is vast, see, e.g., D. Novak, *Natural Law in Judaism* (Cambridge: 1998); A. Sagi, "Natural law and halakha–a critical analysis," 13 *Jewish Law Annual* (2000), 147-96.

normativity[11] – the law prior to the Sinaitic revelation that was partially or fully adopted by pre-Mosaic biblical figures – and the Rabbinic construction of Noahide law.

David Novak, one of the leading theorists in this field, argues that the talmudic construction of Noahide law represents a Rabbinic version of a moral theory of natural law, mainly because the Noahide laws seem to represent rational moral principles that the Rabbis believed to be universally binding. He dismisses the Rabbinic derivation of the Noahide laws from Scripture (as opposed to nature) as mere allusions to positive law, and maintains that the Noahide laws function more like general, speculative, and non-prescriptive principles derived from nature by moral reasoning.[12]

Devora Steinmetz has significantly refined the natural law interpretation of the Noahide code, by demonstrating that the Babylonian Rabbinic discussion of the Noahide laws reflects two alternative traditions regarding the content and nature of the prohibitions. Aside from content-related differences, she observes that one talmudic tradition grounds the Noahide laws in divine legislation and explicit commandments given to Adam, while a second tradition links the Noahide laws to non-legal verses pertaining to the Noah narrative, and defines the prohibited acts as destructive violations of the natural order.[13] Steinmetz further maintains that the second tradition represents a classical view of natural law, according to which there are normative ethical principles that are essentially derivable from the natural order. Interestingly, however, rather than maintaining that the first tradition corresponds to a positive-law conception of Noahide law, she defines this tradition in terms of present-day conceptions of natural law. Despite the use of command terminology and exegetical derivation from Scripture, Steinmetz argues that the Noahide laws of the first tradition are connected to the origins of human society and thus not entirely dependent on positive legislation.[14]

Steinmetz situates the divide between the naturalistic Noahide law and the positive Sinaitic law in the status of sexual partnerships

11 On pre-Mosaic normativity, see Steven R. Wilf, *The Law before the Law* (Lanham MD: 2008).

12 Novak, n. 10 above, 149-54.

13 Steinmetz, n. 1 above, 26-30.

14 Ibid., 31-33.

between siblings, which are prohibited to Jews but permissible to non-Jews.[15] Since incest between siblings is perceived as essential for the beginning of human society (how else could humanity have evolved from a single couple?), from a natural law perspective there is nothing wrong with such relations. Hence within the province of Noahide law, there is no prohibition against brother–sister relations. For those who are commanded by Sinaitic law to eschew sexual unions between siblings, however, they are indeed prohibited.[16]

The conceptualization of Noahide law in terms of natural law theory has been critiqued, most recently by Christine Hayes, who reaffirms the positive nature of Noahide law, deeming it "every bit as particular as Jewish law itself."[17] The Rabbinic derivation of the Noahide laws from Scripture cannot be a mere veneer for natural principles, since the hermeneutic mechanism chosen by the Rabbis reveals something of the prescriptive nature of these laws and their link to authoritative command and revelation. Hayes further stresses that the Noahide laws are variable and unstable, and do not apply universally.[18] Not only are there significant disagreements in the Rabbinic texts regarding the content of Noahide law, but the standards of criminal liability and punitive

15 Ibid., 40-52. Below, we will see that this characterization is apt vis-à-vis the Babylonian Talmud's outlook, but does not reflect the Palestinian Rabbinic discourse.

16 Ibid., 50-51.

17 C. Hayes, *What's So Divine about Divine Law? Ancient Perspectives* (Princeton: 2015), 326-70. I would like to thank Hayes for generously sharing her unpublished work with me. See also Wilf, n. 11 above, 62.

18 While Hayes acknowledges the existence of two alternative theories of Noahide law in the Babylonian Rabbinic tradition, as pointed out by Steinmetz, she contends that the discussion is not "genuinely dialogical," inasmuch as the second tradition, which grounds Noahide law in the natural order, is not considered a real alternative. Not only does the talmudic discussion privilege the first tradition, but certain elements of the second tradition are reinterpreted and revised so as to make them consistent with the dominant position, which views the Noahide laws as commanded. Furthermore, Hayes maintains, contra Steinmetz, that the dominant first tradition conceives of Noahide law as revealed, commanded, and accessible through Rabbinic exegesis, not as a set of rational principles inherent in human nature. In other words, the dominant Rabbinic perception of Noahide law takes it to be positive law: its norms, like those of Mosaic law, were imparted to the nations via divine legislation.

measures for crimes that fall under the Noahide legislation differ for Jews and non-Jews.[19]

Although I agree that the differential application of certain rules of Noahide law highlights certain particularistic features of this system, and the fact that it is a system of positive law, this does not necessarily undermine the universality (or at least inclusiveness) of Noahide law. As we will see, despite such disparities, the Noahide system (in its Palestinian representation) reflects a tendency to standardize and systematize the observance of various ethical principles, and to bridge the gap between Jews and non-Jews.

I contend that characterization of the Noahide system in terms of universality and particularism should be further nuanced by attending to its Palestinian and Babylonian expressions. As we will see, the discussions in the Babylonian Talmud and Palestinian Rabbinic works manifest significantly different, though not completely dichotomous, approaches to the standardization of ethical conduct. We will see that, at least with respect to the Noahide law's sexual prohibitions, the Palestinian sources tend to apply inclusive and nearly universal standards of sexual behavior to Jews and non-Jews alike (with very few exceptions), whereas the Babylonian Talmud exhibits a distinctly particularistic approach that gives rise to fundamental differences between Jewish and non-Jewish norms.

All Rabbinic accounts are in agreement that Noahide law encompasses norms pertaining to sexual conduct, and that there are at least some differences between the norms governing Jews and non-Jews; in this sense, the laws are not universal. That there are differences between the sexual norms that apply to Jews and non-Jews is not a novel notion introduced by the Babylonian Talmud, as such differences are already attested in Palestinian Rabbinic works. Thus, for example, tAvoda Zara 9:4 asserts that sexual relations with a betrothed woman are forbidden to Jews but permitted to non-Jews, and Sifre Deuteronomy 76 (Finkelstein edition, 141-42) holds that relations with a beautiful war captive are permitted to Jews but not non-Jews. Notwithstanding this shared characteristic of Rabbinic writings – namely, disparities between sexual

19 Thus, e.g., the mode of punishment for idolatry and blasphemy differs for Jews and non-Jews (Steinmetz, n. 1 above, 33-34). As for substantive (as opposed to punitive) legal differences, tAvoda Zara 9:4 maintains that a Jew is not liable for murder, theft, or robbery when the victim is a non-Jew, whereas a non-Jew in the converse situation is liable.

norms applicable to Jews and those applicable to non-Jews – we will see that the Palestinian Rabbinic discussions of the Noahide laws of sexual misconduct seek to extend the levitical prohibitions to non-Jews and reduce the gap between the ethical standards governing Jews and those governing non-Jews. By contrast, the Babylonian Talmud attempts to intensify the normative gap between Jews and non-Jews by 'othering' the sexual norms of non-Jews, for example, by tolerating incestuous relationships between non-Jews even within the nuclear family, though these unions are explicitly prohibited by the levitical statutes.

Before turning to the Rabbinic treatment of the Noahide laws of prohibited sexual partnerships, a brief discussion of the biblical material is in order. This will enable us to see how, in their divergent constructions of the Noahide and Sinaitic systems of sexual prohibitions, the Rabbis of Palestine and Babylonia utilized different discursive and exegetical possibilities inherent in the biblical text. Specifically, they adduced, on the one hand, the sharp contrast between the sexual conduct of the Israelites and that of the Canaanites and Egyptians, and on the other, the relationship between the levitical lists of sexual abominations and pre-Mosaic normativity.

3. Biblical foundations

The Holiness legislation (H), the redaction of which is generally assumed to postdate the composition of P,[20] contains two separate lists of sexual prohibitions, one in Leviticus 18 and the other in Leviticus 20.[21] The prohibitions listed in Leviticus 18 are mainly formulated as

20 The main components of the Pentateuch's priestly writings are the Priestly source (P) and the Holiness legislation (H). Scholarship on the date and provenance of P and H is extensive; see, e.g., M. Paran, *Forms of the Priestly Style in the Pentateuch: Patterns, Linguistic Usages, Syntactic Structures* (Hebrew), (Jerusalem: 1989), 7-11; J. Milgrom, *Leviticus 1-16: A New Translation with Introduction and Commentary*, Anchor Bible 3 (NY: 1991), 1-67; idem, n. 8 above, 1361-64; I. Knohl, *The Sanctuary of Silence: A Study of the Priestly Strata in the Pentateuch* (Hebrew), (Jerusalem: 1992), 11-16; B.J. Schwartz, "Introduction: The strata of the priestly writings and the revised relative dating of P and H," in S. Shectman and Joel S. Baden (eds.), *The Strata of the Priestly Writings: Contemporary Debate and Future Directions* (Zurich: 2009), 1-12; C. Nihan, *From Priestly Torah to Pentateuch: A Study in the Composition of the Book of Leviticus*, Forschungen zum Alten Testament 2, 25 (Tübingen: 2007), 215-31, 379-94.

21 A third and more concise list appears in Deuteronomy 27:2-23.

imperatives ("Thou shalt not uncover the nakedness of . . ."), whereas those listed in Leviticus 20 are formulated casuistically ("If a man takes/ lies with . . ."). Traditional and critical commentators alike have long attempted to uncover the nature of the relationship between the two lists. One of the exegetical explanations for this reiteration is that Leviticus 18 lists sexual prohibitions, whereas Leviticus 20 lists punishments for the very acts prohibited in Leviticus 18. This suggested connection is expressed in numerous Rabbinic texts, where, regarding a prohibited act, a verse from Leviticus 18 is invoked as a prooftext for the admonition against that act, whereas the parallel verse from Leviticus 20 serves as a prooftext for the punishment incurred.[22]

> "The man who lies with his father's wife has uncovered his father's nakedness; both of them shall be put to death; their blood is upon them" (Lev. 20:11). . . . We have learned about the punishment, but we have not learned about the prohibition. For that reason it is written: "You shall not uncover the nakedness of your father and the nakedness of your mother" (Lev. 18:7).[23]

Not unlike the rabbis, several critical commentators have argued that the two lists are complementary and were probably issued by the same group of priestly authors. Baruch Schwartz has convincingly demonstrated, however, that the differences between the two lists are highly significant, and that it is therefore likely the lists were issued by different groups of priests.[24] Twelve of the prohibitions mentioned in Leviticus 18 are repeated in Leviticus 20, but five prohibitions are absent from the latter. Moreover, Leviticus 18 is not dependent on the punishments set down in Leviticus 20, as it specifies not only prohibitions, but also a collective punishment, exile – the land will "vomit out" its inhabitants (18:28) – and an individual punishment, divine extirpation (Lev. 18:29). While the prohibitions in Leviticus 20 are based on the idea of holiness – קדש (*k-d-sh*) – this lexical root is completely absent

22 It is an established talmudic principle that "the scriptural text does not punish without having issued an admonition" (bZevahim 106b; bYoma 81a; bKeritot 3b; bSanhedrin 56b). See the discussion in I.Z. Gilat, "Exegetical creativity in interpreting the biblical laws on capital offenses," 20 *Jewish Law Annual* (2013), 46-47.

23 Sifra, Mekhilta de-arayot 9-12 (Vatican 66; cf. Weiss edition, 92b); see also bSanhedrin 54a; bMakot 5b; jSanhedrin 7:6 (33b).

24 Schwartz, n. 8 above, 137-44. Cf. H. Schultz, *Das Todesrecht im Alten Testament*, BZAW 114 (Berlin: 1969), 130. Milgrom 2000, n. 8 above, 1765-68, provides a useful summary of both positions.

from Leviticus 18. Instead, Leviticus 18 invokes the notion that certain "abominations" (*toevot*) cause the land to vomit out its inhabitants. Many other differences in content, language, and style likewise lead to the conclusion that the lists in Leviticus 18 and 20 comprise two distinct priestly versions of the sexual prohibitions.[25]

Whatever the relationship between the lists, the purpose of the levitical account of the sexual prohibitions, when examined as a whole, is to define and safeguard the holiness of Israel (Lev. 20), in contradistinction to the abominations that characterize the conduct of the Egyptians and Canaanites (Lev. 18:3, 24, 27). It would seem, however, that two different construals of the levitical contrast between the holiness of Israel and the abominations practiced by the surrounding nations are plausible, depending on whether Israel's holiness is deemed to be ascribed or achieved.[26] On the one hand, the biblical contrast can be construed as suggesting, though this is not patently manifest in the text, that Israel has an inherent holiness which renders it ontologically distinct from the surrounding nations, whose conduct is abominable.[27] On the other hand, it follows logically from the biblical account that, seeing as the Canaanites and the Egyptians were punished by God for their sexual abominations (Lev. 18:25, 27), they are, at least in principle, governed by the same prohibitions and moral restrictions that govern the Israelites. On this reasoning, had the Canaanites followed these rules, they would have been able to remain in the land of Canaan. There is nothing inherent, therefore, about Israel's holiness; rather, the Israelites are enjoined to strive for a state of achieved holiness. Accordingly, the

25 On efforts to pin down the relationship between the lists, see Schwartz, ibid., 143-44.

26 On this distinction, see, e.g., Knohl, n. 20 above, 177-80; N. Koltun-Fromm, *Hermeneutics of Holiness: Ancient Jewish and Christian Notions of Sexuality and Religious Community* (Oxford: 2010), 31-51; M. Himmelfarb, *A Kingdom of Priests: Ancestry and Merit in Ancient Judaism* (Philadelphia: 2006).

27 This ideology reaches its fullest biblical development in Ezra-Nehemiah, in the doctrine of the holy seed, which underscores the ontological and genealogical differentiation between Jews and non-Jews. H, on the other hand, focuses on the moral shortcomings of the seven nations, and does not explicitly address their lack of ascribed holiness. In terms of the reception of the biblical text, however, it would seem that several ancient exegetes interpreted the seven nations' sexual abominations as reflecting an inherent inability to reach a state of holiness. See S. Olyan, *Rites and Rank: Hierarchy in Biblical Representations of Cult* (Princeton: 2000); C. Hayes, *Gentile Impurities and Jewish Identities* (Oxford: 2002).

sexual prohibitions, like various other religious and moral precepts in the Holiness legislation, are applied inclusively (although not universally, since the laws in H are connected to the land and obligate only its inhabitants, Israelite and non-Israelite alike). In what follows, I will argue that these alternative interpretations of the nature of Israel's holiness – ascribed or achieved – and the applicability of the levitical prohibitions to other nations, underlie the differences between the Palestinian and Babylonian Rabbinic discourses on the Noahide laws of sexual conduct.

Despite the Bible's explicit claim that the Egyptians and Canaanites are guilty of abominable sexual misconduct,[28] it is widely acknowledged that this accusation is fictitious, and serves rhetorical purposes only. Recent studies have concluded that there is no extra-biblical evidence whatsoever to support the existence of widespread incest among the Canaanites and/or the Egyptians. With the exception of royal incest, which was practiced by the Egyptians kings to preserve the royal lineage, there is no evidence of incest or other forms of sexual depravity from ancient Egypt. We have no extant law codes from Canaan, but the Mesopotamian and Hittite laws supply ample evidence that fornication, incest, homosexuality, and bestiality were criminalized and punished, and it is reasonable to assume that the Canaanites were no different from their neighbors in this regard.[29] The historical inaccuracy of the biblical accusations aside, it

28 Leviticus 18:24, 20:23. A negative view of the surrounding nations, who are depicted as guilty of illicit sexual unions and promiscuity, is also found in Genesis 9:22-27, 19:4-9, 19:30-38, 39:7-20; Ezekiel 16:26, 23:19-20. In other places, however, we find the view that the Philistines and the Egyptians were careful not to commit adultery, see Genesis 12:10-13, 20:2, 20:11, 26:7. On this internal biblical discrepancy, see Schwartz, n. 8 above, 157-60.

29 Schwartz, ibid. In the past, scholars sought to corroborate the biblical charges of Egyptian and Canaanite sexual misconduct by adducing ancient Near Eastern mythic accounts of incest among gods. The fact of the matter, however, is that the same cultures that tell these stories about godly incest explicitly forbid incest among humans, and several ancient Near Eastern law codes set down sexual restrictions similar to those in the Hebrew Bible. In light of this, the fanciful notion of ritual fornication that supposedly existed among the Canaanites has been largely abandoned in the scholarly literature. See Schwartz, 155-62; T. Frymer-Kensky, *In the Wake of the Goddesses: Women, Culture, and the Biblical Transformation of Pagan Myth* (NY: 1992), 199-202. For Hittite parallels, see W.H. Pickett, The Meaning and Function of T'B/TO'EVAH in the Hebrew Bible (PhD dissertation, Hebrew Union College, 1985), 131-50.

seems clear that the depiction of the reprehensible sexual conduct of the Egyptians and Canaanites is indeed primarily rhetorical, allowing Israel's holiness to be defined against the foil of the sexually-promiscuous other.

In addition to the priestly lists of sexual prohibitions, the Bible contains several stories involving incest, which are largely at odds with the levitical prohibitions. In violation of the law forbidding marriage to one's half-sister (Lev. 18:19, 20:17; Deut. 27:22), Abram claims that Sarai, his wife, is his father's daughter from a woman other than his mother (Gen. 20:12). Tamar, who appeals to her half-brother Amnon not to rape her, insists that David, their father, would not deny her to him in marriage (2 Sam. 13:13). These sources clearly see nothing prohibited, and no moral problem, in marrying a half-sister from the same father. While the levitical legislators forbid marriage to one's aunt (Lev. 18:12-14, 20:19-20), the Bible relates that Amram married his aunt Jochebed, who bore him Moses and Aaron (Exod. 6:20). Similarly, H forbids marriage to the sister of one's wife while that wife is still alive (Lev. 18:18), but Jacob is said to have been married to Leah and Rachel at one and the same time (Gen. 29:21-30).[30]

In what follows, we will see that these biblical 'violations' of the levitical statutes were creatively utilized by the Rabbis, in both Palestine and Babylonia, in their attempt to reconfigure the system of Noahide laws of sexual prohibitions in light of the Sinaitic regulations. My account will highlight links between the Palestinian Rabbinic account of the Noahide laws and Greco-Roman rhetoric regarding incest, on the one hand, and between the Babylonian Rabbinic account and the Pahlavi rhetoric, on the other hand.

4. The Sinaitic and Noahide codes of sexual conduct

For the most part, the Rabbinic discussion of sexual prohibitions reflects the content of the biblical system.[31] Though the Rabbis introduced the

30 B.A. Levine, *Leviticus, The JPS Torah Commentary* (Philadelphia: 1989), 253-54. Similarly, no moral critique is voiced in the Genesis account of Lot's seduction by his daughters after the destruction of Sodom (Gen. 19: 30–8), though later we learn that their descendants, the Moabites and Ammonites, are excluded from the congregation of the Lord (Deut. 23:3).

31 Aharon Shemesh argues that the mishnaic lists of those liable to the death penalty (mSanhedrin 7:4) and those liable to divine extirpation (*karet*) (mKritot 1:1), which enumerate and categorize the sexual prohibitions,

innovative category of *isur mitzva* or *shniyot laarayot*[32] – extensions of the biblical prohibitions that are meant to safeguard and protect these prohibitions – their discussion of the levitical prohibitions generally mirrors the biblical account. Moreover, the Rabbis, like the priestly legislators, constructed detailed lists sorting the sexual prohibitions and stipulating their relative severity and the penalties incurred for their violation.[33]

---

essentially accord with the levitical lists; see his *Punishments and Sins: From Scripture to the Rabbis* (Hebrew), (Jerusalem: 2003), 113. Granted, the list of those liable to the sanction of flogging (mMakot 3:1), which is applied to all sexual transgressors who are not liable to the death penalty, is entirely a Rabbinic innovation (Shemesh, 178). But the discontinuity associated with the punishment of flogging is not related to sexual offenses in particular, as the Rabbis apply this sanction to other prohibitions as well.

32 See, e.g., mJebamot 2:3-4; tJebamot 3:1, 6:4-5; jJebamot 2:3 (3d); bJebamot 20a-b; bKetubot 35b-36a; bSanhedrin 53a-b. And see the discussion in Satlow, n. 6 above, 44-52.

33 Shemesh (n. 31 above, 101-107) observes that the list of the thirty-six transgressors who are liable to divine extirpation (*karet*) according to mKritot 1:1 is probably the original Rabbinic list, on which the other mishnaic lists depend. These include the lists of transgressors liable to the death penalty and those liable to the sanction of flogging (mSanhedrin 7:4; mMakot 3:1). The first half of the list in mKritot 1:1 covers sins involving sexual violations, the second covers all the other prohibitions. The list is structured according to a clear taxonomy. The Mishnah first addresses sexual transgressors who are liable to death by stoning (a man who has relations with his mother, his father's wife, his daughter-in-law; homosexuality; a man who has relations with an animal; a woman who has relations with an animal). It then lists sexual transgressors who are liable to death by burning (one who has relations with a woman and her daughter); then sexual transgressors who are liable to death by strangling (one who has relations with a married woman). The Mishnah then lists sexual transgressors who are liable to divine extirpation (*karet*) but not to death imposed by the court (one who has relations with his sister, his father's sister, his mother's sister, his wife's sister, his brother's wife, the wife of his father's brother, a menstruant). Lastly, the Mishnah addresses other sins that do not involve sexual violations, see Shemesh, 102.

Interestingly, mMakot 3:1 enumerates seven sexual transgressors who are not liable to the death penalty, while the numerous transgressions associated with eating non-kosher food are all grouped together under the same category of "one who eats carrion, or unfit flesh (*treifot*), or detestable creatures, or creeping things" (mMakot 3:2). This appears to highlight the importance the Mishnah ascribes to classifying the sexual prohibitions in particular.

Significantly, the levitical and Rabbinic discussions of sexual prohibitions have another important feature in common: both seem to define the sexual prohibitions against the backdrop of a reconstructed 'other.' In the Bible, Israel's sexual holiness is contrasted to the sexual abominations practiced by the Canaanites and Egyptians, and in the Rabbinic literature, the Sinaitic legislation is paralleled by a system of sexual regulations that the Rabbis applied to non-Jews. The inherent connection between the Noahide sexual regulations and the biblical portrayal of the Canaanites and Egyptians is, in fact, explicitly acknowledged by the Rabbis.[34]

The Rabbinic contrast between the Sinaitic and Noahide codes of sexual behavior is also informed by the tension manifest in Scripture between the levitical lists of sexual abominations and various narratives concerning pre-Mosaic figures, which casually depict sexual conduct that is explicitly prohibited by the priestly legislators. Indeed, we will see that the divergent Rabbinic construals of the Noahide laws of sexual misconduct hinge on the derivation of these norms from either the levitical lists or the pre-Mosaic narratives.

As I will demonstrate, the Rabbinic classification of the specific sexual unions prohibited to non-Jews was by no means unanimous. We will see that the Babylonian Talmud systematically minimizes the sexual prohibitions applying to non-Jews, tolerating sexual intercourse even within the nuclear family, whereas the Palestinian Rabbinic works present a much more stringent position with regard to sexual restrictions on non-Jews, and generally prohibit sexual intercourse within the nuclear family.

Moreover, the Babylonian Talmud and the Palestinian Rabbinic works exhibit divergent approaches to Noahide law and the possibility of its derivation from Sinaitic law. For the most part, the Palestinian Rabbinic works reflect the idea that the laws of sexual misconduct are 'universal' in the sense that they apply to Jews and non-Jews equally (with only a few exceptions). They take the Noahide rules to be directly derivable from the levitical lists of sexual prohibitions, and as a result,

34 The Palestinian Talmud, e.g., puts forward the following argument: "R. Hila states in the name of R. Shimon b. Lakish: 'It is because of these abominations that the Lord your God is driving them out before you' (Deut. 18:12) – this serves to teach us that the Holy One, blessed be He, does not punish unless He first issued an admonition [hence we see that non-Jews are admonished not to have sexual relations with their sisters]" (jJebamot 11:2 [12a]).

diminish the differences between the Sinaitic and Noahide standards of sexual conduct. The Babylonian Talmud, on the other hand, increases the gap between the Noahide and Sinaitic regulations by detaching the Noahide laws from the levitical regulations and promoting relatively lenient standards, derived from pre-Mosaic norms, of sexual conduct among non-Jews.

The disparity between the Babylonian Rabbinic particularism and the Palestinian Rabbinic inclusiveness can be understood in terms of ascribed vs. achieved holiness. In line with the notion of achieved holiness, the Palestinian sources invoke the biblical punishment meted out to the Canaanites and the Egyptians to emphasize that non-Jews are essentially governed by the same levitical laws of sexual conduct that govern Jews. Jews and non-Jews alike should aspire to a state of holiness by avoiding the levitical abominations. By contrast, the Babylonian Talmud understands Israel's holiness as ascribed, and therefore contends that the levitical prohibitions apply only to Jews, to maintain their inherent state of holiness.

If the nature of Israel's holiness is at stake, then the particularistic construal of sexual standards in the Babylonian Talmud does not necessarily reflect a positive-law approach to the laws of sexual conduct that rejects naturalistic categories. On the contrary, the Babylonian position appears to reflect some sort of 'ontological particularism,' according to which the Jewish people's holiness (and the related standards of sexual conduct) is ascribed and thus inherent. Non-Jews lack this 'ontological' holiness, and hence do not have to abide by the levitical standards of sexual conduct.

The Babylonian Talmud's particularistic approach to the prohibitions can, however, also be understood as ensuing from a positive-law approach, on which the standards of sexual conduct for Jews and non-Jews reflect no underlying 'ontological' difference, but rather the simple fact that different laws were set down for each group, and the levitical prohibitions apply only to Jews. As we will see, this interpretation of the Babylonian position is informed by the Pahlavi discourse on *xwēdōdah*, especially its rhetorical justification in terms of moral and cultural relativism.

A detailed comparison of the Babylonian Talmud's account of the Noahide sexual prohibitions with Palestinian Rabbinic parallels reveals a distinctive Babylonian approach to non-Jewish incestuous practices, an approach that can be fully understood only against the backdrop of the contemporaneous Iranian culture. Moreover, the Babylonian discourse seems to indicate that the Babylonian Rabbis sought to engage, intellectually, with the Zoroastrian practice and doctrine of *xwēdōdah*. To grasp the novelty of the Babylonian Talmud's discussion, however, we must first consider the discussions in the Palestinian Talmud and other Palestinian Rabbinic works. Comparing the perspectives of the two Rabbinic centers will enable us to better appreciate the distinctive and innovative aspects of the Babylonian Rabbinic discussion,[35] as well as its broader Iranian underpinnings.

5. The *sugya* in the Palestinian Talmud

Both Talmuds record a dispute between prominent Tannaitic authorities regarding the permissibility of sexual partnerships between siblings. We will see that the example of sexual unions between siblings, adduced by Steinmetz to argue for an essential divide between Sinaitic law, which she sees as positive, and Noahide law, which she sees as natural, reflects only the Babylonian account of the Tannaitic dispute. The Babylonian account deems sibling incest completely or partially permissible for non-Jews, but prohibited to Jews. The Palestinian Talmud, on the other hand, records a fundamentally different version of the dispute, according to which sibling incest is either completely prohibited to non-Jews, or at least severely restricted, thus bridging the gap between Sinaitic and Noahide law.

The Tannaitic dispute concerns the legal status of non-Jews and converts to Judaism as regards their obligation to refrain from certain

35 The question of the literary relationship between the Talmuds has been long debated, and cannot be systematically addressed here. Suffice it to say, however, that a careful study of the differences between the Babylonian and Palestinian accounts of the Noahide laws is crucial for pinpointing the material in the Babylonian Talmud that is novel and distinctively Babylonian. On the different approaches to the relation between the Talmuds, see, e.g., S. Friedman, *Talmudic Studies: Investigating the Sugya, Variant Readings and Aggada* (NY and Jerusalem: 2010), 40-44; Y. Sussmann, "Once more on y. Nezikin" (Hebrew), in Y. Sussmann and D. Rosenthal (eds.), *Talmudic Studies* 1 (Jerusalem: 1990), 55-134; M.S. Jaffee, "The Babylonian appropriation of the Talmud Yerushalmi: redactional studies in the Horayot tractates," in A.J. Avery-Peck (ed.), *The Literature of Early Rabbinic Judaism: Issues in Talmudic Redaction and Interpretation* (Lanham MD: 1989), 3-27; A.M. Gray, A Talmud in Exile: The Influence of Yerushalmi Avodah Zarah on the Formation of Bavli Avodah Zarah (PhD dissertation, Brown University, 2005), 1-43.

sexual partnerships. Converts, who are deemed to have no legal connections to their biological relatives, are not required to observe the restrictions on incest that govern Jews. They are, however, obliged to observe the laws prohibiting next-of-kin intercourse that apply to non-Jews, lest their conversion be perceived as decreasing their holiness. The *sugya* in the Palestinian Talmud, found in tractate Jebamot, reads as follows:

> A proselyte, [if he married] his sister, whether by his father or by his mother, must divorce her – [these are] the words of R. Meir. R. Judah says: his sister by his mother, he must divorce, by his father, he may keep. [If he married] his mother's sister, he must divorce her, his father's sister, he may keep her – [these are] the words of R. Meir. R. Judah says: his mother's sister by her mother, he must divorce her, his mother's sister by her father, he may keep her. [As to] all other forbidden relatives, if he married [one of them], [the court] does not force him to divorce [that relative]. It says only "if he married" – [from this we can infer that] it is forbidden *ab initio*.
>
> A non-Jew, [if he married] his sister, whether by his father or by his mother, must divorce her – [these are] the words of R. Meir. R. Judah says: his sister by his mother, he must divorce, by his father, he may keep. [If he married] his mother's sister, he must divorce her, his father's sister, he may keep her – [these are] the words of R. Meir. R. Judah says: his mother's sister by her mother, he must divorce her, his mother's sister by her father, he may keep her.
>
> R. Hanin said: It is clear to us that R. Meir's position is corroborated by the verse: "Therefore a man shall leave his father and his mother" (Gen. 2:24), [that is to say,] one who is close to him by his father and who is close to him by his mother. R. Bivi inquired: But if so, then his father's sister should be forbidden, since she is close to his father, and his mother's sister should be forbidden, because she is close to his mother. R. Shimon son of R. Eivo raised an objection: Is it not written: "And Amram took Jochebed his father's sister as his wife" (Exod. 6:20)? But can it be possible that the Israelites had a practice that even Noahides did not [engage in]?! R. Hila says: One who is close to him by his father and one who is close to him by his mother. They raised an objection to R. Meir's view: Is it not written: "And yet indeed she is my sister; she is the daughter of my father, but not of my mother" (Gen. 20:12)? R. Meir answered them: Does that constitute a proof?! No, [for Scripture continues]: "And she became my wife."
>
> What is the decision? R. Jose said: All prohibited relations, for which the court imposes capital punishment, Noahides are admonished against. But all prohibited relations, for which the court does not impose capital punishment, Noahides are [not] admonished against. They raised an objection: But is there not his sister, for [relations with] whom the court does not impose capital punishment, yet with whom Noahides are admonished

against [having relations]?[36] [As we learn from the following, for] R. Hila states in the name of R. Shimon b. Lakish: "It is because of these abominations that the Lord your God is driving them out before you" (Deut. 18:12) – this serves to teach us that the Holy One, blessed be He, does not punish unless He first issued an admonition [hence we see that non-Jews are admonished not to have sexual relations with their sisters].

R. Idi said before R. Jose in the name of Rav Hisda: A slave is permitted [to have relations with] his sister. He said to him: Did you learn [this ruling] even with regard to [his sister] by his mother? Yes indeed, he replied. He said to him: Did we not learn: "And a bondwoman who was released from slavery together with her sons [is just like a proselyte]" (mJebamot 11:2)? This applies only to *halitzah* and levirate marriage. R. Pinhas said before R. Jose in the name of R. Jose: A slave who had relations with a bondwoman[37] is liable to bring a sin-offering.[38]

The dispute between R. Meir and R. Judah, and other parts of the *sugya*, are paralleled in Genesis Rabbah 18:5.[39] Although there are sev-

36 MS Leiden reads "for [relations with] whom the court imposes capital punishment, yet with whom Noahides are not admonished against [having relations]" (הרי בית דין שליש' ממיתין עליה ואין בני נח מוזהרין עליה), but this is probably a scribal error, since incest with one's sister is punished, not by death imposed by the court, but by divine extirpation, as clearly stated in the Bible.

37 According to MS Leiden, which reads אמה. The printed editions, however, read אמו (his mother), referring to next-of-kin relations between a slave and his mother.

38 jJebamot 11:2 (12a).

39 "Therefore shall a man leave his father and his mother" (Gen. 2:24). It was taught: If a man became a proselyte, and he was [previously] married to his sister by his father or to his sister by his mother, he must divorce her – [according to] the words of R. Meir. But the Sages maintain: He must divorce his sister by his mother, but may keep his sister by his father, because paternity does not apply to non-Jews. They raised an objection to his view: Is it not written: "And yet indeed she is my sister; she is the daughter of my father [but not of my mother]" (Gen. 20:12)? He [Abraham] answered them in accordance with their own ideas, was his reply. R. Hanan said: This is corroborated for us by the verse: "Therefore a man shall leave his father and his mother" (Gen. 2:24), which means [he must divorce] she who is related to his father and she who is related to his mother. R. Abbahu raised an objection: Is it not written: "And Amram took Jochebed his father's sister as his wife" (Exod. 6:20)? R. Shimon, the son of R. Abin, said: But can it be possible that before the giving of the Torah, the Israelites had a practice that even Noahides did not [engage in]?! Said R. Ila: This was resolved for us by the verse: "Therefore a man shall leave his father and his mother," which means [he must divorce] a woman who is related to him through his

eral differences between the two versions, it is noteworthy that on both accounts, the Tannaitic positions being debated are essentially the same. According to R. Meir, a non-Jew is forbidden to have sexual intercourse with his half-sister, whether she is his sister on his father's side or his mother's side. R. Judah (or, in the case of the Babylonian Talmud, as we will see below, the Sages), on the other hand, is more lenient on this matter, and concludes that, although a half-sister on the mother's side is forbidden, a half-sister on the father's side is permitted. Below, we will see that this stringent interpretation of the Tannaitic dispute was not preserved in the Babylonian Talmud, which attributes to both authorities a much more lenient position.

After a short discussion about the dispute between R. Meir and R. Judah,[40] the Palestinian Talmud introduces a third Tannaitic position, which seems to parallel the position of R. Meir recorded in tractate Avoda Zara of the Tosefta. The Toseftan passage reads as follows:

> Concerning prohibited [sexual] relations, how so? All prohibited relations for which a Jewish court imposes capital punishment, Noahides are admonished against. But for all prohibited relations for which a Jewish court issues an admonition, [Noahides[41]] incur capital punishment[42]: these are the words of R. Meir. But the Sages say: Many prohibited relations for which a Jewish court does not impose capital punishment, Noahides are admonished against. One who has prohibited relations with a Jew is judged by Jewish law.[43] One who has prohibited relations with[44] a Gentile is judged by Gentile law [lit., the laws of the nations]. And [with respect to prohibited relations] you have only [one difference in practice between Jewish law and Gentile law, namely,] the case of the betrothed maiden.[45,46]

---

father and a woman who is related to him through his mother [i.e., a sister, not an aunt]. (Genesis Rabbah 18:5 [Theodor–Albeck edition, 165-66])

40 There are several textual problems with the Palestinian accounts, which make the discussion that follows the dispute between R. Meir and R. Judah somewhat difficult to follow. The anonymous discussion is quite similar in all three sources (Genesis Rabbah and the two Talmuds); it will be discussed below.

41 The printed editions add "Noahides" (בני נח).

42 MS Erfurt omits the clause: "But for all prohibited relations for which a Jewish court issues an admonition, [Noahides] incur capital punishment."

43 MS Erfurt omits the clause: "One who has prohibited relations with a Jew is judged by Jewish law."

44 MS Erfurt reads: "With respect to these prohibited relations" (באלו העריות) here rather than "One who has prohibited relations with" (בא על עריות).

45 For which Jewish law imposes capital punishment, but Gentile law does not.

46 tAvoda Zara 9:4, according to MS Vienna.

Despite the overall similarity, there are several differences between the Tosefta's account of this tradition and the account found in the baraita in the Palestinian Talmud.[47] R. Jose, who introduces the baraita in the Palestinian Talmud, is most likely a fourth-century Palestinian Amora (either R. Jose b. Zevida or R. Jose b. R. Bun) who is quoting an anonymous Tannaitic source.[48] The Tannaitic position reflected in this tradition is thus presented anonymously in the Palestinian Talmud, whereas the Tosefta attributes it to the Tanna R. Meir. The Tosefta, moreover, provides an alternative to R. Meir's position, attributing it to the Sages.[49] While the Palestinian Talmud initially omits the position of the Sages, the subsequent anonymous discussion implicitly invokes the omitted position.

More importantly, the Tosefta (quoted above according to MS Vienna and the first printed edition) is profoundly different from the baraita quoted in the Palestinian Talmud. The Tosefta presents the criminal liability of Jews and non-Jews for sexual transgressions in terms of an inverse relationship. Sexual transgressions for which a Jewish court imposes capital punishment, non-Jews are merely admonished against, whereas for sexual transgressions which Jews are merely admonished against, non-Jews receive capital punishment. According to the

47 The synoptic problem, i.e., the problem of the relationship between parallel baraitot in the Tosefta, the Palestinian Talmud, and the Babylonian Talmud, is one of the most complicated issues in the critical study of the Rabbinic literature. It has been studied extensively, and several models of the relationship between parallel baraitot have been proposed. On the models proposed by Epstein and Albeck, see E.S. Rosenthal, "Hamoreh" (Hebrew), *PAAJR* 31 (1963), 52. For a developmental model, see S. Friedman, "Uncovering literary dependencies in the talmudic corpus," in S. Cohen (ed.), *The Synoptic Problem in Rabbinic Literature* (Providence: 2000), 35-57; idem, "The baraitot in the Babylonian Talmud and their parallels in the Tosefta" (Hebrew), in *Atara L'Haim: Studies in the Talmud and Medieval Rabbinic Literature in Honor of Professor Haim Zalman Dimitrovsky* (Jerusalem: 2000), 163-201; idem, "Towards a characterization of Babylonian baraitot: Ben Tema and Ben Dortai" (Hebrew), in Y. Elman et al. (eds.), *Netiot LeDavid: Jubilee Volume for David Weiss Halivni* (Jerusalem: 2004), 195-274.

48 In other words, the Tanna R. Jose b. Halafta is probably not the source of this tradition, according to the Palestinian Talmud. On the identity of R. Jose (in cases where his father's name is not specified) in the Palestinian Talmud, see H. Albeck, *Introduction to the Talmud, Bavli and Yerushalmi* (Hebrew), (Tel Aviv: 1969), 334-36.

49 The alternative position has parallels in Sifra, Kedoshim, parasha 10; jKidushin 1:1 (58b); bSanhedrin 57b.

Palestinian Talmud, on the other hand, non-Jews are accountable only for sexual transgressions for which a Jewish court imposes capital punishment, but not for sexual transgressions for which a Jewish court does not impose capital punishment.

To be sure, this version of the Tosefta hardly makes sense, since the Sages' position does not correspond to R. Meir's statement in its present form. Significantly, the second clause of R. Meir's statement ("But for all prohibited relations for which a Jewish court issues an admonition, [Noahides] incur capital punishment") is completely omitted in the Erfurt manuscript of the Tosefta. If R. Meir's original statement included only the first clause ("All prohibited relations for which a Jewish court imposes capital punishment, Noahides are admonished against"), then it would be logical for it to be countered by its inverse ("All prohibited relations for which a Jewish court does not impose capital punishment, Noahides are not admonished against"), as is indeed found in both Talmuds.

One of the implications of R. Meir's position, which is not explicated in the Tosefta, is that sexual partnerships between siblings, which are punished by divine extirpation and not by capital punishment, are completely permissible to non-Jews. In the Palestinian Talmud, this lenient position is questioned, on the assumption that sibling relations cannot possibly be permissible for non-Jews. It is argued that since the Torah informs us that the Canaanites were driven out of the land of Canaan because they engaged in sexual abominations, it must have been the case that they were strictly prohibited to so act.[50]

The *sugya* in the Palestinian Talmud concludes with the statement that non-Jewish slaves are permitted to have relations with their sisters, even when they are related on the mother's side. Although this leniency concerns slaves in particular, the slave here seems to represent a 'limiting case' of the category of non-Jews. Whereas some Tannaitic authorities permit non-Jews to have relations with their half-sisters; a slave, according to the tradition at the end of the *sugya* in the Palestinian Talmud, is permitted to have relations with both his sister by his mother and his sister by his father. Interestingly, this statement is transmitted in

50 According to this logic, however, the **entire** list of sexual prohibitions should apply to Jews and non-Jews alike. Indeed, this logic seems to underlie the Palestinian approach, on which the laws prohibiting incest have broad application, and there is little difference, if any, between the Sinaitic and Noahide systems in this regard.

the name of Rav Hisda, a prominent Babylonian authority of the second generation, who studied at Sura.

Rav Hisda's lenient position is contrasted to a statement attributed to R. Jose: "A slave who had relations with his mother is liable to bring a sin-offering."[51] Although there is no explicit acknowledgement in the Palestinian Talmud of the Babylonian provenance of Rav Hisda's statement,[52] it seems to represent a Babylonian Rabbinic position which is then contrasted to a Palestinian Rabbinic position forbidding a slave to have relations with his mother.

The manner in which these statements are contrasted suggests that the Palestinian Talmud might wish to reject the lenient Babylonian Rabbinic position and instead invoke a local Rabbinic tradition. Although Rav Hisda's statement in the Palestinian Talmud addresses sexual partnerships between siblings, whereas R. Jose speaks of relations with one's mother, it is plausible that the redactors of the Palestinian Talmud sought to contrast the fundamental Babylonian and Palestinian positions as to the Noahide sexual laws. Indeed, the Babylonian Talmud, which should, perhaps, be considered more reliable when it comes to the authenticity of statements putatively made by Babylonian authorities, attributes to Rav Hisda the position that a slave is permitted to have relations with his mother and his daughter. Were we to accept the Babylonian Talmud's version of Rav Hisda's statement over the Palestinian Talmud's, then the disagreement between Rav Hisda and R. Jose, is, in fact, over the very same issue.

6. The *sugya* in the Babylonian Talmud

Although preserving the same Tannaitic traditions addressed in the Palestinian Talmud *sugya*, the *sugya* in the Babylonian Talmud, in tractate Sanhedrin, is profoundly different from its Palestinian counterpart.

51 Admittedly, MS Leiden of the Palestinian Talmud preserves a version that reads אמה, thus addressing, not the case of next-of-kin relations between a slave and his mother (אמו), but a completely different case, namely, relations between a slave and a bondwoman (אמה). The Leiden version, however, does not make much sense in the context of a *sugya* that addresses next-of-kin relations, and the original text may well have been corrupted or misinterpreted. It is plausible, e.g., that a scribe expanded the contracted form "אמ'" as אמה rather than אמו.

52 By using the phrase תמן אמרין ("There, they say. . .") or the like.

It has been taught in accordance with the view of R. Johanan: All prohibited relations for which a Jewish court imposes capital punishment, a Noahide is admonished against. But those for which a Jewish court does not impose capital punishment, a Noahide is not admonished against: these are the words of R. Meir. But the Sages say: [There are] many prohibited relations (between Jews) for which a Jewish court does not impose capital punishment, and a Noahide is admonished against. One who has prohibited relations with a Jew is judged by Jewish law, one who has prohibited relations with a Noahide is judged by Gentile law. And [with respect to prohibited relations], we have only [one difference in practice between Jewish law and Gentile law, namely,] the case of the betrothed maiden.[53] . . .

Now, does R. Meir claim that all prohibited relations for which a Jewish court imposes capital punishment, a Noahide is admonished against? Surely it has been taught: A proselyte,[54] who was not conceived in sanctity but was born in sanctity, possesses kin on his mother's side but not on his father's side. How is this so? If he married his sister by his mother – he must divorce her; by his father – he may keep her; his father's sister by his [i.e., the father's] mother – he must divorce her; by his father – he may keep her; his mother's sister by her [i.e., the mother's] mother – he must divorce her; by her father[55] – R. Meir says that he must divorce her, but the Sages say that he may keep her; for R. Meir held that in every case of prohibited relations on his mother's side, he must divorce her; on his father's side, he may keep her. He is permitted [relations with] his brother's wife, his father's brother's wife, and all other prohibited relations are permitted to him. This includes his father's wife. If he married a woman and her daughter, he remains married to one and must divorce the other. But *ab initio*, he must not marry them. If his wife died, he may marry his mother-in-law; and there are some who learned that his mother-in-law is prohibited to him.

Rav Judah[56] said: there is no difficulty here; one dictum by R. Meir is in accordance with R. Eleazar's view, and the other dictum by R. Meir is in accordance with R. Akiva's view. For it has been taught: "Therefore a man shall leave his father and his mother" (Gen. 2:24) – R. Eleazar said: His father [means] his father's sister[57]; his mother [means] his mother's sister. R. Akiva said: His father [means] his father's wife; his mother [means] his mother, literally. "And he shall cleave" [means] but not to a male; "to his wife" [means] but not to his neighbor's wife; "and they shall be as one

53 For which Jewish law imposes capital punishment, but Gentile law does not.

54 As per MSS Florence, Karlsruhe and Munich 95 (גר). Cf. the Yemenite MS, which reads "a non-Jew" (גוי).

55 MS Florence adds "he may keep her."

56 MS Karlsruhe reads "Rav Joseph."

57 As per MSS Florence, Karlsruhe and Munich 95; the copyist of the Yemenite MS seems to have skipped the words "his father's sister" (אחות אביו) by way of homeoteleuton.

flesh" – this applies to those that can become one flesh, thus excluding cattle and beasts, which cannot become one flesh with man. . . .

Come and hear: "And Amram took Jochebed his father's sister as his wife" (Exod. 6:20). Does this not mean his father's sister by his mother? No, it means his father's sister by his father.

Come and hear: "And yet indeed she is my sister, the daughter of my father (but not of my mother)" (Gen. 20:12). Does not this prove that the mother's daughter is forbidden? Now, was she his sister[58] at all? She was his brother's daughter, and therefore, whether by his father or mother, she is permitted to him. He [i.e. Abraham] declared to him [Abimelech] the following: I am related to her fraternally [i.e., she is my brother's daughter], but on my father's side [i.e., through my brother by my father], not on my mother's side.

Come and hear! Why did Adam not marry his daughter? So that Cain could marry his sister, "for I said, the world shall be built up by grace" (Ps. 89:2). But if it weren't for the purpose of building up the world by grace, would she not be forbidden? Once it was permitted, it remains permitted.

Rav Huna said: "A non-Jew is permitted to have relations with his daughter." Should you ask, if so, why did Adam not marry his daughter? So that Cain could marry his sister, as it is written: "the world shall be built up by grace" (Ps. 89:2). And there are some who say: Rav Huna[59] said: "A non-Jew is forbidden to have relations with his daughter," the proof being that Adam did not marry his daughter, so that Cain could marry his sister.[60] But that proof is fallacious: the reason was so that the world would be built up by grace.[61]

Rav Hisda[62] said: "A [non-Jewish] slave [owned by a Jew] is permitted [to have relations] with his mother and permitted [to have relations] with his daughter,"[63] for he is no longer regarded as a non-Jew, but not yet regarded as a Jew.[64]

In both Talmuds, the dispute between R. Meir and R. Judah (or R. Meir and the Sages) concerning sexual partnerships between non-Jews,

58 MSS Florence and Karlsruhe add "daughter of his father" (בת אביו).

59 MSS Florence and Karlsruhe read "Rav Judah."

60 "So that Cain could marry his sister" is omitted in MSS Florence, Karlsruhe, and Munich 95.

61 This is the reading in the Yemenite MS. Cf. MSS Florence, Karlsruhe, and Munich 95, which read "So that Cain could marry his sister."

62 MS Florence reads "Huna."

63 MS Florence reads "is permitted [to have relations] with his mother and with his sister."

64 bSanhedrin 57b-58b, according to the Yemenite MS of tractate Sanhedrin. For a description of this MS, see M. Sabato, A Yemenite Manuscript of Tractate Sanhedrin and Its Place in the Text Tradition (PhD dissertation, Hebrew University of Jerusalem, 1996).

or converts, and their sisters, father's sisters, or mother's sisters, is juxtaposed to a third Tannaitic tradition, according to which a non-Jew is permitted to engage in certain incestuous relationships, as long as a Jewish court does not impose capital punishment (on Jews) for such an act. While the third Tannaitic position is presented anonymously in the Palestinian Talmud, the Babylonian Talmud attributes this position to R. Meir (in accordance with the Tosefta), whose seemingly contradictory statements are subsequently juxtaposed and contrasted in the *sugya*.

The dispute between R. Meir and his interlocutors regarding sexual partnerships with one's sister, father's sister, or mother's sister is presented differently in the different Rabbinic works. First, Genesis Rabbah addresses only the case of the convert, whereas the Palestinian Talmud addresses two cases: that of the convert and that of the non-Jew. The Babylonian Talmud addresses only the case of one who was conceived as a non-Jew but was born a Jew. The legal status of non-Jews and converts, however, is rather similar in this regard, insofar as converts, like non-Jews, are permitted to have sexual relations with some of their biological relatives.

Second, the Palestinian Talmud and Genesis Rabbah maintain that, according to R. Meir, relations with one's sister, whether by his father or by his mother, are strictly forbidden, whereas according to R. Meir's interlocutor, they are forbidden only in the case of a sister by one's mother. The Babylonian Talmud, on the other hand, maintains that according to R. Meir, relations with one's sister on one's father's side are permissible, while R. Meir's interlocutor permits both types of sisters. As we will see, it is not merely by chance that the more stringent version of the Tannaitic dispute appears in the Palestinian sources, and the more lenient version in the Babylonian Talmud.

As R. Meir addresses several cases (one's father's sister and mother's sister) and not only the case of a sister, it is not entirely clear precisely what it is that the Babylonian Talmud sees as the contradiction that calls for reconciliation. A probable interpretation of the contradiction is the following, though I would not rule out the plausibility of other interpretations. In one source, R. Meir upholds the most lenient position, arguing that a sexual relationship for which a Jewish court does not impose capital punishment on Jews, is permissible for non-Jews, from which it follows that sexual relations with one's sister are **completely permissible** for non-Jews; but in another source, R. Meir maintains that one who marries his sister on his mother's side must divorce her immediately. In response to this alleged contradiction in R. Meir's position, the Babylonian Talmud attributes the more lenient position to R. Meir's teaching that is in accordance with R. Akiva, while the more stringent position is attributed to R. Meir's teaching that is in accordance with R. Eleazar.

After resolving the contradiction in R. Meir's position, the Babylonian Talmud makes several attempts to provide exegetical support for one or another position in the dispute between R. Akiva and R. Eleazar regarding the permissibility of non-Jewish incestuous practices.[65] It first questions the stringent stance by invoking the case of Amram, the father of Moses and Aaron, who married his aunt. But it rejects this attempt, arguing that Amram's aunt was his father's sister by [Amram's father's] father, and not by [Amram's father's] mother, in which case all the Tannaitic authorities (according to the version of the baraita recorded in the Babylonian Talmud) concur that relations with her are permissible for a non-Jew. The Babylonian Talmud then mentions Abraham, who asserts that he married his sister on his father's side, implying that relations with one's sister on one's mother's side are prohibited. But it rejects this inference as well, suggesting that Abraham was in fact married to his niece, not to his biological sister. The former is permissible, of course, even for Israelites, and is practiced by some Jews to this very day.[66] The third attempt at finding biblical support invokes a midrash according to which the reason Adam did not marry his daughter was so that Cain, his son, would be able to do so. From this midrash the Babylonian Talmud deduces that, were it not for the mandate expressed in the verse "the world shall be built up by grace," Cain's marrying his sister would have been prohibited. This attempt, too, is rejected, since it can be argued that "once it was permitted, it remains permitted."

The notion that "once it was permitted, it remains permitted" appears to be the conclusion of the Babylonian Talmud's discussion of

65 Some of the biblical prooftexts are similarly discussed in the Palestinian Talmud and Genesis Rabbah.

66 On the Rabbinic acceptance of marriage to a niece, see mNedarim 8:7, 9:10; jJebamot 13:2 (13c); bJebamot 62b; bGitin 17a; bSanhedrin 76b. In this respect, there appears to be no difference between the Palestinian and Babylonian sources. On a Qumranic-Rabbinic dispute over this issue, see A. Shemesh, "The laws of incest in the Dead Sea Scrolls and the history of halakhah," in A.I. Baumgarten et al. (eds.), *Halakhah in Light of Epigraphy* (Göttingen: 2011), 81-99.

brother–sister unions, thus affirming the position of R. Meir in the name of R. Akiva that non-Jews are not held liable for sexual transgressions for which a Jewish court does not impose capital punishment on Jews. In contrast to the inconclusiveness of the Palestinian Rabbinic discussions of the issue, the Babylonian Talmud appears to accept this lenient stance as normative.[67] The redactors' lenient conclusion can be further deduced from the remainder of the *sugya*, which is completely absent from the Palestinian Rabbinic works.

After discussing the case of sexual relations with one's sister, the Babylonian Talmud turns to the case of sexual relations with one's daughter. This case is addressed by Rav Huna, a prominent authority of the second generation of Babylonian Sages. Two differing versions of Rav Huna's position are attested.[68] According to the first version, "A non-Jew is permitted to have relations with his daughter," while according to the second, "A non-Jew is forbidden to have relations with his daughter." Notwithstanding the contradictory versions of Rav Huna's statement, the lenient position of the anonymous redactors of the Babylonian Talmud is unmistakable.

The more lenient version of Rav Huna's statement is challenged by the fact that Adam refrained from marrying his daughter. This challenge is resolved, however, by the claim that Adam only refrained out of "grace" toward his son, and not because it was forbidden. The more stringent version of Rav Huna's position, on the other hand, is initially inferred from Adam's reluctance to marry his daughter. This explanation is subsequently rejected, however, since Adam refrained

67 It must be stressed that the attempt to identify the 'bottom line' or 'conclusion' of a talmudic *sugya* can be quite challenging. Given the discursive nature of the Babylonian Talmud, it often remains uncertain whether a putative conclusion indeed functions as such, or simply represents a discursive possibility, with both sides of the debate remaining viable options. In the case of the question under discussion, however, the thrust of the *sugya* is consistent.

68 According to MSS Florence and Karlsruhe, the stringent position, which forbids father–daughter sexual relations, is attributed to Rav Judah, and is not presented as a different version of Rav Huna's statement. If this version is accurate, then the matter of father–daughter relations seems to have been a matter of dispute between the two major Babylonian Rabbinic circles, Rav Huna representing the Sura tradition, and Rav Judah the Pumbeditha tradition. While a choice between the variant readings cannot be made with complete confidence, I have followed the generally more reliable Yemenite MS of tractate Sanhedrin.

out of "grace," and not because it was forbidden. In conclusion, then, the lenient position is upheld by the Babylonian redactors, whereas the stringent position is straightforwardly rejected, as Adam would have legally married his daughter were it not for his solicitousness toward his son.

Lastly, after addressing the leniency regarding marriage to one's sister and daughter, the Babylonian Talmud discusses the matter of sexual relations between a non-Jewish slave and his mother.[69] Here too we witness a remarkable difference between the Babylonian and Palestinian Talmuds. Although a somewhat similar statement is attributed by both Talmuds to Rav Hisda, a contemporary and colleague of Rav Huna, there is one key difference. While the Palestinian Talmud attributes to Rav Hisda the view that a non-Jewish slave is permitted to have sexual relations with his sister – a position that was essentially accepted by certain Tannaitic authorities for all non-Jews – the Babylonian Talmud attributes to Rav Hisda the position that a non-Jewish slave is permitted to have sexual relations with his mother! There is no Tannaitic position that permits a non-Jew to have sexual relations with his mother, a practice for which Jewish courts impose capital punishment.

To conclude, the Babylonian and Palestinian works reveal a significant disparity regarding the applicability of the levitical sexual prohibitions to non-Jews. In contrast to the Palestinian Rabbinic works, which generally extend the levitical prohibitions to non-Jews (with only minor exceptions), the Babylonian Talmud takes an approach that systematically tolerates incestuous partnerships between non-Jews, especially first-degree incest: mother–son, father–daughter, and brother–sister.

7. The Zoroastrian doctrine of *xwēdōdah*

Before contextualizing the Babylonian Rabbinic approach by adducing the Iranian practice of incestuous partnerships, I will first provide a more detailed description of the Zoroastrian doctrine that governed this practice. Since *xwēdōdah* is one of the most important religious doctrines in Zoroastrianism, it is relevant to many different aspects of the

69 As I suggested, the Rabbis take the slave to represent a 'limiting case' of the category 'non-Jewish.'

religion, and invoked in a variety of contexts.[70] The doctrine is adduced in theological contexts, legal traditions, epic and mythical narratives, wisdom and moral teachings, polemical and apologetic treatises, and other forms of Pahlavi literature. These texts and traditions address the religious merit and reward for carrying out *xwēdōdah*, and punishment for neglecting to do so; the justification, logic, and benefits of *xwēdōdah*; numerous legal details specifying how it is to be carried out; the mythical and historical prototypes of *xwēdōdah*, and so on.[71]

70 The Pahlavi corpus is largely religious – i.e. Zoroastrian – in nature, as most Pahlavi works are presented as integral parts of the Avesta and Zand (the traditional translation-cum-commentary on the Avesta). Certain Pahlavi works – e.g., the *Pahlavi Videvdad*, the Pahlavi commentaries on the *Hērbedestān* and *Nērangestān* – can be considered Zand proper, in the sense that they accompany, translate, and interpret an original Avestan text. Many other Pahlavi works – such as the *Dēnkard* – are typically presented as reproducing, paraphrasing, or summarizing the contents of the Avesta and Zand. The vast majority of the Pahlavi literature is thus comprised of works taken to be divinely-inspired translations, interpretations, paraphrases, or summaries of divine revelation. A common introductory formula in Pahlavi literature is *pad abestāg paydāg* ("it is manifest, revealed, in the Avesta"), attributing a divine and authoritative tone to the content. For surveys of the extant Pahlavi corpus, see M. Boyce, "Middle Persian literature," in B. Spuler and I. Gershevitch (eds.), *Handbuch der Orientalistik*, vol. 4.2.1 *Iranistik: Literatur* (Leiden and Köln: 1968), 31-66; J. de Menasce, "Zoroastrian Pahlavi writings," in E. Yarshater (ed.), *The Cambridge History of Iran* 3(2) (Cambridge: 1983), 1166-95; J.C. Tavadia, *Die mittelpersische Sprache und Literatur der Zarathustrier* (Leipzig: 1956); C. Cereti, *La Letteratura Pahlavi: Introduzione ai testi con riferimenti alla storia degli studi e alla tradizione manoscritta* (Milano: 2001); M. Macuch, "Pahlavi literature," in R.E. Emmerick and M. Macuch (eds.), *The Literature of Pre-Islamic Iran*, A History of Persian Literature: Companion Volume 1 (London: 2008), 116-96.

71 The main Pahlavi texts on *xwēdōdah* are *Dēnkard* 3.80, in J. de Menasce (ed. and trans.), *Le troisième livre du Dēnkart*, Bibliothèque des oeuvres classiques persanes 4; Travaux de l'Institut d'études iraniennes de l'Université de Paris 5 (Paris: 1973), 85-86; *Pahlavi Rivāyat* 8, in Williams, n. 3 above, 2:11-17; *Rivāyat of Ēmēd son of Aš̌wahist* 22, 27-30, in N. Safa-Isfehani, *Rivāyat-i Hēmīt-i Ašawahistān: Edition, Transcription and Translation, A Study in Zoroastrian Law*, Harvard Iranian Series 2 (Cambridge MA: 1980), 156-58, 190-98; *Hērbedestān* 2.9, 6.7, in F.M. Kotwal and P.G. Kreyenbroek, *The Hērbedestān and Nērangestān* (Paris: 1992–2009), 1:32-33, 45; *Pahlavi Rivāyat of Āturfarnbag* 20.1-2; 143.1-4, in B.T. Anklesaria, *The Pahlavi Rivāyat of Āturfarnbag and Farnbag-srōs* (Bombay: 1969); *Mādayān ī Hazār Dādestān* 44.8-14; 104.9-14; 105.5-10; 18.7-12, in M. Macuch (ed.), *Rechtskasuistik und Gerichtspraxis zu Beginn des siebenten Jahrhunderts in Iran. Die Rechtssammlung*

A systematic survey of the treatment of *xwēdōdah* in the Pahlavi literature is beyond the scope of this article. Various aspects of the doctrine have, however, received scholarly attention, and a comprehensive article on the subject, written by Prods Oktor Skjærvø, was recently published in *Encyclopaedia Iranica*.[72] In the present article, I will adduce the Pahlavi sources on *xwēdōdah* only insofar as they illuminate the talmudic discussions of Noahide law.

Beyond the Pahlavi works, there are several non-Zoroastrian sources that provide important information about the Iranian custom. The overwhelmingly polemical tone of these sources' discussions of the Iranian practice has been noted by scholars. In nearly all non-Zoroastrian accounts of *xwēdōdah*, the Zoroastrian custom is rejected, repudiated, and harshly criticized. A critical stance on Iranian incestuous practices is found in Greco-Roman,[73] Christian,[74] Islamic,[75] Indian-Buddhist,[76] and Chinese-Buddhist[77] sources from the fifth century BCE onward.[78]

The polemical context in which *xwēdōdah* was discussed in antiquity and the early medieval period emerges from Zoroastrian sources as well. One of the most important Zoroastrian sources on *xwēdōdah* – chapter 80 in the third book of the *Dēnkard* – bears the title: "About how a Jew lamented to a Zoroastrian priest (*hērbed*), seeking to know the reason for the sin of performing *xwēdōdah* and the priest's answer as exposed

des Farroḫmard i Wahrāmān, Iranica 1 (Wiesbaden: 1993). Although the term itself is not mentioned in the Sasanian law code *Mādayān ī Hazār Dādestān* ("The Book of a Thousand Judgments"), the practice clearly emerges from this text, and appears to be of great importance in Sasanian family law. See M. Macuch, "Incestuous marriage in the context of Sasanian family law," in M. Macuch et al. (eds.), *Ancient and Middle Iranian Studies: Proceedings of the 6th European Conference of Iranian Studies, Held in Vienna, 18-22 September 2007* (Wiesbaden: 2010), 133-48.

72 Skjærvø, n. 4 above.

73 For Greco-Latin sources, see n. 4 above.

74 Frye, n. 3 above, 449-50; Slotkin, n. 3 above, 614-15; Mitterauer, n. 7 above, 231-50.

75 Frye, ibid., 450-51; van Gelder, n. 6 above, 36-77.

76 J.A. Silk, "Putative Persian perversities: Indian Buddhist condemnations of Zoroastrian close-kin marriage in context," *Bulletin of SOAS* 71 (2008), 433-64.

77 Ibid.

78 For a comprehensive discussion of various non-Zoroastrian sources on *xwēdōdah*, see Skjærvø, n. 4 above.

in the Tradition."[79] While it remains unclear whether this description is a portrayal of an actual encounter or merely a literary construction, it is clear that it reflects a genuine tension that existed between Zoroastrians and non-Zoroastrians over the doctrine of *xwēdōdah*.

Jean de Menasce has argued that the Zoroastrian anti-Jewish polemic that emerges from the third book of the *Dēnkard* reflects a ninth-century Zoroastrian encounter with Islam, and the mention of Jews in this work is merely a literary projection.[80] I contend, however (with Shaul Shaked), that polemical and apologetic excursuses such as these reflect not only the anxieties of Zoroastrians under the Abbasid Caliphate, but also concerns that can be dated back to the Sasanian period.[81]

One of the apologetic arguments in favor of *xwēdōdah* advanced by the Pahlavi authors is that moral standards are not absolute and universal, but rather relative and dependent. Since many non-Zoroastrian critics of the Zoroastrian custom have stressed that next-of-kin partnerships are universally unnatural, unethical, and immoral, the Pahlavi authors attempted to dispute these claims by suggesting that though next-of-kin partnerships might be considered an abomination in one culture, they can be deemed praiseworthy and meritorious in another. This logic is somewhat inconsistent with another Pahlavi argument, which stresses that *xwēdōdah* is (universally) derived from mythical prototypes, but this sort of inconsistency is rather common in the context of religious apologetics.

The notion of cultural and moral relativism is most clearly articulated in *Dēnkard* 3.80.

> If someone says that, in spite of all this that he adduces, there is still something ugly to imagine, they should know that ugliness and beauty are mostly so, not in themselves, but in people's actions, appearances, beliefs, and dispositions (*xōg*).

79 This translation is based on P.O. Skjærvø, *The Spirit of Zoroastrianism* (New Haven and London: 2011), 202. Cf. S. Shaked, "Zoroastrian polemics against Jews in the Sasanian and early Islamic period," in S. Shaked and A. Netzer (eds.), *Irano-Judaica* 2 (1990), 86.

80 J. de Menasce, "Jews and Judaism in the third book of the *Dēnkard*," *K.R. Kama Oriental Institute Golden Jubilee Volume* (Bombay: 1969), 45-48.

81 Shaked, n. 79 above, 2:85-104. For a recent reassessment of this issue, see S. Thrope, Contradictions and Vile Utterances: The Zoroastrian Critique of Judaism in the Škand Gumānīg Wizār (PhD dissertation, University of California, Berkeley, 2012), 33-41.

> There are many ugly children who, to their parents' mind, are mostly beautiful. And there are many with beautiful bodies who, to the minds of "the others," are mostly ugly.
>
> Similarly, when, according to the Tradition of our enemies, someone walks about in the town naked, we hold it to be ugly, but the town of those whose skin is naked calls those beautiful, while those who are dressed (?) seem ugly to them.
>
> To our mind, someone with a completely flat nose is ugly, while *they* consider a high nose ugly and say: "Gee, he has a wall between the eyes!" To them people with blemishes are beautiful.
>
> Ugliness and beauty are so, not in themselves, but in people's actions, appearances, and beliefs and are bound to change with place and time.
>
> For our ancestors, to whom a shaved head was ugly – and it was laid down in the law as a sin worthy of death – rather did not order people's heads to be shaved according to [what is today] the custom of the land. Currently, a wise man will consider it beautiful and even a good deed, and it is not obvious to him that it is ugly.[82]

As we are about to see, in its discussion of the Noahide sexual prohibitions, the Babylonian Talmud seems to reflect the Pahlavi rhetoric of moral relativism. Whereas the Palestinian Rabbinic sources maintain, on the whole, that non-Jews are obligated to follow the sexual restrictions outlined in Leviticus 18 and 20 – thus blurring the distinction between Sinaitic and Noahide law and upholding an inclusive approach to sexual morality – the Babylonian Talmud emphasizes that distinction by deeming various forms of incest that were forbidden by the levitical code to be permissible for non-Jews.

Another Pahlavi rhetorical motif that seems to resonate in the Babylonian Talmud's discussion of Noahide sexual prohibitions is the notion that sexual morals are derived from mythical acts of incest.[83] There are three mythical prototypes of *xwēdōdah* that provide the models for human normativity: (1) sexual union between a father and his daughter is linked to the relationship of Ohrmazd and his daughter Spandarmad (Earth), which produces Gayōmard[84]; (2) sexual union between a son and his mother is linked to the relationship of Gayōmard with his

82 *Dēnkard* 3.80.30-35 (Dresden edition, 57-58; Madan edition, 78); the translation is based on Skjærvø 2011, n. 79 above, 206-207, with slight modifications, but cf. de Menasce, n. 71 above, 89. On cultural relativism and *xwēdōdah*, see also *Dissoi Logoi*, 2.15, in Thomas M. Robinson (ed.), *Contrasting Arguments: An Edition of the Dissoi Logoi* (NY: 1979), 108-111.

83 See Skjærvø, n. 4 above; Williams, n. 3 above, 2:132-33, n. 4.

84 *Dēnkard* 9.38.6; 5.18.3; 3.80.4-6; *Pahlavi Rivāyat* 8a (Williams, ibid., 2:10-11); Skjærvø, n. 4 above.

mother Spandarmad (Earth), which produced Mašī and Mašyānī[85]; (3) sexual union between siblings is linked to the sexual relationship of the first human couple, Mašī and Mašyānī.[86]

The first prototype of *xwēdōdah* (father–daughter) is described in the *Pahlavi Rivāyat*:

> And (concerning) Ohrmazd on the performance of *xwēdōdah* (it is) manifest that when Zarathustra sat before Ohrmazd, and Wahman, Ardwahišt, Šahrewar, Hordad, Amurdad, and Spandarmad were sitting around Ohrmazd and Spandarmad sat at his side and she put her hand upon (his) neck, Zarathustra asked Ohrmazd: "Who (is) this who is sitting at your side to whom you are so friendly, and she is also friendly to you? You who are Ohrmazd do not turn your eyes from her, and she does not turn (hers) from you; you who are Ohrmazd do not let her from (your) hand and she does not let you from (her) hand"?
>
> And Ohrmazd said: "This is Spandarmad, who is my daughter and my Queen of Paradise, and the Mother of Creation."[87]

While incest between divine or semi-divine figures is a common motif in world mythology, the attribution of the practice of *xwēdōdah* to Ohrmazd functions in a rather distinct manner. The interesting point in the Pahlavi account of this mythical episode is not the fact that a god united sexually with his daughter, but rather, that this act provides a mythical prototype for human conduct. Thus, instead of challenging the statutory prohibition of incest found in other cultures by invoking tales of mythical acts of incest, in Zoroastrianism the mythical acts of incest are portrayed as exemplifying desirable human conduct.

The second mythical prototype of *xwēdōdah* (mother–son) is discussed in the following tradition.[88]

85 *Dēnkard* 3.80.7 (trans. Skjærvø 2011, n. 79 above, 203). See also *Pahlavi Rivāyat* 8a (Williams, ibid., 2:10-11).

86 *Pahlavi Rivāyat* 8a6-8 (Williams, ibid., 2:10); *Dādestān ī Dēnīg* 36.69, in M. Jaafari-Dehaghi, *Dādestān ī Dēnīg, Part 1: Transcription, Translation and Commentary*, Studia Iranica 20 (Paris: 1998), 136-37; *Dādestān ī Dēnīg* 65; *Dēnkard* 7.1.9-10.

87 *Pahlavi Rivāyat* 8a2-4 (Williams, n. 3 above, 2:10, with slight modifications). Cf. *Dēnkard* 3.80.4-6: "He himself (Ohrmazd) is the father of all, and Spandarmad, the Earth, is the female one of the creation. He created Gayōmard male . . . also now whenever a father creates a male from his daughter this is called the *xwēdōdah* of father and daughter" (Skjærvø 2011, n. 70 above, 203).

88 Alongside the 'official' Zoroastrian account of mother–son incest between Spandarmad and her son Gayōmard, so-called "Zurvanite" accounts

> Let me also say this as exposed in the good Tradition that, when Gayōmard passed on, his semen (*šusr*), which is called seed (*tōhmag*), was enveloped (*parwand-*) by Spandarmad, the Earth, who was his mother, and from it there came into being Mashī and Mashiyānī,[89] Gayōmard and Spandarmad's son and daughter, which is called the *xwēdōdah* of mother and son.[90]

The third mythical prototype of *xwēdōdah* is that of brother and sister. Several Pahlavi sources consider Mašī and Mašyānī, the first human couple (lit., mortal man and woman), to be the first humans to engage in *xwēdōdah*. Their intercourse is considered the prototype for brother–sister union. Let me cite two key passages, one from *Pahlavi Rivāyat* 8a6-8, the other from *Dēnkard* 3.80:

> Ohrmazd said: O Zarathustra, the best thing to have been introduced by/to mankind would have been this, (that) if, since the primal creation, when Mašī and Mašyānī practiced thus, you would also have practiced thus. Since, when mankind altered that thing, if they had not altered it, just as Mašī and Mašyānī practiced *xwēdōdah*, people would have practiced (it) in that manner.[91]

> Mashī and Mashyānī, desiring offspring, had intercourse in the manner of males and females and produced children, which is called the *xwēdōdah* of brother and sister. A great family (*dūdag*) was born from them, who, having paired up, became husbands and wives. And, so, all humans who have been or are came from the original seed (*tōhm*) of *xwēdōdah*.[92]

---

report that Ohrmazd had sexual intercourse with his mother, the wife of Zurvan. See, e.g., *The Syriac Acts of Ādur-hormizd and Anāhīd*, in P. Bedjan (ed.), *Acta Martyrum et Sanctorum* (Paris and Leipzig: 1890-1897), 2:36; R.C. Zaehner, *Zurvan: A Zoroastrian Dilemma* (Oxford: 1955), 435-36; Thāwdhūru Abū Qurrah, *Maymar fī wujūd al-khāliq wa-al-dīn al-qawīm*, edited and annotated by Ignatius Dick, trans. as Theodorus Abu Qurra, *Traité de l'existence du créateur et de la vraie religion* (Jūniyah, Lebanon: 1982), 201-203. I thank Prods Oktor Skjærvø for these references. And see the discussion in Williams, n. 3 above, 2:132-33, n. 4.

89 On Mašī and Mašyānī and the origins of mankind, see *Bundahišn* 14 and *Dēnkard* 7.1, both translated in Skjærvø 2011, n. 79 above, 108-12.

90 *Dēnkard* 3.80.7 (translation based on Skjærvø, ibid. 203, with slight modifications).

91 *Pahlavi Rivāyat* 8a6-8 (Williams, n. 3 above, 2:10, with slight modifications); cf. *Dādestān ī Dēnīg* 36.69 (Jaafari-Dehaghi edition, 136-37); *Dādestān ī Dēnīg* 65; *Dēnkard* 7.1.9-10.

92 *Dēnkard* 3.80.8 (trans. in Skjærvø 2011, n. 79 above, 204, with slight modifications); see also *Dēnkard* 7.1.10 (trans. in Skjærvø 2011, 111):

> And they [Mashī and Mashiyānī] praised Ohrmazd's work of creation and went about their duties. They did the will of the Creator and laid the foundation of much activity that was to benefit the world, especially

8. Explaining the differences

The differences between the Babylonian Talmud and Palestinian Rabbinic works reflect divergent approaches to the universality of sexual ethics. The Palestinian sources understand the sexual prohibitions to be (nearly) universal, in the sense that they apply to Jews and non-Jews alike. Although there are several differences between the prohibitions that apply to Jews and those that apply to non-Jews – notably one's paternal half-sister, with whom non-Jews are permitted to have relations, according to several Tannaitic authorities, but Jews are not – the differences are relatively minimal. The Babylonian Talmud, on the other hand, exhibits a particularistic and exclusive approach, on which many of the levitical prohibitions do not apply to non-Jews (including prohibitions against incestuous unions between first-degree relatives), because the prohibitions applicable to non-Jews are derived independently from pre-Mosaic normativity.

The inclusive or exclusive application of the biblical prohibitions must not be confused with the question of whether a given body of law should be conceived as natural or positive. While the inclusive approach adopted by the Palestinian Rabbinic works is best understood in terms of natural-law ethical theories, the particularistic approach adopted by the Babylonian Rabbis is compatible with both natural-law and positive-law accounts. One way to understand the Babylonian approach is in terms of a theory of ontological and 'natural' particularism that invokes Israel's inherent holiness.

In line with the inclusive notion of 'achieved holiness,' the Palestinian sources adduce the punishment incurred by the Canaanites and Egyptians to argue that non-Jews are essentially governed by the same sexual prohibitions as Jews. Jews and non-Jews alike are required to aspire to a state of 'achieved holiness' by refraining from the same sexual abominations. The Babylonian Talmud, on the other hand, understands Israel's holiness as inherent, and thus takes the levitical prohibitions associated with this state of holiness to apply only to Jews. Although this is a particularistic approach to sexual morality, it is not deduced from a positive-law understanding of the prohibitions, but rather from a natural-law theory of the 'ontological' or 'ascribed' holiness unique to Israel. On this interpretation of the Babylonian Rabbinic position, the

---

xwēdōdah, the most pious of deeds for giving birth, for establishing lineages, and for the creatures of the world to go forth in large numbers.

difference between the Sinaitic and Noahide legal systems is not that one system is positive law and the other natural law, but rather, two different dimensions of natural law are involved. Noahide law can be seen as natural in the sense that it is anchored in the natural beginnings of humanity in the pre-Sinaitic era, whereas Sinaitic law can be seen as natural in the sense that it reflects an inherent, ontological state.

Alternatively, the particularistic approach to sexual ethics adopted by the Babylonian Talmud is also amenable to a positive-law interpretation, which assumes a theory of moral relativism: the levitical laws of incest are binding for Jews, but they are not binding for non-Jews, who have their own standards of sexual behavior. On this reading, both the Sinaitic and the Noahide codes are positive law, in the sense that they do not apply universally, but pertain to a particular group.

Beyond these internal considerations, the Babylonian Talmud's systematic leniency vis-à-vis Noahide engagement in incest must be read in the light of the Zoroastrian practice and doctrine of *xwēdōdah*. As we have seen, the practice of *xwēdōdah* was familiar to foreign observers from the West to the East. If knowledge of the Zoroastrian practice reached Greco-Roman and Indian-Buddhist authors, it is implausible that the Babylonian Rabbis, who were far more familiar with contemporaneous Zoroastrian practices, were unaware of this practice.

I further wish to emphasize that the redactors of the Babylonian Talmud (and perhaps some of the Sages mentioned in the talmudic discussion) were aware not only of the practice of next-of-kin partnerships, but also of its underlying doctrine, and the rhetoric in which it was couched. The Babylonian Rabbinic discussion's focus on first-degree incest (father–daughter, mother–son, and brother–sister) appears to engage the Zoroastrian doctrine, according to which these three types of *xwēdōdah* in particular are considered highly meritorious.[93] This fact is by no means trivial, as the sexual prohibitions in Leviticus include other restrictions that we might have expected to be the focus of Rabbinic attention in the context of Noahide law. The systematic consideration of father–daughter, mother–son, and brother–sister partnerships in the Babylonian Talmud seems to reflect a perspective that goes beyond the internal Rabbinic discussion and engages the Pahlavi rhetoric.[94]

93 *Dēnkard* 3.80.3 (Skjærvø 2011, n. 79 above, 203; de Menasce, n. 71 above, 85-86); *Pahlavi Rivāyat* 8c1, 8d (Williams, n. 3 above, 2:11-12).

94 Admittedly, discussion of the 'sister' is intertwined with that of the 'aunt.' This, however, seems to be the result of the original setting of the baraita,

Regarding siblings who are related only on the father's side or only on the mother's side, the *Pahlavi Rivāyat* asserts the following tradition.

> When a sister and a brother are of the same father and of a different mother, it is in the usual way (*ōh*)[95] for them, and it is in the usual way when they are of the same mother and of a different father.[96]

It is possible that the Babylonian Rabbinic discussion of sexual relations with one's half-sister on the paternal or the maternal side mirrors this Zoroastrian concern. The Palestinian Talmud suggests that R. Meir forbade unions with one's sister, whether paternal or maternal, and R. Judah forbade relations only with one's maternal sister, whereas the Babylonian Talmud argues that both authorities were in fact more lenient on this issue. According to the Babylonian Talmud, R. Meir permits relations with one's paternal sister, while R. Judah permits relations with either type of sister. Interestingly, then, while the Pahlavi texts seek to include one's half-sister as a sexual partner under the rubric of meritorious *xwēdōdah*, the Babylonian Talmud seeks to exclude one's half-sister from the list of partners prohibited to Noahides.

The profound difference, according to the Babylonian Talmud, between the Sinaitic and Noahide codes of sexual ethics calls to mind an important aspect of the Pahlavi rhetoric. As we saw, one of the most interesting justifications for *xwēdōdah* is the notion of moral and cultural relativism. Alongside the notion of mythical prototypes of *xwēdōdah* that set an example for human normativity, the Pahlavi authors did not hesitate to invoke the idea of moral relativism, arguing that '*xwēdōdah* may be abominable in your eyes, but it is beautiful in ours.' In line with this notion, and in stark contrast to the Palestinian Rabbinic rhetoric of universal sexual standards, the Babylonian Talmud advocates a classification of incest that reflects moral relativism: 'Incest may be wicked for Jews who were commanded to be holy at Sinai, but it is perfectly acceptable for non-Jews.'

---

not its Babylonian redaction. The talmudic redactors begin the discussion with the Tannaitic dispute over brother–sister relations, proceed to Rav Huna's statement regarding father–daughter relations, and conclude with Rav Hisda's statement addressing mother–son relations.

95 On the meaning of the particle *ōh*, see P.O. Skjærvø, "On the terminology and style of the Pahlavi scholastic literature," in C. Bakhos and R. Shayegan (eds.), *The Talmud in Its Iranian Context* (Tübingen: 2010), 194-99.

96 *Pahlavi Rivāyat* 8d5 (Williams, n. 3 above, 2:12, with slight modifications).

Admittedly, the correspondence between the Babylonian Talmud's discussion of Noahide incest and the Pahlavi discussion of *xwēdōdah* is somewhat uneven. To state an obvious difference, whereas incestuous relations are, according to the Babylonian Rabbinic reconstruction of Noahide law, merely **permissible** (that is, tolerated), the Zoroastrian sources speak of *xwēdōdah* as meritorious and praiseworthy. Thus despite the fascinating affinities between the Babylonian and Zoroastrian discussions, it must be borne in mind that these discussions are centered on fundamentally different religious categories.

Though the Babylonian Talmud's legal discourse reveals a surprisingly lenient approach to non-Jewish incest, the Babylonian Rabbinic authorities were constrained by the discursive and legal framework established by the antecedent Palestinian Rabbinic culture, a framework that addressed next-of-kin partnerships in terms of the forbidden/permissible dichotomy. Viewed against this shared Rabbinic heritage, the fact that the Babylonian Rabbis diverge significantly from rulings of their Palestinian counterparts to permit next-of-kin partnerships between non-Jews, while at the same time displaying awareness of the Pahlavi discourse, is remarkable.

The non-legal traditions pertaining to pre-Mosaic instances of incest provide the Babylonian Rabbis with an opportunity to express an affirmative stance on next-of-kin partnerships among non-Jews. In line with the Zoroastrian rhetoric of mythical prototypes that set an example for human norms of conduct, the Babylonian Rabbis similarly adduce examples of pre-Mosaic biblical figures to prove that certain types of incest are permissible for non-Jews. Unlike the Palestinian Rabbinic literature, which characterizes the sexual norms that govern non-Jews as in essence derived from the levitical statutes, the Babylonian Rabbinic discussion is couched in rhetoric that has a significant affinity to the Pahlavi account.

9. Incest riddles

A related *sugya* touching on the issue of Noahide sexual prohibitions, bJebamot 97b, concerns a set of riddles about unions that are incestuous in multiple ways, resulting in overlapping family relationships. Contextualizing the riddles, none of which are found in Palestinian Rabbinic works, by adducing Pahlavi texts on *xwēdōdah*, demonstrates that their content reflects the Babylonian Rabbis' intellectual engagement with Zoroastrian doctrinal subtleties.

While the literary genre of 'incest riddles' is already familiar from the ancient Greek literature, and similar riddles are attested in medieval Christian and Muslim sources (see below), the talmudic riddles in bJebamot 97b are intrinsically connected to the Rabbinic legal discourse on the Noahide sexual prohibitions. As we will see, the talmudic discussion of the riddles, like the talmudic legal discourse, reflects a tolerant approach, on the part of the Babylonian Rabbis, to non-Jewish incestuous practices. Moreover, the discussion of the riddles, I will demonstrate, reflects a talmudic response to specific nuances of the Zoroastrian doctrine of *xwēdōdah*.

"אח מאב דלאו מאם דהוא בעלה דאם ואנה! ברתה דאיתתי"[97] – אמ׳ ראמי בר חמא הא דלא כר׳ יהודה. "אח הוא בר הוא אחתיה אנא דהאי דדארי אנא"[98] – משכחת לה בגוי הבא על בתו.[99] "שלמא לך בר דבת[100] אחתיך אנא" – משכחת לה בגוי הבא על בת בתו. "דלאי דדלו דולא דיפול להו[101] סתר פתר דהאי דדרינא אכתפיה הוא ברי ואנא בת אחוא!" – משכחת לה בגוי הבא על בת בנו. "[ביא] ביא[102] מאח דהוא אב והוא בעל והוא בר בעלה והוא[103] בעלה דאם ואנא ברתה דאיתתיה ולא קא יהיב פיתא[104]

97 דאיתתי – omitted in MS Moscow 594.

98 MS Pesaro: דדרינא; MS Moscow 594: דד(ל)[ר]ינא אכתפא; MS Moscow 1017: [דדרינא] אכיתפאי; MS Oxford 367: דדיירנ׳ אכתפאי; MS Vatican 111: דדרינא אכתפאי.

99 MS Moscow 594 adds: והוליד ממנה בן; MS Vatican 111 adds: והוליד בן.

100 דבת – omitted in MS Oxford 367.

101 MS Moscow 1017: ליפוק לכו; MS Moscow 594: נ?פול להו; MS Oxford 367: לינפול להו; MS Vatican 111: ל[י]פול בכו; MS Pesaro: ליפול בכו.

102 This appears to be a Greek loanword (βία) denoting an act of force or violence. See A. Kohut (ed.), Nathan b. Yehiel of Rome, *Aruch Completum* (Vienna: 1878-1892), 2:45; M. Jastrow, *Dictionary of the Targumim . . .* (NY: 1926), 160; H.G. Liddell and R. Scott, *A Greek-English Lexicon*, 9th ed. with supp. (Oxford: 1968), 314; I. Wartski, *Leshon Hamidrashim* (Jerusalem: 1970), 198. On other uses of this term in Rabbinic sources, see S. Fraade, "Moses and Adam as polyglots," in R.S. Boustan et al., *Envisioning Judaism: Studies in Honor of Peter Schafer on the Occasion of his Seventieth Birthday* (Tübingen: 2013), 188. See also M. Sokoloff, *A Dictionary of Jewish Babylonian Aramaic of the Talmudic and Geonic Periods* (Ramat-Gan: 2002), 201 s.v. בייא.

103 MS Oxford 367 adds: בר, probably by way of interpolation from the previous clause.

104 A Geonic responsum preserves the version פיתפא, which is explained by the Gaon as מזונות (alimony, sustenance). See L. Ginzberg, *Genizah Studies in Memory of Dr. Solomon Schechter*, vol. 2: Geonic and Early Karaitic Halakha (NY: 1929), 177. Eli Ahdut notes, however, that this is an Iranian loanword meaning "food ration" ("Jewish–Zoroastrian polemics in the Babylonian Talmud" (Hebrew), in *Irano-Judaica* 4 (1999), 34 n. 74). See Sokoloff, n. 102 above, 908 s.v. פיתפא; J.N. Epstein, *Studies in Talmudic Literature and Semitic Languages*, edited by E.Z. Melamed (Hebrew), (Jerusalem: 1988), 2: 819-820. On the Iranian word, see C. Bartholomae, *Altiranisches Wörterbuch* (Berlin:

לאחוה[105] יתמי בריה ברתיה" – משכחת לה בגוי הבא על אמו והוליד ממנה בת[106] וחזר הזקן ובא עליה והוליד ממנה בנים ודריא להו.[107] "אנא ואת אחי אנא ואבוך אחא ואנא ואמך אחי" – משכחת לה בגוי הבא על אמו והוליד ממנה שתי בנות וחזר ובא על אחת מהן והוליד ממנה בן ודריא ליה אחתא דאימיה[108] ואמ' ליה הכי. "אנא ואת בני אחיות[109] ואנא ואבוך בני אחי ואנא ואמך בני אחי"[110] – הא בהיתירא נמי משכחת לה. ראובן שיש לו שתי בנות ואתא שמעון נסיב חדא מנייהו ואתא בריה דלוי[111] נסיב חדא נסיב! חדא![112] מנייהו וקאמ' ליה בריה דשמעו' לבר ברי דלוי הכי.

"He is a brother by the father but not by the mother, and he is the husband of the mother, and I am the daughter of his wife" – Rami b. Hama said: Such [a relationship is] not [legally possible], according to R. Judah's view.

"He whom I carry is a brother and a son and I am his sister" – this is possible where a non-Jew had relations with his daughter.

"Greetings to you son; I am the daughter of your sister" – this is possible where a non-Jew had relations with his daughter's daughter.

"Ye water-drawers who draw [water], a riddle has befallen you that defies solution.[113] He whom I carry on my shoulders is my son and I am the

---

1979 [1904]), 905-906 s.v. *pīhwā*; D.N. MacKenzie, *A Concise Pahlavi Dictionary* (Oxford: 2002 [1971]), 68 s.v. *pih*; S. Shaked, *The Wisdom of the Sasanian Sages* (Colorado: 1979), 267.

105 MS Vatican 111 adds: מאב.

106 All other textual witnesses add: וחזר ובא על אותה הבת. I suspect that the scribe of MS Munich 141 skipped this line by way of homeoteleuton. Alternatively, he might have found this clause redundant and decided to omit it.

107 דריא להו – omitted in MSS Moscow 1017, Oxford 367, and Pesaro.

108 דאימיה – omitted in MSS Moscow 1017, Vatican 111 and Pesaro. MS Oxford 367 has: אידך אחתא.

109 MSS Moscow 1017, Oxford 367, Pesaro: אחי.

110 ואנא ואמך בני אחי – omitted in MS Oxford 367, by way of homeoteleuton.

111 דלוי – omitted in MS Moscow 1017.

112 These words were probably erroneously duplicated by the scribe of MS Munich 141.

113 This translation follows Rashi's commentary on bJebamot 97b s.v. ליפול לכו: "to the workers, who irrigate the fields, I present this riddle . . . an enigmatic and secretive riddle has befallen you"

(לבני פועלין המשקין את השדות אני שואלת חידה זו. . . הרי נפלה לכם חידה סתומה ומוסתרת להפתר).

The expression ליפול לכו/בכו, which appears in most textual witnesses, is explained by Rashi as referring to a riddle that "befalls" the water-drawers. Similarly, R. Nathan b. Yehiel of Rome, in *Sefer Haarukh* (Kohut edition, n. 102 above, 3:64 s.v. דל), suggests the following explanation: "People who draw water, that is, those who draw profound insights, I ask that you solve the [following] enigma"

(בני אדם הדולין מים, כלומ' דולי חכמות עמוקות, אשאל לכם פתר סתור).

A somewhat different explanation is suggested in a Geonic responsum (Ginzberg, n. 104 above, 177):

daughter of his brother" – this is possible where a non-Jew had relations with the daughter of his son.

"I submit a complaint! For there is a brother who is a father and a husband and the son of the husband and the husband of the mother, and I am the daughter of his wife, and he provides no food for his orphan brothers, the children of his daughter" – this is possible where a non-Jew had relations with his mother and from her begot a daughter; then the grandfather had relations with her and from her begot sons and he carries them [perhaps in his arms or on his shoulders].

"I and you are brother and sister; I and your father are brother and sister, and I and your mother are sisters" – this is possible where a non-Jew had relations with his mother and from her begot two daughters, and then he had relations with one of these and from her begot a son. The mother's sister carries him, and she addresses him thus.

"I and you are the children of sisters, I and your father are the children of brothers, and I and your mother are the children of brothers" – this indeed is also possible in the case of a lawful marriage; Reuven had two daughters, and Shimon came and married one of them, and then came the son of Levi and married the other. The son of Shimon can thus say this to the son of the son of Levi.[114]

The passage contains a set of seven riddles, which portray multiple incestuous encounters that result in overlapping family relationships. The solutions to these riddles attempt to decipher the exact sequence of incestuous events that generated these complicated relationships. That incest should be the topic of talmudic riddles is not surprising,

---

"<. . .> דלו דולא סתר פתר פיר ' אשה העוברת <. . .> שהם דולין מים להשקות את <. . .> להן ריב ומצה יפול ביניהם שזה <. . .> שא הוא בני ואני בן אחיו משכחת לה <. . .> בא על בת בנו כדמפרש בגמרא."

Ginzberg, 168-69, interprets the Gaon's suggestion innovatively: "you, weavers, who weave the strings, dismantle the strong weaving" (אתם האורגים שמארגים החוטים סתרו האריגה החזקה). However, his creative construals of דולא as "woven cloth" and of סתר פתר as "unweaving" are challenged in E.S. Rosenthal, "Was Rav the son of the brother of R. Hiya also the son of his sister?" (Hebrew), in S. Lieberman et al. (eds.), *Hanoch Yalon Jubilee Volume on the Occasion of his Seventy-Fifth Birthday* (Hebrew), (Jerusalem: 1963), 303-304 n. 53. Rosenthal seems to suggest that the woman in the riddle addresses the water-drawers, saying that enmity (ריב ומצה) will befall them, for "he whom I carry on my shoulders is my son and I am the daughter of his brother." Rosenthal humbly concludes, however, that "For the time being, we must admit – as there is no use in entertaining new suggestions – that the words of this poor woman remain inaccessible to us, like an unsolved riddle that awaits solution." Sokoloff, n. 102 above, 835 s.v. סתר פתר, is likewise uncertain about the meaning of this phrase.

114 bJebamot 97b, according to MS Munich 141.

since incestuous relations that result in overlapping family relationships appear to have prompted intellectual curiosity in other cultures as well. Several examples of riddles involving incest are mentioned in ancient Greek works, and numerous examples are attested in medieval Christian and Muslim sources.[115] Despite the universal interest in incest riddles, the content of the talmudic riddles suggests a more specific connection to Zoroastrian ideology.

Nearly a decade ago, in an article on Jewish–Zoroastrian polemics, Eli Ahdut briefly addressed the riddles in bJebamot 97b.[116] According to Ahdut, the talmudic riddles reflect a direct polemic against the Zoroastrian practice of *xwēdōdah,* insofar as the Rabbinic engagement can be seen as an attempt to ridicule the Zoroastrian custom. Underlying Ahdut's argument that if the Rabbis devise riddles about incest, this must be for the polemical purpose of ridiculing an abhorrent practice, is the premise that incest is universally wrong. Indeed, this underlying premise reflects a deeply-entrenched and pervasive bias in Rabbinic and general scholarly culture.

Although I agree with Ahdut that the riddles reflect Babylonian Rabbinic awareness of the practice of *xwēdōdah,* I am inclined to disagree with his interpretation of the passage and the conclusions that should be drawn from it. According to Ahdut, the passage seeks primarily to ridicule and critique the institution of *xwēdōdah* as part of a broader

115 See especially van Gelder, n. 6. above, 138-43. A particularly interesting 13th-century riddle, which alludes to the Zoroastrian custom of next-of-kin marriages, reads as follows:

I have a maternal aunt, and I am her maternal uncle.
I have a paternal aunt, and I am her paternal uncle.
As for the woman whose paternal uncle I am,
the mother of my father is her mother.
Her father is my brother, her brother is my father,
and I have a maternal aunt who is thus described.
Where is the lawyer who has the various kinds
of expertise and knowledge in this matter?
Who will explain to us her relationship clearly
and reveal what worries our mind.
For we are no Zoroastrians or unbelievers,
we follow the divine law of Ahmad (i.e., Muhammad).
(cited in van Gelder, 140)

The last sentence of this riddle evokes the solution of the last of the seven riddles in bJebamot 97b, according to which "this indeed is also possible in the case of a lawful marriage."

116 Ahdut, n. 104 above, 34-36.

Jewish–Zoroastrian polemic in the Babylonian Talmud, a polemic his article charts. I contend, however, that in the passage in question – bJebamot 97b – there is in fact no negative or cynical tone, and no polemic or critique is apparent. The fact that the Babylonian Talmud resolves one of the riddles by saying that it refers to "a non-Jew who had relations with his daughter" does not necessarily imply that this practice is viewed negatively by the redactors. On the contrary, in the talmudic discussion of Noahide sexual prohibitions, we saw that there is an explicit statement, ostensibly made by the third-century Babylonian authority Rav Huna, to the effect that "A non-Jew is permitted to have relations with his daughter."[117] We also saw that this lenient position is accepted by the redactors of the *sugya* in question, who go out of their way to permit first-degree incestuous relations between non-Jews, permitting a non-Jew to have relations with his daughter, sister, and, in the case of a slave, even his mother. Keeping in mind the insights garnered from our analysis of other talmudic *sugyot* enables us to thoroughly reframe and contextualize the import of the riddles in bJebamot 97b.

Although the incest riddles appear only in the Babylonian Talmud, they are consistent with a broader Rabbinic interest in situations of multiple criminal counts. In their legal discussions, the Rabbis often seek to define the legal criteria for individuating criminal charges. They often consider distinct categories of transgression, individual bodies, and separate states of unawareness to be sufficient for such individuation. In a *sugya* concerning liability on multiple criminal counts in the case of incestuous relations (bMakot 14a),[118] the Babylonian Talmud relates the following:

117 bSanhedrin 57b-58b.

118 The Talmud devotes a lengthy discussion (bMakot 13a-14b) to a Tannaitic dispute over the question of whether sinners who are liable to the death penalty or to divine extirpation (*karet*) are also subject to the sanction of flogging. R. Ishmael argues that both those liable to the death penalty and those liable to divine extirpation are subject to flogging. R. Akiva argues that only those liable to divine extirpation are subject to flogging, while those liable to the death penalty are not. A third position is attributed to R. Isaac, according to whom even those liable to divine extirpation are not subject to flogging. R. Isaac deduces his position from the fact that Leviticus 18 prescribes divine extirpation for all sexual transgressors. Seeing that Scripture has already declared all sexual offenders liable to divine extirpation, what is the objective of reiterating, in Leviticus 20, that the penalty of divine extirpation (*karet*) is incurred for transgressing the prohibition against relations with one's sister? According to R. Isaac, the redundancy

> What would be the purpose of the reiteration of the penalty of divine extirpation (*karet*) in the case of [one who has relations with] his sister? To indicate separate liability for his sister, his father's sister, and his mother's sister. But is that not obvious? Are they not distinct persons, [relations with whom] fall under different categories [of transgression]? [Rather, the reiteration is intended to indicate] separate liability in the case of one who has relations with his sister, who is also his father's sister and his mother's sister. And how could such a case be possible? R. Ada b. Ahava said: [It is possible] in the case of a sinner who is the son of a sinner.[119] And this last point, where does R. Isaac derive it from? He deduces it by an a fortiori argument, as was taught: R. Akiva said: I [once] asked Rabban Gamaliel {and R. Joshua} at the fair held at Emmaus, where they had gone to buy an animal for the [marriage] feast of Rabban Gamaliel's son: If one has relations with his sister, who is also his father's sister and his mother's sister, what is the extent of his offence? Would he be liable only once for the various counts or for each count separately? And they said: This question we have not heard, but we have heard the following: If one has relations with his five wives [i.e., five different women] when they are menstruating, in one [continuous state of] unawareness, [upon discovering what he has done] he is liable for each act separately. And this yields an a fortiori argument: if, in the case of the menstruants, though each error is [a transgression] of the same sort, he is nonetheless liable for each act separately, he should be all the more liable on each count separately where the transgression falls under three different categories! And what does the other side say? The a fortiori argument is invalid, for how can one argue from the case of the menstruants, which involves several distinct persons [to this case, where there is only one person involved]?[120]

The *sugya* in bMakot 14a addresses a case of someone who had relations with a woman who was simultaneously his sister, his father's sister, and his mother's sister. Unlike the *sugya* with the riddles, however, here the Babylonian Talmud is not concerned about solving intellectual puzzles, but rather has practical legal concerns regarding the individuation of criminal charges. Although similar cases are already addressed in the Mishnah,[121] the Babylonian discussion of this issue in particular differs from earlier Rabbinic accounts and attests to an intensification of this line of thought in Babylonian

---

indicates that only *karet* is incurred, and not both *karet* and flogging. The passage quoted here addresses the Talmud's question about how R. Ishmael and R. Akiva would interpret the reiteration of the *karet* penalty in the case of the prohibition relating to one's sister.

119 Cf. bKritot 15a, and the discussion on p. 105 below.

120 bMakot 14a, according to MS Yad Harav Herzog.

121 See mKritot 3:5-6.

Rabbinic culture. In the Babylonian Talmud, R. Akiva inquires about someone who has relations with "his sister, who is also his father's sister and his mother's sister," whereas the parallel passages in the Mishnah and Sifra discuss the case of one who has relations with "his sister, and his father's sister and his mother's sister in one [continuous state of] unawareness." In other words, the Tannaitic works attribute to R. Akiva a question concerning the individuation of multiple counts of incest without alluding to the case of overlapping familial relationship in a single individual. The parallel passage in the Sifra reads:

> R. Akiva said: I [once] asked Rabban Gamaliel and R. Joshua at the fair held at Emmaus, where they had gone to buy an animal for the [marriage] feast of his son: If one has relations with his sister and his father's sister and his mother's sister in one [continuous state of] unawareness, what is the extent of his offence? Would he be liable only once for the various counts or for each count separately? They said to him: This question we have not heard, but we have heard the following: If one has sexual relations with his five wives [i.e., five different women] when they are menstruating, in one [continuous state of] unawareness, [upon discovering what he has done] he is liable for each act separately. And we see that this yields an a fortiori argument.[122]

The Babylonian Talmud explicitly states its reason for diverging from the earlier Rabbinic accounts. In the case of one who had relations with three different women while in a single continuous state of unawareness, it is obvious that he is liable for each count separately, since these are "distinct persons, [relations with whom] fall under different categories [of transgression]." In other words, the Babylonian Talmud has shifted the discussion from the case of distinct persons and distinct sorts of transgressions, to a case of prohibited relations with just one woman, but one who, being his sister, his father's sister, and his mother's sister, is related to him in three distinct ways, each of which renders relations with her prohibited. In line with the riddles of bJebamot 97b, the Babylonian Talmud's emphasis on 'overlapping relationships' in bMakot 14a underscores a heightened concern about this issue, above and beyond the cases discussed in Palestinian Rabbinic works.

Significantly, although mKritot 3:5-6 addresses a similar case in which a single sexual act with just one woman results in multiple

122 Sifra, Dibura De-Hova, parasha 1:8, according to MS Vatican 66. Cf. mKritot 3:7.

transgressions, since she is related to him in several ways, it is the Babylonian Talmud that delves into the complex sexual scenario that led to this situation of overlapping relationships. According to R. Ada b. Ahava, the case of a woman who is "his sister, who is also his father's sister and his mother's sister" must involve "a sinner who is the son of a sinner." This case is further explicated by R. Ada b. Ahava in bKritot 15a. A man had relations with his mother and gave birth to two daughters (who are also his sisters). This man then had relations with one of his daughters/sisters, from which union a son was born. Now, if this son has relations with the other daughter/sister from his father, he is in fact having relations with his sister, who is also his mother's sister and his father's sister, all at the same time.

In contrast to the neutral tone of the riddle *sugya* in bJebamot 97b about the overlapping family relationships generated by incestuous partnerships among non-Jews,[123] in the *sugya* in bKritot, R. Ada b. Ahava refers to the (Jewish) perpetrator as "a sinner who is the son of a sinner." E.S. Rosenthal has suggested that this "sinner who is the son of a sinner" is the same transgressor as the one described in the enigmas of bJebamot 97b, where he is referred to by the designation "non-Jew," using *lishna maalya*, euphemistic or 'politically correct' language, to avoid using a realistic description of his true nature (sinner, reprobate, etc.).[124] Use of the term "non-Jew" to denote a Jewish sinner is attested once more in the Rabbinic literature, in bSanhedrin 54a, where Rav Judah asserts that a "non-Jew" who has relations with his father is liable on two separate counts, namely, relations with one's father and homosexual relations. The talmudic redactors explicitly interpret "non-Jew" in this instance as referring to a Jewish sinner: "as to use of the term 'non-Jew' – that is a euphemism (*lishna maalya*)."

It is difficult to claim, however, that this extremely rare usage of the term "non-Jew" in the Rabbinic literature as a euphemism for a Jewish sinner is what the authors of the talmudic riddles had in mind. While Rav Judah in bSanhedrin 54a addresses a perpetrator who is liable for the serious transgressions of homosexual relations and the uncovering of one's father's nakedness, no transgressions are alluded to in the riddles of bJebamot 97b. That sugya depicts only legal enigmas and their respective solutions. Were the Babylonian Talmud using the term

123 Two of the riddles refer to relations not prohibited to Jews; see below at n. 126.

124 Rosenthal, n. 113 above.

"non-Jew" to designate a Jewish sinner, one would expect to find this usage referred to explicitly, as it is in bSanhedrin 54a. It is thus more plausible that the riddles of bJebamot 97b refer to non-Jewish incestuous relationships. The non-critical tone of the riddles simply reflects the Babylonian Talmud's general halakhic attitude to Noahide incest.[125]

It should be noted that some of the riddles in bJebamot 97b do not refer to incestuous relations between non-Jews, but to relations that are permissible for Jews. The last riddle is explicitly said to be "also possible in the case of a lawful marriage." It appears, then, that the riddles which refer to incestuous relations that are forbidden to Jews should be interpreted as pertaining to encounters between non-Jews, while the riddles that refer to relations that are permissible for Jews should be interpreted as pertaining to encounters between Jews. This does not mean, however, that non-Jews are criticized, ridiculed, or are in any way prohibited from engaging in such relations.[126]

10. Zoroastrian connections

Given that the 'incest riddle' genre is widely-attested in Greek, Christian, and Muslim literature, it cannot simply be assumed a priori that the riddles in bJebamot 97b were a response to the Sasanian practice of *xwēdōdah*. But it is possible to show that the creators of the talmudic riddles manifest a thoroughgoing familiarity with the doctrinal discourse about *xwēdōdah* reflected in the Pahlavi texts. In other words, it is not the mere fact that the Babylonian Talmud preserves a set of 'incest riddles' absent from Palestinian Rabbinic works that suggests a Zoroastrian impetus for their composition. Rather, the details of the riddles'

125 I suspect that, like Ahdut, Rosenthal seeks to read the entrenched assumption about the universality of incest taboos into the talmudic text. This assumption, however, is straightforwardly incompatible with Babylonian Rabbinic culture's tolerant attitude to non-Jewish acceptance of incest.

126 Admittedly, an alternative interpretation of "also possible in the case of a lawful marriage" could be suggested, namely, that the riddle can refer to Jews and non-Jews alike, just as the other cases can be seen as sinful for Jews and non-Jews alike. But in light of the fact that most of the riddles explicitly speak of "non-Jews" and are not formulated in general terms, it is more plausible that the constellation depicted in the last riddle is lawful **even** for Jews. Furthermore, the lack of any pejoratives or negative epithets to denote the non-Jews engaged in the relations in question supports my interpretation of the passage.

wording suggest Rabbinic awareness of, and reaction to, specific doctrinal and rhetorical elements found in the Pahlavi texts.

The notion of overlapping blood-relationships achieved by engaging in *xwēdōdah* is described in the following Pahlavi texts:

> It is likewise with a son born from a father and his daughter. It is crystal clear to be seen in this age that he is very happy and joyful who has a child from his child. What happiness, sweetness, and joy he experiences from a son whom a man has with his own daughter **and who is also the mother's brother!**
>
> And if it is a child born from a son and his mother **he is also the father's brother**. This is the road to more joy and bliss. And there is no harm from it greater than the benefits from it, nor any blemish greater than the beauty of it.[127]

> Assuredly, a daughter who was born of (his own) mother [and is thus his daughter and his sister], when the father practices (*xwēdōdah*) with the daughter who was born from his own copulation [with his mother], then it is superior to that when he is not her brother.[128]

The connections between the talmudic riddles and the Pahlavi rhetoric of *xwēdōdah* should be sought, however, not just in the general notion of overlapping family relationships achieved by multiple incestuous unions, but in the riddles' rhetorical elements. Consider the fascinating complaint that appears in one of the riddles in bJebamot 97b: "I submit a complaint! For there is a brother who is a father and a husband and the son of the husband and the husband of the mother, and I am the daughter of his wife, and he provides no food for his orphan brothers, the children of his daughter." It is significant that the complaint addresses neither the incestuous partnership in itself, nor the resulting overlapping relationships, but rather the fact that, despite the existence of multiple blood relationships that tie the addressee of the complaint to his orphan brothers, he is unwilling to provide food for them.

It may be the case, therefore, that this riddle echoes the Zoroastrian rhetoric of *xwēdōdah*. Alongside other justifications of the custom (see §7 above), the Pahlavi texts argue that by uniting sexually, relatives and members of a nuclear family can multiply and strengthen the ties (*paywand*) and connections that already exist between them. This rationale is expressed, for instance, in *Dēnkard* 3.80.3:

127 *Dēnkard* 3.80.21-22 (Madan edition, 76; Dresden edition, 56); translation based on Skjærvø 2011, n. 79 above, 205 (emphasis added).

128 *Pahlavi Rivāyat* 8d4 (Williams, n. 3 above, 2:12, with slight modifications). See also Ahdut, n. 104 above, 36.

> For that tie (*paywand*) to be immeasurably firmer, people of the same species should unite with their closest relatives and those who are close relatives with those to whom they are most closely tied. And the most closely tied relationships are the following three relationships involving being tied together: father and daughter, son and birth mother, and brother and sister.[129]

The *Pahlavi Rivāyat* similarly argues that had mankind followed the prototypical example of Mašī and Mašyānī, "never would a brother have been abandoned in love by his brother, nor a sister by her sister."[130] The text continues:

> For all penury, hatred of parents, and lack of love came to mankind on that account, when men came to them from a different town, and from a different province, or from a different country, and they married, and when they took their wives away, the fathers and mothers (i.e. of the women) wept, with these (words): "They are taking our daughter into captivity."[131]

We can see that, seeking to counter the "rule of exogamy" (namely, if men are forbidden to marry women from their own group, they will

129 *Dēnkard* 3.80.3 (Dresden edition, 53-54; Madan edition, 73); trans. based on Skjærvø 2011, n. 79 above, 203. In another passage, the author gives the example of how one's love for his sister can be increased and strengthened by engaging in *xwēdōdah* with her. See *Dēnkard* 3.80.18-19 (Dresden edition, 55; Madan edition, 75-76); trans. Skjærvø 2011, 204.

130 *Pahlavi Rivāyat* 8a8 (Williams, n. 3 above, 2:10).

131 Ibid. 8a9 (2:11, with slight modifications). Cf. the following description of exogamous marriage from *Dēnkard* 3.80.26-28 (trans. Skjærvø 2011, n. 79 above, 205):

> On the other hand, in the case of wives from outside, one can see their subservience and helplessness; how eager they are to serve their husbands so that they do not commit any offense; the patience they muster against the husband's harshness, and many other things. Nor are they happy in this way, for, when it comes to covering themselves with ornaments, wearing excellent garments, having servants, making up their faces and wearing perfumes, and living in large mansions, and all the other things affected by ladies of the house, then, when she does not get what she wants and she has no other recourse, she calls him bad names and heaps upon him foulness and bad language. She has accumulated by trickery the things she owns. Secrets she divulges. Night and day she bickers and finds fault with him, she attacks his parents' household, drags her husband to court, and incites the town against him. She will say: "Release me from this marriage!" and many other various bad, harmful, evil, ugly sins connected with this."

marry women from outside),[132] which would undermine the tradition of *xwēdōdah*, the Pahlavi authors maintained that marriages contracted with foreigners cause sorrow and displeasure to everyone involved, whereas consummation of *xwēdōdah* increases the natural love and affection one already possesses for his next-of-kin. Interestingly, this justification is not only recorded in Zoroastrian sources, but confirmed by Ovid in the *Metamorphoses*. As Skjærvø notes, according to Ovid, there are "peoples (*gentes*), among whom sons join with their mothers and daughters with their fathers so that their sense of duty/devotion (*pietas*) is increased by their double love (*geminato amore*)."[133]

Viewing the complaint in the fifth riddle of the *sugya* in bJebamot against the backdrop of this argument is highly illuminating. The talmudic argument is phrased as a personal complaint: despite the existence of multiple blood-relations that tie the addressee of the complaint to his orphan brothers, he has failed to protect them and provide for their needs. Insofar as the purpose of *xwēdōdah* is to enable one to better protect and care for family members, the talmudic riddle could be seen as subversive. It is not clear, however, whether the Babylonian Talmud is criticizing this Pahlavi justification of *xwēdōdah* by arguing that multiplying family ties between relatives does not necessarily lead to heightened attentiveness to their needs, or whether the Babylonian Talmud is actually receptive to the Pahlavi rhetoric, invoking it to reproach one who fails to live up to his commitments despite the existence of multiple ties. Either way, the riddles in bJebamot 97b, like the *sugyot* about the Noahide sexual prohibitions, echo important aspects of contemporary Zoroastrian discourse on *xwēdōdah*.

132 See, e.g., C. Levi-Strauss, *The Elementary Structures of Kinship*, trans. J.H. Bell and R. von Stumer (Boston: 1969), 19, 51, 481; B. Malinowski, *The Sexual Life of Savages* (Boston: 1987 [1927]), 425, 433.

133 Skjærvø, n. 4 above, citing Silk, n. 76 above, 447 n. 42, which adduces Ovid, *Metamorphoses*, 10.331-334.

Aggregation of Estimates when Decision by Majority is not Possible

Itay Lipschits* and Mordechai E. Schwarz**

1. Introduction

The majority principle is a basic decision-making rule in many legal systems. It gives rise to such procedural rules as creation of panels with an odd number of judges to ensure a majority opinion, and, less

* College of Law and Business, Ramat-Gan

** Department of Management and Economics, Open University Institute for Policy Analysis frequently, mandating that a debate be held before a decision is handed down, to ensure that both views have been duly considered. Decision rules are, however, also needed for cases in which no opinion can muster a majority. The issue addressed in this article was pondered by the Sages of Jewish law between the years 200-600 CE, as recorded in a *sugya* in tractate Baba Batra of the Talmud, and seems likely to challenge twenty-first century scholars as well. The *sugya* discusses how to determine the value of an asset as an aggregate of three different appraisals by professional assessors. According to the majority principle, it is clear that if two of the assessors agree on one value, while the third assessor disagrees, the decision is in accordance with the majority opinion. The problem arises when each of the assessors specifies a different value. For cases in which three assessors who appraise an asset specify values of 80, 100, and 120, three different methods of aggregation were suggested by Tannaitic Sages. These methods yield three different results: 100, 90, and $93\frac{1}{3}$. It was decided that the method yielding the result 100 would be the legally authoritative method. But the Babylonian Talmud's justification for this ruling, and for its rejection of the other methods, is surprising: the Amoraic Sages did not determine which method was 'correct,' but ruled that an alternative approach that R. Huna put forward as the correct ruling twice in the course of the *sugya* was obscure and incomprehensible. It was this argument that inspired us to explore the methods that were not accepted as legally authoritative, especially the most challenging of the methods, namely, the one that yields $93\frac{1}{3}$.

This article seeks to examine the proposed Tannaitic decision rules, and in particular, to decipher the obscure third method, for which we suggest three different interpretations. The Tannaitic views address a specific case, that of appraisal by three assessors who set values that are symmetrically distributed around the mean. We will generalize the Tannaitic views, applying them to appraisals with values other than those mentioned in the baraita of the assessors, especially when the distribution is not symmetrical, and also generalize the method set down as legally authoritative, so as to render it applicable to cases of more than three appraisals. Lastly, we will examine the controversy among the decisors over how the decision rule is to be implemented in practice, and suggest an interpretation of the controversy.[1]

1 Some of the insights presented in this article are the fruit of collaborative study with Nobel Laureate Robert J. Aumann.

2. The *sugya* of the assessors (bBaba Batra 107a-b)

A baraita in tractate Baba Batra discusses the appraisal of assets:

> Our Rabbis taught: Three went down to appraise. One says, [its value is appraised] at a *mane* [100 *zuz*] and two say, at 200 [*zuz*]; one says, at 200 [*zuz*] and two say, at a *mane* [100 *zuz*]: the one, being in the minority, is overruled (*batel yahid bemiuto*).[2] One says, at a *mane* [100 *zuz*], one says, at 20 [*sela*] [80 *zuz*], and one says, at 30 [*sela*] [120 *zuz*]: it is adjudged at a *mane* [100 *zuz*]. R. Eliezer b. Zadok says, it is adjudged at 90 [*zuz*]. Others say, they appraise between them and divide it by three (*meshalshin*).[3]

Following the baraita, a debate ensues in the Talmud:

> He who says, we adjudge it at a *mane* [100 *zuz*], adopts the middle course (*milta metziata*). R. Eliezer b. Zadok says, it is adjudged at 90 [*zuz*]. His view is that the land is worth 90 [*zuz*]. He who says 20 [*sela*] [80 *zuz*], errs by 10 downward, and he who says a *mane* [100 *zuz*], errs by 10 upward.
>
> On the contrary (*aderaba*), [why not say that] the land is worth 110 [*zuz*], and he who says a *mane* [100 *zuz*], errs by 10 downward. And does he who says 30 [*sela*] [120 *zuz*], err by 10 upward? Nevertheless, [adopt an aggregated appraisal based on] the first two [appraisals], which do not exceed a *mane* [100 *zuz*].
>
> Others say, they appraise between them and divide it by three. Their view is that the land is worth $93\frac{1}{3}$. He who says 20 [*sela*] [80 *zuz*], errs by $13\frac{1}{3}$ downward. He who says a *mane* [100 *zuz*], errs by $13\frac{1}{3}$ upward. By rights he should have said more [i.e., aggregated the appraisal higher], and the reason he did not is that he thought, It is enough; I already exceeded my colleagues by a lot.
>
> On the contrary, [why not say that] the land is worth $113\frac{1}{3}$, and he who says a *mane* [100 *zuz*], errs by $13\frac{1}{3}$ downward. He who says 30 [*sela*] [120 *zuz*], errs by $13\frac{1}{3}$ upward. By rights he should have said more, but he thought, It is enough; I already exceeded my colleagues by a lot.
>
> Nevertheless, adopt the first two, which do not exceed 100 [*zuz*]. Rav Huna said: the law is in accordance with the others' view. Rav Ashi said: we do not understand the rationale of the others, shall we decide the law in

2 On this expression, see Saul Lieberman, *Tosefta Kifshuta*, Sota, 660. In Lieberman's opinion, it appears only with regard to assessors and judges; he therefore concludes that when it is mentioned with regard to witnesses, it refers to disqualified witnesses.

3 bBaba Batra 107a-b. The baraita also appears, with certain differences, in tKetubot 11:2. The main difference between the two versions is in the formulation of the view of the "others," which the Tosefta puts as follows: "They appraise it between them and divide them [in the printed editions: it] by three." On the various meanings of the term "divide by three" (*meshalshin*), see n. 24 below.

> accordance with their view?! The judges of the exile taught: they appraise between them and divide it by three.
>
> Rav Huna said: the law is in accordance with the view of the judges of the exile. Rav Ashi said: we do not understand the rationale of the judges of the exile; shall we decide the law in accordance with their view?!

Neither the baraita and nor the *sugya* clarify why the appraisal was needed, but according to most of the Early Authorities, the appraisal was needed for repayment of a debt.[4]

4 See *Hidushei Ri Migash*, bBaba Batra 107a, which explains the *sugya* as discussing the case of a debtor who has only land. The Rashbam ad loc. s.v. *shlosha*, interprets it as a case of assets belonging to orphans from which it is necessary to pay out the maintenance due the orphans' deceased father's wife and daughters. This is also the view of R. Isaac b. Abraham of Narbonne-Carcassonne (Ri Karkusha), who notes that some ask, why would it be necessary to get an appraisal, rather than selling the asset at an auction? He offers two answers to this question. One refers to a situation in which market prices are liable to change, and the appraisal will take these anticipated changes into consideration. The second is that the sale of the assets would be the type of sale where no public announcement of the impending sale is made, as is the procedure when sales are intended to fund maintenance payments (*mezonot*) and burial expenses (see bKetubot 100b); see R. M.J. Blau, *Shitat Hakadmonim*, Baba Batra (NY: 1981), 17. R. Abraham b. Isaac of Narbonne (Rabad II) offers a similar interpretation, cited in Blau, 235: "Where a public announcement is made, appraisal is not germane." R. Menahem Hameiri queries the relevance of appraisal in cases where a public announcement of the sale is made, and leaves the question open, but implicitly, it turns out that an appraisal takes place even where an announcement is made (*Beit Habehira*, bBaba Batra 107a s.v. *shuma*).

The Ritba quotes the Rashbam's interpretation, with which he disagrees, arguing that in the case of a sale for the purpose of paying maintenance for the wife and daughters, the price is set according to the going market rate, because the wife and daughters have no legal entitlement to the land, see *Hidushei Haritba*, Baba Batra (Mosad Harav Kook edition, 819). The Ritba quotes the explanation given by the Ri (Migash, according to the editor of the Mosad Harav Kook edition) that this is an appraisal for the purpose of paying a *ketuba* claim or repaying a debt. In support of this view, Lieberman notes that from the specific place where the baraita is found in the Tosefta, it appears that the assessors are appraising the field for the woman herself, who wishes to use it, see *Tosefta Kifshuta*, Ketubot, 359. Yet another interpretation, which the Ritba takes to be the main explanation, is that the case refers to a transaction between a buyer and a seller who have agreed that the price would be set by three assessors. (See bAvoda Zara 72a: "When [an item] has been appraised by three [we determine the price accordingly], even if two of the three agree [about the price].") R. Bezalel

3. The assessors' legal status

Three assessors are required for an appraisal in light of the requirement that a lay court (*beit din shel hediotot*) have a minimum of three judges.[5] The three who "went down to appraise" so that the asset could be sold are not judges, but individuals with knowledge or experience in appraising[6]; we will henceforth refer to them as "assessors."

Before discussing aggregation of the assessors' appraisals, it will be helpful to consider a preliminary question about the assessors' legal status. Are assessors like witnesses, and thus subject to the rules of evidence? Or are assessors akin to judges, and thus subject to the procedural rules operative in the courtroom? Or might it be the case that they

---

Ashkenazi, in *Shita Mekubetzet*, adduces the Reem's interpretation, according to which, when a debtor has land but no money, the creditor takes over the land in accordance with such an appraisal. It is very surprising that there do not seem to be any Early Authorities who explain the need for the appraisal with reference to estimation of damages (see R. Joseph Rosin, *Responsa Tzofnat Paneiah* [Warsaw edition, 245]) or for valuations of assets for sacred purposes or the second tithe, which are mentioned in the third Mishnah of the first chapter of mSanhedrin.

5 "R. Joseph b. Maniumi said in the name of R. Nahman: A widow does not need a court of expert [judges], but she does need a court of laymen" (bBaba Metzia 32a). And Maimonides rules:

> A widow, whether from engagement or marriage, may take an oath and sell her [deceased] husband's land and [from the proceeds of the sale] collect [the sums specified in her *ketuba*] either in a court of expert [judges], or in a court of non-expert [judges], provided it consists of three trustworthy men who are knowledgeable about appraising land. . . . But if she sells [land] without the participation of the court, a public announcement need not be made, yet nevertheless she does need three who are trustworthy and knowledgeable about appraisal. (*Code*, Laws concerning Marriage 17:13)

The Meiri rules: "And as long as it is only a matter of trust, two are sufficient, but to divide [assets], it needs to be appraised, and wherever you need an appraisal, there are never fewer than three" (*Beit Habehira*, bSanhedrin 17b). The *sugya* we are examining, bBaba Batra 107a-b, specifies that in the case of an appraisal by three assessors, each one is required to do the appraisal on his own. The Talmud also tells us of a procedure of appraisal by ten assessors: "And regarding [valuations of land dedicated to the Temple], nine [Israelites] and a priest (*kohen*), and so too regarding [valuations of] people" (mMegila 4:3). See also n. 18 below.

6 Alfasi explains that in the context of appraisal, the term "lay court" means "men who are trustworthy and proficient at appraisal" (*Rif*, bKetubot 56b).

have a sui generis status, and are akin to neither witnesses nor judges, and when they render a professional determination, it is not testimony but rather an estimate (*umdena*)? The baraita opens by saying that when there are two identical appraisals and a divergent third appraisal, "the one, being in the minority, is overruled." Decision by majority opinion could, perhaps, be interpreted as favoring the testimony of two assessors over the testimony of just one assessor – "the word of one shall not stand against the word of two"[7] – or as applying the procedural rule "incline toward the many," as is done in the courtroom. But from a passage in tractate Temura, it appears that an appraisal is indeed an estimate, and not testimony or a judicial verdict:

> Said Ula: They said [that individuals must refund to the Temple (*hekdesh*) any losses incurred in redeeming consecrated objects] only where two [assessors] made the appraisal, but where three made the appraisal, even if afterwards a hundred assessors disagreed with the three, the appraisal of the three is not revised. But is it so? R. Safra said: Where is it said that a hundred are like two, and two are like a hundred? In matters of testimony. But with regard to estimates (*umdena*), we follow the majority opinion. Moreover, if there are three against three [i.e., three come after the first trio of assessors and give a higher estimate], do we not follow the latter, so that the [interests of the] Temple will always come out ahead? Ula avers: the appraisal requirement is a matter of Rabbinic law (*midivreihem*), and the Rabbis were lenient about it.[8]

This *sugya* reveals that on the one hand, appraisal is unlike testimony, because with respect to appraisal, the majority opinion is followed, whereas with regard to testimony, the operative principle is "two are like a hundred." On the other hand, the *sugya* concludes that were an appraisal required by Torah law, it would be possible to appeal even a three-assessor appraisal, if three other assessors testify that the field is worth more, since in a case of doubt, that which is consecrated to the Temple takes precedence. The finality of three-assessor appraisal follows from the fact that by Torah law, it is possible to de-consecrate, i.e., redeem, something worth a *mane* [100 *zuz*] with a coin of little value (*pruta*); the appraisal process is required only by Rabbinic law. But the possibility of appealing an appraisal proves that appraisal is unlike a

7 This talmudic dictum is stated with reference to the rules of testimony. See, e.g., bShevuot 48a, regarding testimony of two witnesses that is challenged by testimony to the contrary by just one witness.

8 bTemura 27b.

judicial verdict, because in Jewish law there is no appeals instance.[9] The combination of the two special laws governing appraisal – decision by the majority view and the possibility of appeal – implies that the testimony of assessors is not testimony in the usual sense.

In the talmudic literature, testimony with respect to which we do not apply the "two are like a hundred" rule, but rather, we apply the principle of decision by the majority view, is found only in cases where it is possible to rely on the testimony of a sole witness, or that of disqualified witnesses, for "in every case where [the testimony of] one witness has legal effect, a woman and a disqualified witness can also testify."[10] Regarding this type of testimony, R. Nehemia said: "In every case where the Torah relied on one witness – it followed the majority view."[11]

This means that wherever the Torah did not insist that two fit witnesses were required, not only is the testimony of a sole witness valid, but so is that of disqualified witnesses, and the status of the testimony is that of an estimate, where decision is by the majority view. The contrast between the laws of testimony (where "two are like a hundred" and decision is not by the majority view) and the laws of estimation is explicit in the Gemara: "When do the Rabbis say that we follow the majority view? This applies only in the case of estimates, where the more there are, the more experts there are."[12] In other words, with respect to an estimate based on a majority determination, the larger the group of assessors, the higher the likelihood that a decision will be correct.[13] Despite the fact that following the majority is a universal rule derived

9 See Zerach Warhaftig, "Precedent in Jewish law," in H. Ben-Menahem and N.S. Hecht, *Authority, Process, and Method: Studies in Jewish Law* (Amsterdam: 1998), 1-32.

10 Maimonides, *Code*, Laws concerning Witnesses 5:3.

11 bSota 31b; 47b.

12 bShevuot 42a.

13 This intuition, which was proven in 1785, is known as the Condorcet Jury Theorem. It states that if the probability that every member of a deciding body will independently reach a 'correct' decision is greater than $\frac{1}{2}$, then: (a) the probability that the group will reach a correct decision by majority ruling is greater than the probability that an individual 'expert' will reach a correct decision; (b) as the number of the members of the deciding body increases, the probability of the group's reaching a correct decision approaches 1. It must be noted, however, that the Condorcet Jury Theorem applies to decisions about binary problems. For a proof of the intuition with regard to problems where the decision variables are continuous, see Gerlach-Kristen, n. 88 below.

from the verse "incline toward the many" (*aharei rabim lehatot*) (Exod. 23:2), and is valid both in court judgments and in other situations where there is doubt (as in the case of nine shops),[14] in the case of estimation, at least, this is not a rule imposed by scriptural decree (*gzeirat hakatuv*) with no rational basis. Rather, it seeks to maximize the probability of arriving at the value that is as close as possible to the 'real' value.[15]

The assessors are not witnesses in the regular sense because they do not testify about what they have seen, but about an estimate arrived at on the basis of their evaluation and professional knowledge. In contemporary parlance, they are expert witnesses. Nor are the assessors judges, because they do not decide the law, rather, they provide information to the court, and the court makes the decision. Moreover, halakhically speaking, the determination that assessors (and expert witnesses) have the legal status of estimators explains why the Tannaim in the baraita had to decide on aggregation rules for the case where the three appraisals differ. Were the status of the assessors that of witnesses, we would have to regard them as witnesses who contradict each other, and their testimony would have been set aside.[16]

4. The problem

The baraita about the aggregation of three appraisals starts with the simple case in which there is a majority of two against one. In this case there is no controversy among the Tannaim: the minority view is overruled (*batel yahid bemiuto*). It might seem that, given that the problem we are dealing with is not binary (e.g., liable or exempt?; kosher or non-kosher?, etc.), it would have been proper, despite the fact that it is likely the different assessors have similar skills and hence each has the same chance of producing a correct or a mistaken evaluation, to assess the asset using a formula that gives some weight to the minority

14 See bHulin 11a on meat purchased in a locale with a preponderance of kosher shops, and it is not known whether its source is a shop that sells kosher meat or non-kosher meat; one can rely on the fact that the majority of shops are kosher, and permit the meat.

15 This may be what R. Joseph Rosin (the Rogatchover) meant in saying, "In any case, in bBaba Batra 107 concerning estimation, we follow the majority, though the exact meaning of majority [here] is irrelevant" (*Responsa Tzofnat Paneiah*, 1:241 [Warsaw edition, 13]).

16 On the case of a panel of judges who issue three different opinions, see below at nn 113-14.

opinion too.[17] But the baraita states that majority decision is preferred even in the case of appraisers, although their legal status is that of estimators.[18] R. Samuel b. Meir (the Rashbam) and other Early Authorities noted that decision in accordance with the view of the majority

17 E.g., it could have been stipulated that the appraised value would be the weighted average of the assessor's appraisals, in this case: $\frac{2}{3}\times 200+\frac{1}{3}\times 100=166\frac{2}{3}$.

18 See R. Jacob Kamenetsky, *Emet Leyaakov*, Moed, 400, which addresses the problem raised by the *Tosafot* regarding bMegila 23b s.v. *asara kohamim*, and in bArakhin 19b s.v. *o dilma shani*, namely, why have ten appraisers, and not eleven, which would prevent the possibility of a split court (*beit din shakul*)? One of his arguments points out that in the 'three who went down to appraise' baraita, the simple rule regarding a case where two say 200 and one says 100 – the opinion of the assessor in the minority is overruled – is mentioned even though the 'follow the majority' principle is straightforward and goes without saying. Despite its simplicity, it is important to mention it in the context of assessors. In R. Kamenetsky's opinion, in the case of assessors, unlike that of judges who disagree about whether someone is liable or exempt, and the opinion of one judge or the other is true, it is possible that all the appraisals are mistaken, because there is no single truth (i.e., appraisals have a subjective element to them). Hence the baraita's assertion that if the majority has agreed on an opinion, a minority view to the contrary is nonetheless to be totally disregarded, and given no weight, is indeed a novel insight.

The issue of ignoring the minority also arises in light of the talmudic principle that "we do not follow the majority in [disputes over] monetary matters" (bBaba Kama 27b, 46b), which conflicts with the judicial decision-making principle of deciding in accordance with the view of the majority of the judges, ignoring the minority opinion. When there is a majority of judges against a minority, a debate takes place (in mishnaic parlance, negotiation [*masa umatan*]), in which both sides voice their opinions. The debate over how to decide the case strengthens the majority view, in the sense that the minority view has been explicitly considered in relation to the majority view, given a hearing, and rejected; see *Tosafot*, bBaba Kama 27b s.v. *km"l deein holkhin*. It is conceivable that the three who "went down to appraise" also conducted a debate among themselves before firming up their opinions. This is how the Rashbam understood the *sugya*: "They negotiate the matter, and each one knows what his colleague thinks, and after they have negotiated, they set their hearts on stating what appears to them to be the case" (ad loc. s.v. *ubedin hu dilma*). Similarly, R. Joseph ibn Migash rejects appraisal by two assessors (even if their appraisals concur) because "someone can say: maybe, had there been a third with them, he would have disagreed with them and showed them that they are mistaken and they would have adopted his opinion, or one of them would have concurred with his opinion, and the other would have remained alone, and

of assessors is mandated by the scriptural verse that addresses judges, namely, "incline toward the majority" (Exod. 23:2), which might seem to be a scriptural decree. But in light of the above discussion, the other possibility is that the Tannaim understood that when an absolute majority of assessors concurs regarding an exact value, it is likely that the divergent opinion represents 'too big an error,' and therefore ought not to be considered at all, that is, the minority view should be overruled (*batel yahid bemiuto*).

The main question addressed in the baraita is the case where there is no majority for any view, and each of the assessors sets a different value, the example given in the baraita being 80, 100, and 120. But we may nonetheless wish to explore why, in the case of three divergent opinions, we cannot simply apply the rule that the minority view is overruled. In other words, if we assume that "the 100 appraisal is covered by the 200 appraisal" (בכלל מאתיים מנה),[19] then the median value, 100, is covered by the 120 appraisal, and in this case the appraisal of 80 is overruled as the minority opinion. But the claim that the minority view is overruled is stated in the baraita only with respect to the case where there are two identical appraisals, whereas the Talmud's explanation of the Tanna Kama's view in the case in which there are three divergent opinions is that it recommends the "middle course" (*milta metziata*). It seems that the majority view overrides the minority view only when it is unanimous, not when the majority itself is divided.[20] The baraita quotes the opinions of three Tannaim. Two of them specify a numeric value without revealing the rule used to reach the decision. The third opinion is formulated as an obscure rule for reaching a decision. All the opinions offer an alternative to the rule that "the one, being in the

his opinion would not have been relied on" (*Responsa Ri Migash*, #141). And see too *Netivot Hamishpat* 103:1, which rules likewise.

19 bSanhedrin 31a, bBaba Batra 41a.

20 *Tosefta Kifshuta*, Sota, 660, emphasizes the stylistic difference between "the one, being in the minority, is overruled" and "the word of one shall not stand against the word of two." See also R. Zechariah Agmati (Morocco, 12th c.) *Sefer Haner*, 274, quoting the commentaries of the Ri Migash and R. Meir Halevi Abulafia, *Yad Rama* (Jerusalem 1994 edition, 472). The Early Authorities use the expression "the one, being in the minority, is overruled" with reference to the first part of the baraita. In referring to the second part, which deals with the decision between the various assessors' opinions, the expression they use is "the word of one shall not stand against the word of two," which appears to be based on a logical evaluation of the data.

minority, is overruled," which cannot be implemented directly when there are three divergent appraisals.[21]

5. The three Tannaitic views on appraisal

The Tanna Kama's view is that the assessors' controversy is settled by appraising the asset at 100 [*zuz*]. The opinion is not explained in the baraita, and at first sight, it seems that it can be reached in three ways. One way is the simple average that sums the three appraisals and divides the sum by three. The second is setting the value of the asset at the midpoint between the two extreme appraisals of 80 and 120. The third is to use the median appraisal. In the specific example adduced in the baraita (80, 100, 120), each of these calculations yields the same result: 100. In examples with different numbers, however, each method of calculation produces a different result. Let us take a closer look at the three methods.

The first decision method, averaging, takes into account all three opinions, but it is liable to produce a result that does not coincide with the opinion of any of the assessors. Note that this method was not mentioned at all as an interpretive or halakhic possibility.[22]

The second method sets the appraised value at the midpoint between the extreme appraisals, completely ignoring the median appraisal. We would need to clarify why, after selecting three assessors, the median appraisal is ignored, and why it is necessary to

21 This conclusion must be qualified with both the Bah's gloss on the *Rashbam*, which invokes the "the one, being in the minority, is overruled" argument (the formulation in the 1721 Venice edition of the *Rashbam* is the same as that found in the printed editions), and the commentary referred to as Rashi printed around the pages of the *Rif* s.v. *nadon bemane* (51a). The latter reads: "Since both the one who said 30 [*sela*] [120] and the one who said a *mane* [100], agree that it is worth 100, he who said 20 [*sela*] [80] is alone and overruled as a minority." On the identity of the author of this commentary on the portion of Baba Batra for which there is no Rashi commentary, which includes the *sugya* we are examining, see I.M. Ta-Shma, "Rashi–Rif and Rashi–Rosh," in Z.A. Steinfeld (ed.), *Rashi Studies* (Hebrew), (Ramat-Gan: 1993), 209-20; R. Abraham Havatzelet, "Rashi's commentary printed around Rif," *Moriah* 19:1-2 (1993), 106.

22 This exclusion of the simple arithmetic average from consideration in the *sugya* calls for explanation; indeed, the status of the average in halakhic thinking is a subject that merits a study of its own. See below at nn 29 and 82.

select three assessors to begin with if one of the appraisals will not be taken into account. Moreover, in most cases the midpoint cannot be expected to coincide with the opinion of any of the assessors. This means that basically, the appraisals serve as a sample by means of which we evaluate reality, but there is no commitment that any of the appraisals will be accepted.

Deciding in line with the median appraisal appears to ignore the two other opinions, and is based on the appraisal of just one assessor.

The second Tannaitic view adduced in the baraita is that of R. Eliezer b. Zadok, who sets the appraisal at 90. This opinion appears to be arrived at by setting the appraisal at the midpoint between the two lower appraisals, 80 and 100, so this opinion, too, utterly ignores one of the appraisals, namely, 120.

The third opinion, that of "the others" – an epithet for the Tanna R. Meir[23] – does not give a number, but rather formulates a decision rule: "they appraise between them and divide it by three (*meshalshin*)." The literal meaning is that the appraisal should be "between" the assessors, that is, some intermediate value should be reached, and then somehow divided.[24]

Let us now examine these views in greater detail.

23 On the Talmud's explanation for its use of this epithet to refer to R. Meir, see bHorayot 13b.

24 The term *meshalshin* has a number of meanings in the Rabbinic literature:

(a) to divide equally. See mBaba Batra 3:4; mMakot 1:3; bBaba Batra 56a; bBaba Batra 146a.
(b) to divide into three. "They divided the day into three, a third for Torah, a third for prayer, a third for labor" (Ecclesiastes Rabbah 9). This is how the Rashbam interprets the term in our *sugya*: "it should be adjudged by [dividing it into] thirds."
(c) to divide proportionately, not evenly. "Said Rav Hisda: This was taught only if he who bid forty stands by his bid, but if he who bid forty does not stand by his bid, then we divide it (*meshalshin*) between them" (bArakhin 27b); and see *Rashi* ad loc.
(d) to consign to a third party (bGitin 40b, Rashi ad loc.). It may be that here the word would be pointed differently, rendering its pronunciation *mashlishin*.
(e) to repeat three times, as in tNegaim 8:2.

And see *Tosefta Kifshuta*, Ketubot, 359-60.

5.1 The Tanna Kama

The Tanna Kama's opinion – that the value of the asset is set at 100 – is explained in the Babylonian Talmud as a "middle course" (*milta metziata*), that is, a midpoint. This explanation seems to be compatible with all three methods of calculation presented above: median (*hetzion*), average, and midpoint between the extreme points. The Rashbam and Maimonides disagreed about the interpretation of the term "midpoint."

Maimonides adduces the Tanna Kama's ruling as law, and brings the example of the three appraisals from the baraita, where the value of the asset is determined to be 100. But he also adds his own example to illustrate how, in his view, the Tanna Kama's figure of 100 should be understood: "One says 100 and one says 90 and one says 130. It is adjudged at 110, and in this way it is always assessed between them."[25]

In other words, according to Maimonides we must ignore the median (100) and determine the appraised value according to the point that is midrange between the two extremes: $110 = \frac{130+90}{2}$. Maimonides' interpretation of "middle course" (*milta metziata*) is that it is arrived at by taking the midpoint (*milta metziata*) between the two extremes.[26] But this method raises difficulties: (a) In what way are the extreme appraisals that determine the aggregated appraisal preferable to other appraisals of the item's value? (b) The method is open to manipulation (it is not strategy-proof), and anyone who puts forward an extreme appraisal knows that she can tilt the aggregated appraisal.[27]

The Rashbam's interpretation of the Tanna Kama's opinion raises a difficulty. The Rashbam starts with an explanation similar to that given by Maimonides: "The value that decides between the two [extremes] is reached by adding 5 [*sela*] [20 *zuz*], to the lower appraisal and subtracting 5 [20] from the higher."[28] The Rashbam appears to be deciding between the two extreme appraisals, and the fact that his determination

25 *Code*, Laws concerning Creditor and Debtor 22:14. In the printed editions, the word "always" is absent, but in most MSS it appears as quoted here, or at the end of the sentence; see n. 35 below.

26 This is also the Meiri's ruling in *Beit Habehira* ad loc. (Sofer edition, 470).

27 "We are dependent on one assessor, who can exaggerate, and we will take his opinion into account for the sake of [reaching] a middle course (*milta metziata*), contra the majority" (*Tosefta Kifshuta*, Ketubot, 359).

28 *Rashbam*, bBaba Batra 107a s.v. *milta metziata*.

coincides with the median appraisal (100) is coincidental.[29] But immediately after that, he states:

> And the law is that it should be adjudged in accordance with the view of the one who said a *mane* [100], since both the one who said 30 [*sela*] [120] and the one who said a *mane* [100], agree that it is worth a *mane* [100]. {Hence the one who said 20 [80] is alone and overruled as a minority. And both the one who said 20 [80] and the one who said a *mane* agree that it is not worth more than a *mane*, and the one who said 30 [120] is alone and overruled as a minority.}[30] And in my opinion, the same is true if he said 28 *sela* [112], which is not so much in the middle.[31]

In this statement, the Rashbam takes the thrust of the law to be that the determinative appraisal is the median appraisal (100), basing this ruling on the majority principle, a type of "median voter theorem."[32] On this argument, two assessors – the one who says 100 and the one who says 120 – concur that the asset is worth at least 100, and their opinion prevails over that of the third assessor, who says 80. On the same logic, we can also argue that two assessors, who say 80 and 100 respectively, concur that the value of the asset does not exceed 100, and their opinion prevails over the assessor who appraised it at 120. The median method is thus strategy-proof.

But what is the relation between the two parts of the Rashbam's remarks? We would suggest that at the beginning of his remarks, the

29 As a teenager, Gilad Lipschutz (the author's son), suggested an additional possibility, namely, that the Rashbam is describing a simple method for calculating averages, like that commonly used in elementary school math lessons. Blocks are used to construct three columns, whose heights represent the three appraised values. To arrive at the average, the tall column is shortened by removing blocks, which are added to the short column until the heights are equal, as in the talmudic notion of "leveling the indentations," a procedure for comparing the elevation of a plot of land to the average. If this suggested understanding is correct, the Rashbam was familiar with the concept of the mean, but did not think it was the appropriate principle to apply in the case at hand.

30 The sentences within the brace brackets are in the Bah's gloss ad loc. Prof. Aumann drew our attention to the fact that R. Meir Halevi Abulafia, in *Yad Rama*, commenting on the appraisal *sugya*, endorses the Tanna Kama's view (100) with an argument much like that presented in the Bah's account of the Rashbam's view.

31 *Rashbam*, bBaba Batra 107a s.v. *milta metziata*.

32 On the median voter theorem, see, e.g., J. Hindriks and G.D. Myles, *Intermediate Public Economics* (Cambridge MA: 2006), ch. 4.

Rashbam is giving an interpretation of the term "middle course" (*milta metziata*), or what we have called the midrange (midpoint). Unlike Maimonides, however, he does not take the term to denote a decision-making principle, but just the result of the specific numeric example in question (80, 100, 120). The Rashbam then proceeds to discuss the question of the appropriate decision rule for the context in general, which is not based on the midpoint. Indeed, he concludes by noting: "And in my opinion, the same is true if he said 28 *sela* [112], which is not so much in the middle." In the case of the numbers 80, 112, 120, for instance, the decision will be 112 despite the fact that this is not the midpoint, but the majority principle applies here as well. The Rashbam prefers this interpretation, which seems correct to him, and in order to uphold it, is willing to reject the Talmud's rubric of the "middle course" as a general formula for calculating the aggregate appraisal, taking it, instead, to describe a calculation that is correct only for the specific example in the baraita, but not in general.[33] It could, perhaps, be argued that according to the Rashbam, "*milta metziata*" refers to the median, but in our view, this does not appear to be his interpretation of the Tanna Kama's position.[34]

The advantage of the Rashbam's reading, on which the median value determines the aggregate appraisal, is that the median is, as we said, a strategy-proof decision principle. Moreover, the median represents what can be characterized as a 'sort of' majority that can be invoked when it is not possible to use the principle that the minority view is overruled (*batel yahid bemiuto*). We will see that taking the

33 This insight ensued from our studying the matter together with Prof. Aumann.

34 Another reading of the connection between the two parts of the Rashbam's comments is as follows. It was important for the Rashbam to mention that using the numbers in the baraita yields 100 even without invoking such an artificial majority, as 100 is both the midpoint and the opinion of the assessor who quotes the middle value. If we had only the two extreme appraisals, 80 and 120, this would yield 100 as the middle number. In the specific case of the baraita, the midpoint is agreeable to the assessor who gave 100 as his appraisal. The Rashbam therefore accepts Maimonides' principle of taking the midpoint as the aggregated value in this case, because it does not ignore the middle appraisal. The Rashbam proceeds to explain why, given the numbers used in the baraita, it is also necessary to arrive at 100 using the **artificial majority** principle. The artificial majority principle explains why we ignore the appraisals that are perceived as minority views. By contrast, Maimonides does not explain why we ignore the middle opinion.

median to be the decision principle renders the two parts of the baraita consistent. That is, in the case where two assessors concur, the majority principle is straightforwardly determinative, and the minority view regarding the asset's value is overruled, and in the case where there are three divergent views, the majority principle, expressed by the median, is also determinative.

5.2 R. Eliezer b. Zadok

According to R. Eliezer b. Zadok, the aggregated appraisal should be 90. This opinion is also based on the majority view, viz., the two lower appraisals, 80 and 100, as opposed to the minority view of 120. The difficulty is that the majority appraisals are not in accord with each other, as the assessor who says 80 does not agree to a value greater than 80, and the one who says 100 does not agree to a value less than 100. R. Eliezer b. Zadok's new insight is that as long as the gap between them is no greater than a given critical value, the two appraisals can be viewed as concurring as to the appraisal,[35] and the reason each assessor gave a different number is that every assessor is liable to err.[36] When the gap between the assessors is greater than the critical value, we must assume that the assessors do indeed disagree. R. Eliezer assumes that the distribution of errors for each assessor is symmetrical, and apparently, for the values of the baraita, the critical value is not smaller than 10.

It is thus possible to construe the 80 and 100 appraisals as 'sort of agreeing' on the value of 90, assuming that each assessor was mistaken by 10, one upward, the other downward. Were there only one assessor,

35 When the gap between the appraisals is greater than the critical value, it is not possible to regard them as agreeing on a single value. This also follows from the Rashbam's comment ad loc. s.v. *tishim*: "each one errs by **a little**." But we have to define "a little." R. Eliezer's decision method is limited to cases where the discrepancy between the various appraisals is not too big. The advantage of the Tanna Kama's method is that it is not subject to this limitation. It may be that Maimonides was aware of this – he ruled, as we saw, in accordance with the Tanna Kama's view – and hinted at it when he said "and in this way it is always assessed between them"; see n. 25 above.

36 "And the Tanna Kama maintains that we must say that people do not err at all, therefore take the middle and [ignore] the other two, lest they err. And R. Eliezer b. Zadok believes that people err by 10 . . . and the others believe that one may err by $13\frac{1}{3}$ regarding something worth more than 80" (*Rashbam* ad loc. s.v. *osin shuma*). Notice that in the phrases "do not err at all" and "lest they err," the Rashbam is using the verb "err" in two different senses.

for instance the one who said 80, we would set the 'true' value between 70 and 90, assuming that the critical value is 10. When we have two assessors, and there is some overlap in their 'confidence intervals,' the range of which is determined by the critical value, the value that represents their opinion is the midpoint of the intersection of the two confidence intervals. Assuming a symmetrical distribution, this point is always the middle point between the two opinions. In the 80, 100, 120 example in the baraita, the intersection contains only one point: 90.

The Rashbam explains that R. Eliezer prefers this decision method over the Tanna Kama's, because the Tanna Kama (as the Rashbam interprets his stance) bases the appraisal on a single opinion, that of the median assessor. By contrast, in R. Eliezer's opinion, the appraisal should be based on the majority principle adduced at the beginning of the baraita, which he takes to be the guiding decision principle.

R. Eliezer b. Zadok's view is innovative in two respects:

(a) R. Eliezer assumes that appraisal is not an exact science, and therefore it is fitting to ascribe a 'reasonable' margin of error to each assessor. Contra the Tanna Kama, who believes that the various appraisals should be accepted as is,[37] R. Eliezer does not view the appraisals as 'opinions' between which a choice must be made, but as a 'sample' that serves as the basis from which we seek to approach the 'correct' value as closely as possible.
(b) R. Eliezer performs a 'cluster analysis' on this sample, and rules that the assessors who appraised the asset at 80 and 100 belong to the same cluster, the center of which is 90. This approach makes it possible to apply the majority principle and set the asset's value at 90, because in R. Eliezer's opinion, the majority of the assessors support this appraisal despite the fact that none of them gave this specific value as their appraisal.

The Talmud points to an obvious difficulty raised by this approach: "On the contrary (*aderaba*), [why not say that] the land is worth 110, and he who says a *mane* [100], errs by 10 downward. And does he who says 30 [*sela*] [120], err by 10 upward?" In other words, it would have been possible, based on the same cluster analysis logic, to similarly assign the 100 and 120 appraisals to the same cluster, and invoke the majority

37 "And the Tanna Kama maintains that we must say that people do not err at all" (*Rashbam*, ibid.).

principle to rule that the asset's value is 110, contra the minority opinion of 80. The example in the baraita is symmetrical, and therefore assigning the appraisal at 100 to the same cluster as the 120 appraisal is just as logical as assigning it to the cluster with the 80 appraisal. In the first case, the majority view yields 90, in the second case it yields 110. The Talmud's response to this problem is, "Nevertheless, adopt [an aggregated appraisal based on] the first two [appraisals], which do not exceed a *mane* [100]." In other words, there is a downward asymmetry, hence the appraisal of 90 is preferable to that of 110, because the opinions that form the 90 cluster do not exceed the threshold of 100. The question is: what is the source and logic of the asymmetry?

The Rashbam interprets the asymmetry as follows:

> In other words, according to what they say [the appraisals at 80 and 100], we must say that when [the appraisals are] close to a *mane* [100], they are equal, though not exactly 100; and we do not follow the two higher ones [100 and 120], as they say [a number that is] more than a *mane* [110], because "if you take hold of too much, you have not taken hold of anything" (*tafasta merube lo tafasta*).[38]

The 'if you take hold of too much' principle generates the rule that one is always to choose the lower option.[39] Applying this principle

38 Ibid., s.v. *nekot mihat trei kamai*. And see too *Tosafot* ad loc. s.v. *demitorat mane lo mafki lei*. The main thrust of the *Tosafot*'s opinion, too, is a preference for a lower appraisal over a higher one, and not the threshold of 100, as the two high assessors, who value the asset at 100 and 120, also concur that the value is not lower than the 100 boundary.

39 The source of this law is R. Akiva's statement in Sifra (Metzora, parashat Zavim, 5): "Two days can be interpreted as many days. Said R. Akiva, Regarding everything that can be interpreted broadly or narrowly, if you take hold of too much, you have not taken hold of anything, if you take hold of a little, you have taken hold of it." The scope of the rule is debated in *Tosafot*, bYoma 70a s.v. *naavid arbaa*, a debate that has shaped the two chief ways in which the rule is understood: (1) We invoke the 'if you take hold of too much' rule only where there is hesitancy about choosing between a lesser value and a greater infinite value. But where the greater value is finite, then it must be taken hold of, because "the 100 appraisal is covered by the 200 appraisal" (בכלל מאתיים מנה). In some cases, the 'if you take hold of too much' rule is applied even where the greater value has a limit, namely, when other decision rules apply, e.g., 'when in doubt, opt for stringency' (*safek lehumra*), which in this case is the lesser value. And when it is a monetary matter to which the rule that "the burden of proof is on the one who makes a claim against his fellow" (*hamotzi mihavero alav hareaya*)

in our case will result in a preference for an appraisal of 90 over an appraisal of 110 regardless of the 100 boundary mentioned in the Talmud ("which do not exceed 100"). If so, why does the Talmud mention the threshold of 100? It appears that, in the Rashbam's view, the decision depends on which cluster we assign the appraisal of 100 to, the upper or the lower. Either way, it will be construed as "close to a *mane* [100]," and the difference is whether it is close from above or from below. To resolve this dilemma, the Rashbam needs the 'if you take hold of too much' principle, and this is how he interprets the Talmud's comment about exceeding 100.[40]

An additional question is why the 'if you take hold of too much' rule applies here, since on the Rashbam's interpretation, the appraisal is conducted for the purpose of selling land regarding which there are contradictory interests. The creditors are interested in a low appraisal in order to obtain a larger plot, and the owner of the land is interested in a high appraisal. In such a case, the law is that we adduce the rule that "the burden of proof is on the one who makes a claim against his fellow" (bBaba Kama 46a), and therefore it would seem that one should prefer the higher appraisal to protect the defendant from the creditors. By contrast, in an appraisal made for estimating damages, it is the injured party who makes the claim, and in this case, it is the lesser amount that is called for on the strength of the 'burden of proof' principle.[41]

---

applies, we cannot appropriate money at the higher value, but only at the lower. (2) The prevailing understanding of the rule appears to be the following: even if the greater value is finite, we apply the 'if you take hold of too much' rule. Some of the Later Authorities suggested that the concept of 'holding' (*tfisa*) in terms of which the rule is formulated is borrowed from the monetary context. In other words, the rule is interpreted as meaning: hold on to the minimalist interpretation, for one who debates whether to take hold of the lesser or the greater should take hold of that which is certain, and that is the lesser. This may be what Rashi intended in his comment "and [the rule] is a metaphor" (bSuka 5a s.v. *tafasta merube*). See, e.g., R. Isaac Flexer, *Shearei Yitzhak*, Suka (1999 edition, 31).

40 On this interpretation, the Rashbam takes the phrase "which do not exceed a *mane* [100]" (*mitorat mane lo mafki lei*) to refer to the median appraisal and not to the value of the asset. In other words, assigning the median appraisal to the lower cluster prevents its removal from the class of appraisals that do not cross the threshold (100).

41 See n. 4 above. It appears that on the Ritba's interpretation, mentioned in n. 4 above, in cases, such as that where "[the item] has been appraised by three," that are based on a contractual agreement, we do not apply the principle that "the burden of proof is on one who makes a claim against his

In contrast to the Rashbam, who did not address the 'burden of proof' issue at all, Nahmanides asserts that on the strength of this principle we must always rule that the owner of the land prevails, and therefore "we raise it [the appraisal] by all we can raise it." In his opinion, "this is why we ask 'on the contrary' (*aderaba*) – in order to raise it," referring to the Talmud's question "On the contrary [*aderaba*], [why not say that] the land is worth 110 . . . err by 10 upward?" In other words, this question arises from the 'burden of proof' principle. The Talmud's response – "adopt the first two, which do not exceed 100" – rests on a psychological assumption that the assessors' (indeed, everyone's) conception of value is not continuous, but segmented into discrete orders of magnitude, and a psychological barrier prevents assessors from crossing the threshold of an order of magnitude (such as tens, hundreds, or thousands) from below. As Nahmanides puts it, "People are more competent in [making decisions] between 100 and over-100 than they are vis-à-vis other appraisals [that do not cross the threshold of an order of magnitude], because people are more careful [when crossing the threshold] between 100 and over-100."[42] Therefore, in his opinion, attaching the appraisal of 100 to that of 80, rather than to the appraisal of 120, is preferable, because this cluster will contain two appraisals, neither of which exceeds the threshold of 100, whereas attaching it to the higher appraisal (120) yields a median appraisal that crosses the threshold.[43] But we must still query the basis for this psychological presumption, and why it is deemed to be sufficiently strong to enable the court to take money from a defendant, as per the 'burden of proof' principle.[44] Moreover, Nahmanides' suggestion is applicable only in cases, such as

fellow," as is apparent in the case of the worker's wages (bBaba Metzia 87a). See text below at n. 89, and see too n. 98 below.

42 *Hidushei Haramban*, bBaba Batra (Maarva edition 1993, 127). Many laws are based on psychological assumptions, such as the presumptions that: "no one would dare be so impudent toward his creditor" (bBaba Metzia 3a); "no woman would dare be so impudent toward her husband" (*SA*, EH 17:2); "no one commits a sin unless he stands to profit from it" (bBaba Metzia 5b).

43 On Nahmanides' interpretation, the phrase "which do not exceed 100" refers to the assessors whose appraisals do not cross the 100 threshold (80 and 100). Cf. the Rashbam's interpretation, n. 40 above.

44 It may be that on Nahmanides' understanding, the psychological assumption in question is akin to a halakhic presumption that justifies taking money from a defendant. See, e.g., *SA*, HM 78:1; R. Solomon Ganzfried, *Pnei Shlomo* (Jerusalem 1999 edition, 225): "And Nahmanides, of blessed

that in the baraita, where assignment of an appraisal to one of the clusters involves crossing the threshold of an order of magnitude. It is not clear how Nahmanides would interpret the opinions of R. Eliezer and the others in cases where assigning the median assessor to the higher cluster does not require crossing a threshold.

The Ritba offers a different interpretation. In his opinion, the preference for the appraisal of 90 over that of 110 follows from the fact that it is supported by the majority opinion, whereas the 110 appraisal is supported only by the assessor who assessed the asset at 120. The difficulty with this explanation is that R. Eliezer's opinion is based on the assumption that the assessor's ruling incorporates a deviation from the correct value, and does not reflect a precise valuation to begin with. The Ritba's interpretation, however, assumes, in the second stage of the cluster analysis, that the original appraisals were exact, and it is on this basis that the appraisal of 90 is preferred over that of 110. It appears that the Ritba himself tries to address this difficulty: "Maybe there is no mistake, and [the assessor] does not adopt this appraisal [110], but only the [120] one."[45] But if so, that is, if "there is no mistake" here, the assessor who assessed the asset at 100 does not necessarily accept the appraisal of 90.

In sum, the case described in the baraita is symmetrical. The final appraisal, according to R. Eliezer (and as we will see below, according to the others as well), breaks the symmetry and sets the appraisal below 100. As we have seen, various Early Authorities tried to explain the asymmetry. Nahmanides noted that downward asymmetry is contrary to the reverse asymmetry that follows from the principle that "the burden of proof is on the one who makes a claim against his fellow" (which is to the defendant's advantage). R. Solomon Ganzfried also suggests an argument for upward asymmetry. He contends that the higher cluster should be preferred to the lower, because in clusters of equal radius, the higher the center of the cluster, the lower each assessor's rate of error, expressed as a percentage of the value of the asset.[46]

---

memory, had to accept this forced supposition." R. Ganzfried's analysis of the appraisal *sugya* is brilliant.

45 *Hidushei Haritba*, bBaba Batra (Mercaz Harav Kook edition, 819).

46 This is how R. Ganzfried explains the term "on the contrary" (*aderaba*) that appears twice in the *sugya* in connection with the upper cluster. According to R. Ganzfried, the term *aderaba* indicates a preference for the option being suggested, whereas in the case of a balanced doubt, where neither option

5.3 The others

The third opinion is that of the "others," and it is the only one that does not specify a numeric value, but offers a rule for reaching a decision: "they appraise between them and divide it by three (*meshalshin*)." This is the most challenging of the suggested methods of aggregation.

Two questions arise from the others' proposal: in using the term "between them," who are the others referring to, and what does "divide by three" mean? "Between them" can be interpreted as referring to the three assessors, to the two assessors who gave the extreme appraisals, or to the assessors who can be assigned to the lower cluster, as suggested by R. Eliezer b. Zadok. We will present three proposals for understanding the others' aggregation method, based on different interpretations of the term "between them." The meaning of the term "divide by three" will emerge from each of these proposals.

The symmetry of the talmudic discussion indicates that the Talmud perceives the others' method as an elaboration of R. Eliezer b. Zadok's method. The Talmud challenges both methods with the expression "on the contrary" (*aderaba*), and with regard to both of them, justifies the preference for the lower cluster with the phrase "adopt [an appraisal based on] the first two." Both R. Eliezer and the others conjoin two divergent appraisals to form one cluster. In the center of this cluster is the 'correct' value from which each of the assessors in the cluster deviated. In light of these parallels, these two appraisals are deemed to constitute a majority view that overrules the third appraisal (the minority view). According to both R. Eliezer and the others, the value that determines the final appraisal is the center of the majority cluster that is constructed around the lower value.[47]

According to the Talmud, the differences between the others' method and R. Eliezer b. Zadok's method are as follows:

(a) The others suggest a 'formula' for finding the center of the cluster and for the calculation (of its radius). For the example in the baraita (80, 100, 120), the Talmud specifies that the radius is $13\frac{1}{3}$.

---

is preferred, the Talmud indicates this by using the term "lest" or "maybe" (*dilma*).

47 The Rabad ad loc. explained the methods of R. Eliezer and "the others" (a term that, as pointed out above, denotes R. Meir) as in agreement regarding the following principle: "Therefore we take the average of the first two assessors, who are actually of the same opinion, and this is the method of the others" (quoted in *Shita Mekubetzet*).

(b) The others encounter an interpretive difficulty that induces them to take into account a factor not previously considered. To accept the concurrence of the 80 and 100 appraisals for an asset valued at $93\frac{1}{3}$, we must assume that just as the appraisal at 80 deviated downward by $13\frac{1}{3}$, so the appraisal at 100 could have deviated upward by $13\frac{1}{3}$, and therefore we would have expected an aggregated appraisal of $106\frac{2}{3}$, but such an appraisal was not made. How, then, can we posit a concurrence of the appraisals of 80 and 100 at $93\frac{1}{3}$?

(c) To settle this difficulty, the Talmud suggests that the others' method features an innovation, just as R. Eliezer b. Zadok's method did. The others assume that the assessors' appraisals are affected by strategic considerations: the assessors update their appraisals as new information becomes available, for instance, their colleagues' appraisals. It is thus reasonable to assume that an assessor's initial appraisal, prior to learning of the values assessed by his colleagues, differs from that which he ultimately gives. In the example before us, it is possible that the assessor who assessed the asset at 100 intended to say $106\frac{2}{3}$, but, under the influence of the colleague who assessed the asset at 80, feared he would be exaggerating, and revised his appraisal to 100.[48]

(d) Implicit in the Talmud's account of the others' method is a tacit assumption that there is communication between the assessors. Until now we have considered three independent assessors, each of whom

48 Regarding the others' method, Nahmanides asks: taking 100 as the starting point, why not calculate the point from which every opinion deviates by $13\frac{1}{3}$? Accordingly, we ought to say that the asset's value is $86\frac{2}{3}$ and the assessor who assessed the asset at 80, though initially he intended to specify a value lower than 80, revised his appraisal upward under the influence of the assessor who assessed it at 100 (*Hidushei Haramban*, bBaba Batra [Maarava edition 1993, 127]). In response, the Ramban, the Ritba (*Hidushei Haritba*), and the Ran (quoted in *Shita Mekubetzet*) put forward a psychological assumption: the principle that other views are taken into account ("I already exceeded my colleagues by a lot") is invoked only vis-à-vis upward revisions of the initial appraisal, not downward revisions. For an assessor who assesses the asset at a lower value than his colleagues does not find it hard, is not embarrassed, to voice his appraisal even if it is far from the appraisal above it, and therefore will voice his exact opinion and not revise it upward. R. Solomon Ganzfried sought to respond to the difficulty raised by Nahmanides by adducing the principle of minimizing error, see above at n. 46. He contends that once the preference for the lower cluster has been established, its center must be raised as much as possible in order to minimize each assessor's rate of error. Note that on the Tosafists' interpretation, the issue raised by the Early Authorities does not arise at all; see text at n. 49.

uses private information. But the others' method clearly assumes that the assessor who assessed the asset at 100 is aware that it was assessed at 80 by another assessor. The *Tosafot* maintain that the order of the appraisal is "the two lower ones speak first."[49] R. Haim Shor (Poland, d. 1632), author of *Torat Haim*, suggests an order similar to that of an English (open ascending) auction, "as to the order: at the beginning they ask whether it is worth more by some obvious increment, such as 60 and 70 and 80. And when they ask about [its being worth] more than what was quoted, one of them quits, and when they ask about [its being worth] more than 100, the other quits, and when they ask about [its being worth] more than 120, the third one quits."[50] Thus the appraisals are delivered one by one, from low to high, each being influenced by the one below it.[51] The Rashbam, by contrast, does not specify the order in which the assessors speak, but assumes that the appraisals are common knowledge: "And even though we do not know which one spoke first, they negotiate the matter, and each one knows what his colleague thinks, and after they have negotiated the matter, they set their hearts on stating what appears to them to be the case. And because he knew that his colleague wanted to say 80, he was afraid to say more than a *mane* [100]."[52]

The Talmud asks, regarding the others' method (as it does about R. Eliezer b. Zadok's method): by the same token, why not say that the asset's value is $113\frac{1}{3}$, and let us assume that the assessor who assesses it at 100 deviated downward by the rate we assumed $(13\frac{1}{3})$, whereas the assessor who assessed it at 120 intended to say $126\frac{2}{3}$, but revised his appraisal down to 120. The Talmud's answer, as in its discussion about R. Eliezer's view, is that a method that sets the value on which two assessors concur below 100 is preferable to a method that sets it above 100.[53]

Note that the Talmud does not explain how the deviation, set at $13\frac{1}{3}$, is calculated, or how this calculation is derived from the others' statement, "they appraise between them and divide it by three." The Early Authorities explained that the calculation is derived from the difference

49 *Tosafot* ad loc. s.v. *mistaya deka tefina*.
50 *Torat Haim*, bBaba Batra 107a-b.
51 Could the order be that of a Dutch auction (open descending), in which they ask: who will pay 1000? who will pay 900? and so on? It is evident that this type of bidding does not fit the *sugya*, because in our case the assessor who appraised the asset at 100 clearly revised his appraisal under the influence of the appraisal at 80, which means he knew about it. On classic bidding theory, see Krishna Vijay, *Auction Theory*, 2nd ed. (Burlington MA: 2009).
52 *Rashbam*, 107b s.v. *ubadin hu deleima*.
53 See above at n. 38.

between the extreme appraisals ($120-80=40$) divided equally between the three assessors: $\frac{40}{3}=13\frac{1}{3}$. But it is by no means straightforward how this formula is inferred from the expression "they appraise between them." First and foremost, therefore, we must understand the mathematical logic on which it rests.[54]

6. Proposals for interpreting the others' appraisal method

Given that, as recounted in the *sugya*, the others' suggestion – namely, that 100 is in fact $106\frac{2}{3}$ – is sheer speculation, we must ask how halakhic rulings can be grounded in mere conjecture that lacks any necessity. First of all, how do we know that the assessor who appraised the asset at 100 intended to say exactly $106\frac{2}{3}$? Furthermore, by the same logic, it could be claimed that even the assessor who appraised it at 120 intended to set a higher value, and if so, the basis for the calculation $\frac{40}{3}=13\frac{1}{3}$ is unclear. It seems plausible to say that endorsing the value $93\frac{1}{3}$ is objectively defensible and does not require us to ascribe strategic thinking to the assessors. This number derives directly from what the others said, "we appraise between them and divide it by three"; the strategic argument can be interpreted as merely a 'defense' of the main thesis, viz., that the value is $93\frac{1}{3}$, allowing it to be anchored in a valid decision-making rule. If this suggestion is correct, then in the case of the others' aggregation method, unlike that of R. Eliezer's method, we must distinguish two stages:

> (a) "Others say, they appraise between them and divide it by three. Their view is that the land is worth $93\frac{1}{3}$." The value $93\frac{1}{3}$ is derived from the formula "appraise between them and divide it by three." How the others arrived at this value, and the underlying logic of the calculation, is not explicit in the *sugya*, and requires clarification. But even if we accept the reasoning that yields this specific value, we still lack a valid decision rule that expresses the others' aggregation method, as the others' statement in the baraita is not formulated as a decision rule, but as an obscure mathematical formula.

To this end, the Talmud proceeds to the next stage.

> (b) The value $93\frac{1}{3}$ can be supported by the majority principle as understood by R. Eliezer b. Zadok, by invoking a cluster comprising the appraisals of the majority of the assessors, the center of which is

54 Lieberman, n. 4 above, suggests that the division by three reflects the fact that there are three assessors. On this reasoning, the difference is divided by the number of assessors.

this value. But we must regard majority opinion flexibly, in light of the claim that the appraisal at 100 can also reflect a value of $106\frac{2}{3}$, as noted above.

6.1 Proposal 1

In an attempt to understand the first stage of the others' aggregation method, Prof. Aumann, in the course of our joint study, put forward an analysis, based on the statement in the baraita that "they appraise between them and divide it by three," which also yields the value $93\frac{1}{3}$. On this proposal, the others' aggregation method, contrary to what was stated above, is not an elaboration of R. Eliezer's method, but rather based on the Tanna Kama's method, as understood by Maimonides.

As we saw, on Maimonides' interpretation, the rule for determining the aggregate appraised value is to take the value that is midrange between the two extremes. That is, Maimonides upholds the Tanna Kama's method. The problem with this method, though, is that it completely ignores the median value. The others' aggregation method overcomes this difficulty. The appraisal is set between the extreme appraisals, but we must "divide by three," that is, weight each extreme appropriately. That is, if we accept as our starting point that an asymmetry emerges from the *sugya*, we must adjust the appraisal of 100 downward (despite the fact that it is positioned 'in the middle') and conjoin it with the appraisal at 80. The result is that the appraisal that is to be set between the extremes imparts to the appraisal at 80 twice the weight of the appraisal at 120 (since it encompasses two appraisals, and the weight is to be divided proportionately), in other words, $\frac{2}{3}\times 80+\frac{1}{3}\times 120=93\frac{1}{3}$. On this proposal, the "them" of "between them" is interpreted as referring to the two extreme appraisals.

Computationally, this method is identical to the calculation proposed by the Rashbam in his commentary on the *sugya*. On the Rashbam's interpretation, the range of the appraisal values (120 – 80 = 40) must be divided by 3 and added to the lowest appraisal value, which is not disputed: $80+13\frac{1}{3}=93\frac{1}{3}$.[55] But this method – namely, the others' method as unpacked by Prof. Aumann – unlike the Rashbam's, displays legal as well as arithmetical logic. We must, however, consider

55 It is evident that the Rashbam's calculation and this proposal are equivalent. Let us designate the three appraisals x, y, and z ($x < y < z$). According to the Rashbam, the calculation is $\frac{z-x}{3}+x$, and according to this proposal, it is $\frac{2}{3}x+\frac{1}{3}z$. It is easy to show that $\frac{z-x}{3}+x=\frac{2}{3}x+\frac{1}{3}z$.

whether the legal logic on which the proposal is based is consistent with the Talmud's understanding. According to the *sugya*, a ruling of $13\frac{1}{3}$ appears to be based on ignoring the appraisal of 120, because taking it into account would have to be premised on the assumption that this assessor, too, lowered his original appraisal under the influence of the two assessors who appraised the asset at a value lower than he did.[56] But the present proposal clearly relies on the value as declared by the assessor who assessed the asset at 120.[57]

Pursuing this line of thought, we can provide a similar explanation of R. Eliezer b. Zadok's method as well, an explanation which differs from that suggested in the *sugya*. We can say that the value 90 is not, in fact, the midpoint between 80 and 100. Rather, the value 90 can be taken as deciding between the extremes as follows: $\frac{1}{4}\times 120+\frac{3}{4}\times 80=90$. On this proposal, at the first stage, R. Eliezer calculates the relative weights of the extreme appraisals in a manner that differs from the Tanna Kama's calculation (as Maimonides explains it). In his opinion, it is not possible to assign the same weight to the two extreme appraisals, and 80 must be assigned a weight three times greater than 120. At the second stage, the talmudic explanation validates the ruling of 90 on the strength of the majority principle, since a majority can be mustered around the appraisal at 90. The others disagree with the ratio proposed by R. Eliezer and suggest a ratio of 1 to 2 between the extremes. According to the Talmud's explanation, even on the others' method, $93\frac{1}{3}$ can still be regarded as a value agreed on by the majority. The difficulty, however, is that it is not clear how R. Eliezer arrived at the relative weights in question.

This understanding of the *sugya* has certain advantages. It results in a coherent view of the three Tannaitic opinions, each of which presents a decision based on a point somewhere between the extremes. According to the Tanna Kama, this point is the midrange (on Maimonides' understanding of the Tanna Kama); according to R. Eliezer, this point falls on the line between the extremes, dividing it at a ratio of 1:3; and according to the others, the ratio is 1:2. This understanding offers insight into Maimonides' interpretation of the Tanna Kama's aggregation method, which, unlike the Rashbam's interpretation, takes it to be a division into

56 See *Torat Haim*, n. 50 above, s.v. *aderaba*.

57 An additional question, which is outside the scope of the present discussion, is the following: assuming that we have n assessors producing appraisals $a_1, a_2, \ldots, a_n$ such that $a_1 < a_2 <, \ldots, < a_n$, how would the proposed aggregation method assign weights to these appraisals?

2 of the distance between the extremes. It could be said that reflecting on the correct understanding of R. Eliezer b. Zadok's view, and the others' view – construed as we have proposed here – induced Maimonides to interpret the Tanna Kama's view, too, in light of the Talmud's characterization of that view as a "middle course," viz., a decision in the middle, between the extreme appraisals. But even if we accept this explanation, we must still investigate how the Tannaim arrived at the aforementioned relative weights, and the origin of the disagreement between them as to the appropriate ratio (Tanna Kama – 1:1; R. Eliezer b. Zadok – 1:3; the others – 1:2).

With regard to the cluster analysis, too, the proposed understanding of the *sugya* generates coherence between the three Tannaitic views, even on Maimonides' understanding of the Tanna Kama's view. The Tanna Kama sees all the appraisals as one large cluster, and therefore sets the 'center' of the cluster at the midpoint of the range. In providing a numeric example of his own,[58] Maimonides' intention is to emphasize that the Tanna Kama disagrees with R. Eliezer and the others with regard to every case, and not only in the case of a symmetrical distribution of appraisals around a specific value. In the example he brings (90, 100, 130), the Tanna Kama would, according to Maimonides, set the aggregated appraisal at 110, R. Eliezer, at 95, in the center of the (90, 100) cluster, and the others – on the proposed understanding of the *sugya* – would set it at $90\times\frac{2}{3}+130\times\frac{1}{3}=103\frac{1}{3}$. This value is the center of the $\left(90, 116\frac{2}{3}\right)$ cluster, and expresses the Talmud's estimate that the assessor who assessed the asset at 100 intended to say $116\frac{2}{3}$.

In Figure 1, the appraisal at 100 is the revised appraisal of the assessor who intended to quote $106\frac{2}{3}$, but 'updated' his appraisal after hearing the first assessor's quote of 80. The original discrepancy between the appraisals of the first two assessors was $26\frac{2}{3}$, and the discrepancy after the update is 20.

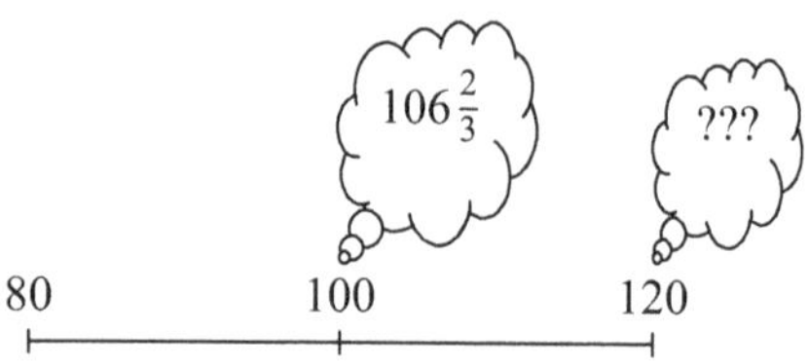

Figure 1

58 See above at n. 25.

In Figure 2, which is based on Maimonides' own example, the original discrepancy between the appraisals was also $26\frac{2}{3}$, but after the update was reduced to 10. On this presentation of the others' method, the revision of the appraisals does not appear to be consistent. In the example illustrated in Figure 1, the discrepancy between the first two assessors' appraisals after the revision (20) is 75% of the original discrepancy, whereas in the example shown in Figure 2, the discrepancy after the revision is 37.5% of the original discrepancy.

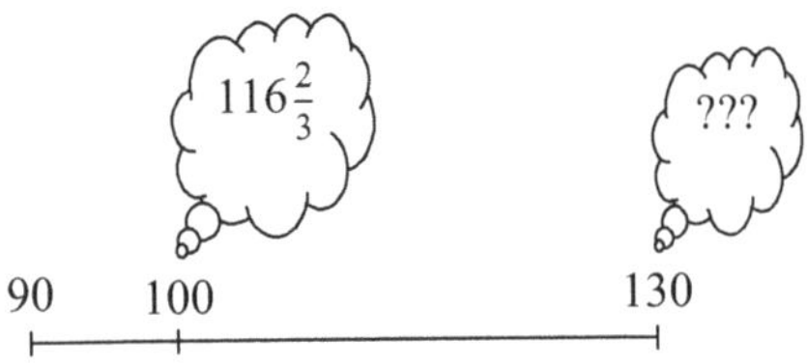

Figure 2

At this point, a general question is in order. According to the Early Authorities, the Talmud's 'guess' that the assessor who assessed the asset at 100 intended to say $106\frac{2}{3}$ is based on a division of the range spanned by the three appraisals. The problem here is that just as we assume that the assessor who assessed the asset at 100 intended to give a higher appraisal, the same must be assumed about the assessor who assessed it at 120, and if so, it is not clear why we divide the 80–120 range, given that 120 is a 'revised' appraisal that does not necessarily represent the third assessor's 'true' opinion. The same is true for the example illustrated in Figure 2.

In our opinion, the biggest problem with this proposal for interpreting the others' method is that if we tilt the weights upward instead of downward, and assign a weight of $\frac{2}{3}$ to the upper extreme of the range and $\frac{1}{3}$ to the lower extreme, we get $\frac{1}{3}\times 80+\frac{2}{3}\times 120=106\frac{2}{3}$. But this calculation is not consistent with the way the *sugya* unfolds, because subsequently the Talmud asks: "On the contrary, [why not say that] the land is worth $113\frac{1}{3}$." In other words, the counter-value adduced by the Talmud differs significantly from the counter-value that ensues from the present proposal. This proposal is thus likely to remain an independent explanation for the others' opinion that is inconsistent with the talmudic interpretation of that method.

6.2 Proposal 2

The authors will now put forward another way to understand the first stage of the others' method (the stage at which the average deviation is established), which differs from the first proposal both in its calculation of the deviation, and its underlying logic. This second proposal also differs, it goes without saying, from the Rashbam's interpretation of the others' aggregation method. Our proposal is to interpret the opinion of the others, "they appraise between them and divide it by three," as applying to R. Eliezer's method. The connection between R. Eliezer's method and that of the others is already manifest in the *sugya*.[59] Based on this connection, we propose that the words "between them" be interpreted as applying to the two appraisals in the lower cluster (80, 100), on which R. Eliezer based his decision. The others, too, in light of R. Eliezer's asymmetry arguments, take the (80, 100) cluster to determine the appraisal, but in their opinion we must **divide by three** between them and not settle for the center of the cluster, as per R. Eliezer's method. In other words, the 100 appraisal is assigned twice the weight of the 80 appraisal: $80\times\frac{1}{3}+100\times\frac{2}{3}=93\frac{1}{3}$.

According to this proposal, although the others agree that the appraisal must be based on the lower cluster, they assign a weight of $\frac{2}{3}$ to the 100 appraisal, taking into account the third assessor, who set an even higher value (120). On the one hand, the others do not take into account a value higher than 100, because it falls outside the selected cluster, and is thus considered an 'error.' On the other hand, they do not entirely ignore the third assessor's view, in the sense that its existence doubles the weight assigned to the extreme appraisal closest to the selected cluster.[60] This decision rule also yields a coherent result in the simple case in which two assessors say 100 and one says 200.[61]

It follows that, according to the aggregation method upheld by the others, the same result is obtained when the appraisals are (80, 100, 120) as when they are (80, 100, 130). In other words, an 'exaggeration' in the highest appraisal does not affect the final result. The Tanna Kama's method, as understood by the Rashbam, has a similar feature: manipulation of the extreme appraisals does not affect the aggregated appraisal. But whereas the Tanna Kama's method is entirely robust, the others' method is only impervious to upward exaggeration.

On this understanding of the others' aggregation method, in the Tannaitic controversy over an appraisal where no two assessors agree on the asset's value, the Tanna Kama's decision rule (on the Rashbam's interpretation) takes the median appraisal to be determinative, R. Eliezer's

59 See above at the beginning of §5.3.

60 This idea may be hinted at in the Rabad's comments quoted in *Shita Mekubetzet*; see n. 47 above.

61 Applying the rule in this case yields $100\times\frac{1}{3}+100\times\frac{2}{3}=100$.

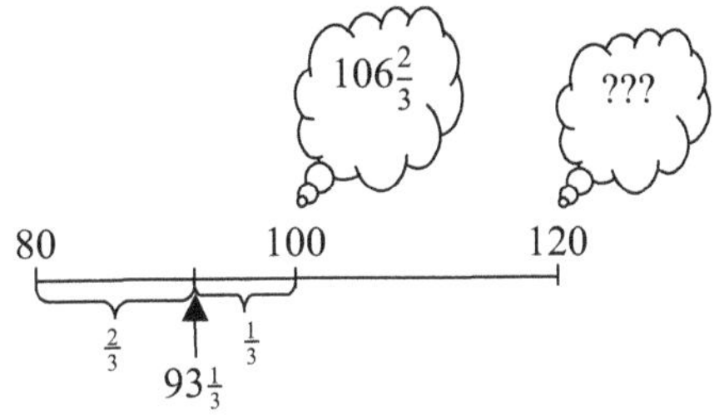

Figure 3

rule takes the two lower appraisals to be determinative, and the others' method, improving on R. Eliezer's, assigns weight to the highest appraisal as well, factoring it into the aggregate of the two lower appraisals.[62]

This account of the others' opinion yields the result $93\frac{1}{3}$ for the example in the baraita (Figure 3). But for the example Maimonides brings (90, 100, 130), it yields a result that differs from the result generated by the calculation based on the Rashbam's interpretation of the others' method and by Proposal 1. The 90–100 range that is disputed by the two lower assessors is divided proportionately, and the result is $96\frac{2}{3}$. The majority principle, as understood by R. Eliezer b. Zadok and the others, can be invoked in support of this value, which can be understood as the center of a cluster that encompasses most of the assessors' appraisals, assuming that the 100 appraisal reflects an initial intent to quote $103\frac{1}{3}$, in line with what the *sugya* states. On this calculation, the discrepancy between the post-revision appraisals is 75% of the original discrepancy, as in the example in the baraita. This result is a general one.[63]

Proposal 2 explains why the extreme points of the range, 80 and 120, can serve to anchor the calculation. Is it not the case, someone might have queried, that the assessor who appraised the asset at 120 also initially intended to say 'more'? On our proposal, had that assessor

62 Again we note that weighting all the appraisals equally, so as to yield a simple arithmetic average, is not even considered; see n. 22 above.

63 Let us designate the original (pre-revision) appraisals of the assessors as $x < y_0 < z_0$ and the appraisals they actually quoted as $x < y_1 < z_1$. The cluster we are interested in is the lower of the two (x, y_1), and the final appraisal is determined by the formula $a = \frac{1}{3}x + \frac{2}{3}y_1$. The discrepancy between the original appraisals in the lower cluster is $\Delta_0 \equiv y_0 - x = 2(a - x) = 2(\frac{1}{3}x + \frac{2}{3}y_1 - x)$, and the discrepancy after the revision is $\Delta_1 \equiv y_1 - x$. The relation between the discrepancies is therefore $\frac{\Delta_1}{\Delta_0} = \frac{y_1 - x}{2(\frac{1}{3}x + \frac{2}{3}y_1 - x)} = \frac{3}{4}$. By contrast, it can be shown that according to Proposal 1, the ratio of the discrepancies is $\frac{\Delta_1}{\Delta_0} = \frac{3(x - y_1)}{2(x - z_0)}$, which means that the ratio depends on z as well (but, using the numbers from the baraita, also equals $\frac{3}{4}$).

tried to tilt the final appraisal upward, he would have said 100, since any upward deviation would only have lowered the final appraisal, for a reason we are about to explain. It follows that if he quoted a value of 120, this is apparently the value he deems correct. Moreover, the assessor who appraised the asset at 120 has no incentive to revise his appraisal, because on our proposal, revisions by the highest assessor will not change the final appraisal.

It can be demonstrated that the others' method is not monotonic: according to our proposal, had the assessor who appraised the asset at 120 said 100, we would have said that the one in the minority (80) is overruled, and set the final appraisal at 100. The fact that this assessor quoted a value higher than 100 lowered the final appraisal, according to our proposed interpretation of the others' method, to $93\frac{1}{3}$. The *Tosafot* point out a similar paradox: had we only two appraisals, one at 100 and the other at 120, the aggregated appraisal would be 110.[64] If so, how is it possible that adding a third opinion that is lower (80) will raise the value of the aggregated appraisal to $113\frac{1}{3}$, as the Talmud assumes in its question about the others' opinion?[65] Nahmanides, who mentions this question with the rubric "some query" (*yesh makshim*), argues that the queriers' basic assumption is in error, because when there are only two appraisals, the final appraisal is determined by the principle that "the burden of proof is on the one who makes a claim against his fellow." By contrast, when there are three appraisals, we follow the majority view.[66]

R. Haim Shor, author of *Torat Haim*, identifies an error on which the question raised in the *Tosafot* rests. On the assumption that the assessors are influenced by their colleagues' appraisals, were it not for the assessor who appraised the asset at 80, the two other assessors would have quoted higher values. He then draws attention to another manifestation of the non-monotonicity of the others' method: if we only had the 80 and 120 appraisals, the final appraisal would be at least 100. Upon adding the 100 appraisal, the final appraisal goes down to $93\frac{1}{3}$. His argument is that if the assessors' skills are assumed to be identical, there is no reason to assume that there is an assessor who makes no mistakes. Hence when there are

64 Ad loc. s.v. *aderaba hai ara*. No solution is suggested by the *Tosafot*, which assumes that all three Tannaitic views concur about this: both R. Eliezer b. Zadok and the others can say that in effect, there is agreement as to the aggregated appraisal of 110, and the Tanna Kama would take 110 as the midpoint.

65 See text above near n. 53.

66 *Hidushei Haramban*, bBaba Batra (Maarava edition 1993, 127).

two assessors, we can ascribe equivalent errors to both. But when we have three or more assessors, we cannot ascribe equivalent error to all, because there is no value on a one-dimensional number line that is equidistant from three or more points. The others thus ascribe error to the three assessors inequivalently.[67] The foregoing discussion endeavored to explain how this inequivalent distribution of error is determined.

This proposal, too, is inconsistent with the Talmud's query, "On the contrary, [why not say that] the land is worth $113\frac{1}{3}$," because tilting the appraisal upward, as per the proposal, would yield $\frac{1}{3}\times 120+\frac{2}{3}\times 100=106\frac{2}{3}$. This proposal is thus also likely to remain an independent explanation of the others' method that is inconsistent with the talmudic interpretation of that method.

6.3 Proposal 3

As noted above, the others' aggregation method is based on R. Eliezer's cluster analysis method.[68] The Talmud's explication of the others' method rests on two assumptions: (1) the error ascribed to each assessor in the lower cluster is $13\frac{1}{3}$; and (2) even professional assessors are influenced by their colleagues' appraisals, and revise their own appraisals accordingly. From the first assumption, the Talmud infers that the center of the lower cluster is $80+13\frac{1}{3}=93\frac{1}{3}$. The value $93\frac{1}{3}$ is not the center of the (80, 100) cluster, but the center of the $\left(80, 106\frac{2}{3}\right)$ cluster. Relying on the second assumption, it is evident that we can ascribe to the assessor who quoted 100 a higher initial appraisal, $106\frac{2}{3}$. In this section, we propose a mathematical formula that elucidates the values given by the Talmud in unpacking the others' method, and the meaning of the expression "they appraise between them and divide it by three."

67 R. Shor's argument explains another perplexing result mentioned by R. Joseph Zundel Hutner: on Maimonides' understanding of the Tanna Kama, if there are three assessors, two of whom quote 100 and one who quotes 130, we would rule in accordance with the majority view and set the appraisal at 100. But if one of the assessors quotes a lower value (90), the final appraisal goes up – according to Maimonides – to 110! (*Hevel Yosef*, Ulam Hamishpat, on *SA*, HM 103, p. 58). According to the explanation in *Torat Haim*, when two assessors quote identical values, we can assume that their appraisal was on target. But when there is no agreement about any value, we must assume that all the assessors erred.

68 See above at n. 47.

R. Eliezer begins with cluster analysis. For the selected cluster, he estimates the error for each assessor in the cluster (in this case, the [80, 100] cluster, with an error of 10), ignoring the assessor who is not in the cluster. The others disagree, and maintain that each assessor's error should be estimated first, and the clusters constructed on the basis of the error estimates. The reasoning here is that all three assessors have identical skills and thus there is no reason to assume at the outset that any assessor errs more than his colleagues.[69] The preliminary stage of error estimation is expressed in the others' statement: "they appraise between them and divide it by three," with emphasis on "between them," referring to **all** the assessors.[70] Our proposal is that the others' error estimate per assessor measures the mean deviation.

Each assessor's mean deviation is expressed as the average distance from the median,[71] that is, the average deviation of the appraisal from

69 "The others think that the error must be ascribed to all three of them, as none is better than his colleague" (*Torat Haim* ad loc.) Based on this opinion, *Torat Haim* resolves an apparent paradox. If we had two appraisals, at 80 and 120, the aggregated appraisal would be 100. Adding an appraisal at 100, the others maintain, lowers the aggregated appraisal to $93\frac{1}{3}$. Since we must ascribe error to each assessor, when there are three assessors error is ascribed to all of them, and there is no reason to say, as follows from the Tanna Kama's method (especially as interpreted by the Rashbam), that the assessor who quoted 100 did not err. See too *Minhat Bikurim* (R. Samuel Avigdor) on tKetubot 11:3.

70 This proposal fits best with the formulation of this dictum in tKetubot 11:2: "They appraise it between them and divide them [in the printed editions: it] by three." As we will see, this proposal is based on two computational stages, as indicated by the formulation in the Tosefta.

71 Since, according to the Rashbam, the preferred measure of the central tendency is the median, the appropriate measure of dispersion – a measure used by the others – is the mean deviation from the median (as opposed to the deviation from the mean), as one of the known differences between the mean and the median is that $\bar{x} = \min_x \sum_{i=1}^{n} (x_i - x)^2$ whereas $med(x) = \min_x \sum_{i=1}^{n} |x_i - x|$. In other words, the mean minimizes the sum of squared deviations (and therefore minimizes the standard deviation), whereas the median minimizes the sum of absolute deviations, and therefore minimizes the mean deviation (from the median). It follows that an explanation of the others' opinion that is based on the measure of mean deviation from the median is consistent with using the median as a measure of the central tendency, as per the Rashbam's understanding of the Tanna Kama's view, even though today, the more accepted measure of dispersion is the standard deviation based on the average of squared deviations, as proposed by Gauss. The measure of mean deviation proposed by Laplace

the median (in absolute values). Let us designate the number of assessors as n; the median appraisal as $med\,(a^i)$; the appraisals of assessors $i=1,2,3$ as a^i; and the mean deviation as md. The mean deviation is given by the formula:

$$md = \frac{1}{n}\sum_{i=1}^{n}\left|a^i - med\left(a^i\right)\right| \qquad (1)$$

One of the two basic assumptions of the others' method is that the assessors take their colleagues' opinions into account and revise their appraisals accordingly. Let us designate the original appraisal of assessor i as a_0^i, and let us assume that the revised appraisal is described by the following formula:

$$a_1^i = \begin{cases} a_0^i\,, & a_1^j \geq a_0^i \\ a_0^i - \beta^i md & a_1^j < a_0^i \end{cases} \qquad (2)$$

where β^i is the 'correction coefficient' of assessor i, which measures the degree to which the assessor took his colleagues' views into account. In our case, given that the assessors' skills are identical, it is reasonable to assume that every assessor ascribes to himself and his colleagues half the potential error (a kind of 'two hold on to the error' situation [see mBaba Metzia 1:1]), and therefore $\beta^i = \frac{1}{2}$, $\forall i$. According to formula (2), assessor i revises his appraisal only if he finds that it is higher than that of another assessor (j). It is possible that assessor i does not know the mean deviation md, so we assume that in the case of a revision, he reduces his original appraisal by βmd at most, and therefore $a_0^i \leq a_1^i + \beta md$. In other words, a_0^i is the upper limit of the estimated value of the original appraisal quoted by assessor i, but in practice it is possible that his original appraisal was lower. The 'reconstructed' cluster is $\left(a_1^i, a_1^j\right)$, and the final appraisal is at the center of this cluster. It is thus clear why the Talmud says "by rights he should have said more," without indicating a precise number.

Inserting the numbers from the baraita into formula (1), we obtain $md = \frac{|-20|+|0|+|20|}{3} = 13\frac{1}{3}$. It follows that, according to formula (2), $a_0^2 \leq 100 + \frac{1}{2}\times 13\frac{1}{3} = 106\frac{2}{3}$, the 'reconstructed' cluster is $\left(80, 106\frac{2}{3}\right)$, and the center of the reconstructed cluster, $93\frac{1}{3}$, is the final appraisal.

measures the mean absolute deviation. Both measures refer to deviations from the mean. Although Gauss's measure has several advantages over Laplace's, it can be assumed that the latter better reflects talmudic thinking, as it is both easier to compute and more intuitive.

The Talmud queries this calculation: "On the contrary (*aderaba*), [why not say that] the land is worth $113\frac{1}{3}$." In other words, if we applied this procedure to the two assessors who quoted the high appraisals, we would obtain a reconstructed cluster of $\left(100, 126\frac{2}{3}\right)$, and the final appraisal would be found at its center, that is, at $113\frac{1}{3}$. The Talmud's reply, "adopt the first two, which do not exceed 100," is identical to the reply it gave in discussing R. Eliezer's method.

The aggregation method suggested by Proposal 3 differs from the other proposed methods, and inputting numbers that differ from those in the baraita will yield different results. For instance, with the numbers suggested by Maimonides (90, 100, 130), the aggregated appraisal calculated according to the Rashbam's interpretation of the others' method will be 100, according to Proposal 1, it will be $103\frac{1}{3}$, and according to Proposal 2, $96\frac{2}{3}$. On Proposal 3, we first calculate the mean deviation from the median (which, for Maimonides' example, is also 100), as follows: $d = \frac{|-10|+|0|+|30|}{3} = 13\frac{1}{3}$. Using the mean deviation, we 'reconstruct' the median assessor's original appraisal, and obtain $a_0^2 \leq 100 + \frac{1}{2} \times 13\frac{1}{3} = 106\frac{2}{3}$. The reconstructed cluster is therefore $\left(90, 106\frac{2}{3}\right)$, and the final, i.e., the aggregated, appraisal (the center of the reconstructed cluster) is $98\frac{1}{3}$.[72]

7. The ruling: the law is in accordance with the Tanna Kama's view

R. Huna's view that the law is decided in accordance with the others' view is adduced twice in the *sugya*, and twice R. Ashi rejects the ruling with the argument: "we do not understand the rationale of the others; shall we decide the law in accordance with their view?!" The second time, R. Huna invokes "the judges of the exile," an epithet for the Amoraim Samuel and Karna ("Rav Huna said: the law is in accordance with the view of the judges of the exile"), but R. Ashi rejects their ruling, despite the prevailing rule that in monetary matters, the law is in accordance with Samuel's view.[73] Apparently, it was clear to the decisors that the choice was between the Tanna Kama's method and that of the others,

72 A calculation similar to that in n. 63 shows that $\frac{\Delta_1}{\Delta_0} = \frac{y_1 - x}{2[(y_1 + \beta md) - x]}$. It is easy to demonstrate that as *md* increases, the ratio decreases.

73 bBekhorot 49b. See E.E. Urbach, *The Halakhah: Its Sources and Development*, trans. R. Posner (Ramat-Gan and Jerusalem: 1986), 334. According to Urbach, this ruling exemplifies R. Ashi's stance, as a matter of principle, on the central role played by rational inference (*svara*) in halakhic decision-making. In other words, even if the great Amoraim decide the law in accordance with the others' view, R. Ashi will not uphold this ruling if he does not understand

and once the others' method was rejected, it was manifest that the law was not to be decided in accordance with R. Eliezer b. Zadok's method, but in accordance with the Tanna Kama's method. Following R. Ashi's ruling, all the decisors concurred that the law is in accordance with the Tanna Kama's view, but disagreed about how to interpret his method, as explained above. The questions that arise from this ruling are as follows:

(a) What does R. Ashi mean by "we do not understand the rationale of the others?"
(b) The law having been decided in accordance with the Tanna Kama's view, how is this view to be understood?
(c) How are we to rule in cases of multiple appraisals, and in cases where the distribution of the appraisals around the mean is not symmetrical?

We discuss these questions in turn.

7.1 Clarification of R. Ashi's argument

Four explanations of the expression "we do not understand the rationale of the others" can be found in the writings of the Early Authorities:

(1) Rabbenu Gershom ad loc. raises two possible doubts about the others' method:
    (a) "Because one may ask the same question that the Talmud asked: On the contrary (*aderaba*)." In other words, the "adopt the first two, which do not exceed 100" argument, which is the basis for preferring the lower cluster even in a symmetrical case, is not convincing, especially when it works against the principle that "the burden of proof is on the one who makes a claim against his fellow."[74] It may be that Rabbenu Gershom had an even stronger objection, namely, how is it possible to say "do not exceed 100" when we assume that the assessor who quoted 100 initially intended to quote a higher value, from which it follows that there is a clear majority for the opinion that the asset is worth more than 100?![75]

---

its rationale. In this vein, see Alfasi's similar explanation of the 'one who was married to three wives' *sugya*, bKetubot 51 (Alfasi pagination).

74 See text above near n. 41.

75 See text above near n. 40. It appears that the Rashbam's understanding of the "*aderaba*" query and the Talmud's "adopt the first two" response provides an answer to this objection.

(b) "'By rights he should have said more' – but the exact sum is not specified." This sentence can be interpreted in several ways. Rabbenu Gershom may be saying that the very assumption that assessors revise their professional appraisals under the influence of their colleagues is just speculation about the nature of a cognitive process taking place in the assessors' minds, and has not been substantiated. Or he may be saying that even if the assumption is acceptable, the others did not explain how they arrived at the rate of revision, and what the assessors wanted to say initially.[76]

(2) The Rashbam interpreted it as "their rationale is unreasonable," and in the same vein, the Ritba wrote, "we do not adequately understand the rationale of the others." From these statements it is apparent that the rationale for the others' method was known and even understood by R. Ashi, but R. Ashi found it flawed, though the flaws were not explained in either the Talmud or the commentaries of the Rashbam and the Ritba.

(3) According to the interpretation given by R. Abraham b. Isaac of Narbonne (Rabad II) (author of *Haeshkol*), the others' method is based on ascribing error to all the assessors, but in his opinion, it is not reasonable to say that they all erred.[77] He adds that this is also the reason R. Eliezer's method is rejected.[78]

(4) R. Ishmael b. Hakhmon explains that the others' method was rejected because it ascribes strategic considerations to the assessors,

76 Note, however, that according to Proposal 3, the value that the assessor intended to quote initially is of no consequence; what matters is the upper limit of the appraisal that can be ascribed to him.

77 Rashbam s.v. *osim shuma*, explains that it was over this very point that the Tanna Kama disagreed with both R. Eliezer and the others. According to the Tanna Kama, it is not necessary to say that all the assessors erred equally. On the contrary, in his opinion it should be assumed that one of the assessors is closer to 'the truth' than his colleagues. The Rashbam's aggregation method – namely, taking the median – serves not only to make a decision (on the basis of the majority principle), but also to identify the assessor who is closest to 'the truth.' We saw that according to both R. Eliezer and the others, the same deviation must be ascribed to all the assessors, on the assumption that their skills are identical. But from what the Rashbam says, it is not clear whether this is indeed the reason R. Ashi rejects the others' method (and R. Eliezer's method) as the basis for determining the aggregate appraisal.

78 N. 4 above.

and says of them that they revise their appraisals under the influence of other assessors, "which is not the way of the God-fearing."[79]

To the above explanations of R. Ashi's objection to the others' method, put forward by Early Authorities, we can add several additional explanations.

(1) R. Ashi's assertion that "we do not understand the rationale of the others" may refer to uncertainty about how the figure of $93\frac{1}{3}$ was calculated. The Talmud assumes that the assessors in the lower cluster err by $13\frac{1}{3}$, and the Early Authorities explain that this value is calculated as follows: $\frac{120-80}{3} = 13\frac{1}{3}$. The Early Authorities do not explain their position, but it is reasonable to say that the range between 80 and 120 contains the correct appraisal, and that the controversy over the asset's value involves appraisals that fall within this range. But it is not clear why division of this range by the number of assessors (3) yields the error to be ascribed to each of them. It is thus plausible that this is what R. Ashi was puzzled about, although we showed above that there are three different calculations that yield a final appraisal of $93\frac{1}{3}$. Even if we assume that R. Ashi was aware of these various possibilities, as long we cannot determine which of the three calculations actually served as the basis for the others' aggregation method, the conclusion that "we do not understand the rationale of the others" is justified. Indeed, if the various calculations are applied to a different set of numbers, each produces different results.

(2) The others' method is based on a hidden assumption, which Nahmanides adduces. He explains why there is no concern that the assessor who quoted 80 intended initially to quote a lower value, but revised his appraisal upward under the influence of the other appraisals. According to Nahmanides, an assessor who appraises the asset "at a lower value is not afraid of his colleagues, but he is embarrassed to overestimate it." In other words, the hidden assumption is that assessors are apprehensive about exaggerating upward, but not downward. R. Ashi may wonder what the basis for this assumption is. Pursuing Nahmanides' line of thought, let us note that if we assume that there is bi-directional revision of appraisals (both upward and downward), the only assessor about whom it

79 H. and M. Hershler (eds.), *Perush Kadmon Lebava Batra* (Jerusalem: 1971), 176.

can reasonably be assumed that he quoted a value representing his initial, i.e., unrevised, opinion, is the one who quoted 100, because had he wished to take his colleagues' opinions into consideration, then on his right was the assessor who quoted 120, and on his left, the one who quoted 80, so it was reasonable to assume that their influences offset each other.

7.2 The Maimonides–Rashbam controversy

The accepted halakhic ruling, agreed upon by all the decisors, is that the court, in determining an appraisal, takes a "middle course," in line with the Tanna Kama's opinion, as interpreted by the Talmud. The expression "middle course" (*milta metziata*) hints at the fact that the court's appraisal should be based on some measure of the central tendency of the assessors' appraisals. Measures of central tendency that were known, it seems, in the ancient world, are the mode, the midrange, and the median. It is likely that Pythagoras and his students, in the sixth century BCE, were familiar with the arithmetic, geometric, and harmonic means, which are known as the "Pythagorean means."[80] Nicomachus of Gerasa (second century BCE) names ten types of mean.[81] It is not clear, however, whether the Sages were familiar with the mean.[82] The decisors who comment on the 'three assessors' *sugya* do not mention the mean.[83]

80 Pythagoras left no written exposition of his views, and most of his teachings are known from relatively late traditions. One of the important sources for Pythagoras' theories is a work by Nicomachus of Gerasa (today Jerash, Jordan), see the next note.

81 Nicomachus of Gerasa, *Introduction to Arithmetic*. trans. M.L. D'Ooge (Annapolis MD: 1926), Book 2, ch. 28. See also T.L. Heath, *A History of Greek Mathematics* (Oxford: 1921), 1:87.

82 D. Hershkovitz and R. Rosenbaum have argued that, in light of the *sugya* in bPesahim 89b, it can be concluded that the Sages were familiar with, and had recourse to, the concept of the weighted average. See D. Hershkovitz, "Mathematical problems in the halakha and in Jewish sources" (Hebrew), *Mispar Hazak* 2000:3 (2002); R. Rosenbaum, *The Wisdom of Fraction Theory: Mathematics from a Jewish Perspective* (Hebrew), (Jerusalem: 2005). In our opinion, Hershkovitz's interpretation, though elegant, need not be adduced vis-à-vis the *sugya* of the assessors. It follows from Chebyshev's inequality that the distance between the median and the mean is no greater than one standard deviation, that is, $\left|\bar{x} - med(\mathbf{x})\right| \leq \sigma$.

83 Let us assume that we have a sample $= \{x_i\}_{i=1}^{n}$. The arithmetic mean is $\bar{x} = \frac{1}{n}\sum_{i=1}^{n} x_i$. To calculate the median, we rearrange the sample so that $x_i \leq x_{i+1}$ and define $k = int\left(\frac{n+1}{2}\right)$ where $int(n+1)$ is the closest integer

According to Maimonides, the "middle course" is the midrange appraisal; according to the Rashbam, it is the median appraisal. The Later Authorities disagreed on whether to rule in accordance with the view of the Rashbam or that of Maimonides. R. Joseph Caro, author of the *Shulhan Arukh*, ruled in accordance with Maimonides' view, whereas R. Joshua Falk Katz, author of the *Sema* (*Sefer Meirat Einaim*), and subsequent Later Authorities, ruled in accordance with the Rashbam's view.[84]

Above, we noted the problems arising from Maimonides' account of the proper method of aggregating appraisals. First, the result is greatly affected by exceptional appraisals, and thus subject to manipulation. Second, the final appraisal is liable to be a value that was not quoted by any of the assessors, which is a problematic result whether we treat the appraisal as testimony or as a kind of judicial proceeding.[85] Another difficulty with Maimonides' view is that it seems to be at odds with the import of the *sugya* taken as a whole, namely, that the aggregated appraisal should reflect an established decision-making rule, and specifically, the majority principle. At the beginning of the baraita, when two assessors quote the same value, the *sugya* asserts "the one, being in the minority, is overruled" (*batel yahid*

---

to $\left(\frac{n+1}{2}\right)$. Then the median is $med(\mathbf{x}) = \frac{1}{2}\left(x_k + x_{n+1-k}\right)$. The midrange is $mid(\mathbf{x}) = \frac{1}{2}\left(x_{max} - x_{min}\right)$.

84 R. Joshua Falk Katz (Poland, 1550-1614), *Sefer Meirat Einayim*, HM 103, 100:5, refers readers to his *Derisha* commentary on *Tur* ad loc. He claims to prove there that the Rif, the Rosh, and the Tur all ruled in accordance with the Rashbam's view. In his *Beer Hagola*, HM ad loc., R. Moses b. Naftali Rivkes (c. 1600-c. 1672) disagrees with R. Falk Katz's remarks in *Sema*, and notes that the Rabad did not express any reservations about Maimonides' view, and that R. Joseph Habiba, author of *Nimukei Yosef*, also upholds Maimonides' view. He also disputes the claim that the Rif, the Rosh, and the Tur all ruled in accordance with the Rashbam's view, noting that he did not see the said passage in the *Derisha*. (Indeed, the extant *Derisha* has no commentary on *Tur*, HM 103). It may, however, conceivably be inferred from the Tur's statement "we follow the one who says 100," that the reference is to the median assessor, as per the Rashbam's view. R. Joseph ibn Lev states that all the decisors disagree with Maimonides (*Responsa Mahari Ben Lev* 2:29). Other Later Authorities who concur with the Sema's view are R. Jonathan Eibeschutz, R. Jacob Lorberbaum, and R. Yehiel Mikhel Epstein.

85 Although in our opinion, appraisal should not be classed as either; see §3 above on the assessors' legal status.

bemiuto). The methods of both R. Eliezer and the others are presented as being based on the decision of a majority of assessors. And the Tanna Kama's method, according to the Rashbam, is also based on the majority principle.

Maimonides' aggregation method, by contrast, is not based on the majority principle,[86] and as R. Jonathan Eibeschutz points out, in certain cases Maimonides' method yields results that are incompatible with it.[87] It may be possible to resolve these problems by assuming that in Maimonides' opinion, an appraisal is neither testimony nor a judicial procedure, but rather a kind of statistical sample of expert evaluations that is used to estimate an asset's value. Maimonides seems to have understood appraisal in this manner, i.e., as a sample, to which he applies his preferred measure of central tendency: the midrange.

86 R. Joseph Zundel Hutner, n. 67 above, however, argues that Maimonides' method should indeed be viewed as a majority-based decision rule. The midpoint of the cluster that contains the two extreme appraisals represents two assessors against the middle one. In his opinion, the Rashbam's method is problematic, because it is based on the principle that "the law is in accordance with the view of the one who tips the scales (*hamakhria*)" [i.e., the one whose view resolves a stalemated debate] (see, e.g., bShabat 39a). But this principle is valid when the 'scale-tipping,' i.e., decisive, opinion turns on a distinction that is relevant to the two opposed, i.e., stalemated, opinions, but not when it introduces a third, new opinion. "A decisive [i.e., scale-tipping] opinion that is based on a third argument is not determinative" (bBaba Kama 116a), and see *Rashi* and *Tosafot* ad loc. In our opinion, Maimonides' method is not based on the majority principle at all. The Rashbam's method, we contend, is based on the majority principle, not the principle that "the law is in accordance with the view of the one who tips the scales," as is apparent from his remarks on the subject. The principle of 'the one who tips the scales,' as it appears in the Talmud, is relevant to controversies that are qualitative in nature, and may itself be grounded, in some sense, in the majority principle.

87 *Urim Vetumim*, 103a. In Maimonides' own example (90, 100, 130), the final appraisal, as Maimonides calculates it, is 110, despite the fact that most of the assessors agree that the asset is not worth more than 100. R. Eibeschutz argues that Maimonides' method is refuted by bKetubot 100a, which explains the force of an appraisal by the court by the fact that the court represents many, whereas according to Maimonides, an individual can skew the appraisal to a value higher than 100.

In the Rashbam's opinion, the Tanna Kama's method involves selecting the median opinion. As noted above, the median method is strategy-proof.[88]

A controversy similar to that between Maimonides and the Rashbam concerning the proper method of aggregation is found in another *sugya*, bBaba Metzia 87a. A baraita in that *sugya* asserts: "He who engages a laborer, and says to him [I will pay you] as one or two townspeople [are paid], must pay him the lower of the wages. This is R. Joshua's view. But the Sages say: It is appraised between them (*meshamnin beineihem*)."[89] The wage defined in the labor agreement reflects the wage paid to one or two residents of the town. Apparently, R. Joshua's method is based on the rule that the burden of proof is on the one who makes a claim against his fellow. But according to the Sages, this rule should not be applied, as is stated in the Jerusalem Talmud: "Said R. Hosheia: this means that custom supersedes law (*minhag mevatel et hahalakha*). Said R. Imi: [usually,] the burden of proof is on the one who makes a claim against his fellow, but this case is exceptional."[90] A worker's wages must be set according to the prevailing rate in the area (the 'custom of the land'), but obviously, there is more than one customary wage rate. The Sages ruled that, this being so, "it is appraised between them" – they aggregate the various rates. Maimonides decides the law in accordance with the Sages' view, interpreting the *sugya* of the laborer's wages as follows: "He who engages a laborer, and says to him [I will pay you] as one or two townspeople [are paid] – takes the lower wage and the highest wage, and appraises between them."[91] It is evident that here

88 When the skills of the assessors are not identical, deciding on the basis of the median is preferable to the mean as well, as has been demonstrated in P. Gerlach-Kristen, "Monetary policy committees and interest rate setting," *European Economic Review* 50 (2006), 487.

89 bBaba Metzia 87a.

90 jBaba Metzia 7:1 (11b).

91 Maimonides, *Code*, Laws concerning Hiring 9:2. In print, the term is "*meshamnin*" (they appraise), but Maimonides, *Commentary on the Mishnah*, mBekhorot 2:6, distinguishes between "*meshamin*" and "*meshamnin*." See also Maimonides' comments on mBaba Batra 7:4 and R. Joseph Kafih's commentary ad loc. The same reading is found in R. Nahum Rabinovich's edition of the *Code*, *Yad Pshuta*, Mishpatim 1, p. 194, as well as in the Makbili edition.

too, Maimonides, consistent with his approach in the assessors' *sugya*,[92] adopts an estimate based on the midrange.[93]

Rashi interprets "appraise between them" (*meshamnin beineihem*) as follows: "not by less and not by more, but like the custom of the land, the intermediate [value]."[94] But in the *Tur*, a different formulation of Rashi's comment is quoted: "They give to them like they give to the intermediate ones."[95] That is, Rashi adduces the rate paid to "the intermediate ones" (*beinoniim*), i.e., the rate paid the average laborer, whereas according to Maimonides, the rate, being based on the midrange, can be a value that does not reflect the rate paid to any worker. It would thus seem that Rashi suggests that the laborer's wage is set according to the median wage, not the midrange.[96] The Ritba is more explicit: "In other words, he pays the intermediate wage, and if there are two intermediate wages, or three, he gives the one in the middle."[97] Clearly, the Ritba did not uphold Maimonides' view, because if the meaning of "interme-

92 More generally, Maimonides tends to uphold Aristotle's 'golden mean' approach – articulated in the *Nicomachean Ethics*, Book II: "virtue is a kind of mean . . . it aims at what is intermediate" (1106b28) – and regards the middle course as the preferred path in many areas. See *Code*, Laws concerning Ethics 1-2; *Introduction to Tractate Avot* (also known as *Eight Chapters*), ch. 4.

93 In so doing, Maimonides adopts Rabbenu Hananel's interpretation (Domb edition, 156). This is also R. Jonathan of Lunel's interpretation, as quoted in *Shita Mekubetzet*. R. Jonathan emphasizes that what is at issue is not the midrange between the highest and lowest rates, but the midrange between the "high customary rate" and the "low customary rate." R. Jacob b. Asher notes that R. Meir Halevi Abulafia, the Rama, also rules this way (*Tur*, HM 331). On the basis of *Magid Mishne*, on *Code*, Laws concerning Hiring 9:2, R. Joseph Caro concludes that Nahmanides and the Rashba also adopt Maimonides' interpretation of "appraise" (*meshamin*) (*Beit Yosef*, *Tur*, HM 331). But from the extant text of *Magid Mishne*, it appears that the reference to Nahmanides and the Rashba was intended to underscore the novelty of their view that the appraisal rule from bBaba Metzia should be applied to additional *sugyot* where the rule is not explicitly mentioned. And this is also the import of Nahmanides' own comments, which do not offer any interpretation of "*meshamin*" at all.

94 *Rashi*, bBaba Metzia 87a. s.v. *meshamnin beineihem*. A similar version appears in the *Rashi* that is printed with the Rif's commentary: "not like the lesser and not like the greater, but like the custom of the land, the intermediate [value] between them."

95 HM 331.

96 This is also how the *sugya* is interpreted by *Lehem Mishne* on Maimonides, *Code*, Laws concerning Hiring 9:2, and *Perisha* on *Tur*, HM 331.

97 *Hidushei Haritba*, bBaba Metzia 87a s.v. *vehahakhamim omrim*.

diate" is the midrange, it is a single value, and there cannot be two or three "intermediates."

In the *sugya* of the wages, like that of the assessors, the Early Authorities disagreed about how to reflect many dispersed values by means of a single value.[98] One faction prefers the median, another faction prefers the midrange. This controversy has halakhic significance primarily when the values are not distributed symmetrically around the mean. The characteristics of these measures serve as indications of the decisors' priorities, and suggest the relevant criteria for generalizing their rulings.

Without relation to the aforementioned views of the decisors, the choice between the median and the midrange, as a universal decision rule, must take into account the risk vs. the prospect inherent in a given rule. What is at issue is not the probability of arriving at 'the truth' or the type and magnitude of error that would occur in a specific case, but rather the risk and prospect inherent in choosing a given rule and applying it to every case.

The suitability of measures of central tendency for representing a given population, and the risk inherent in their use, is evaluated by means of the loss function. The loss function is intended to identify the best-suited measure of central tendency for a given data set in a way that minimizes the loss of data.[99] There are four useful loss functions:

(1) **Number of errors**: Measures the number of observations that are not identical to the selected measure of central tendency (henceforth, the measure). The distance of the observations from the

98 That the controversy among the Early Authorities regarding the *sugya* of the assessors is related to the controversy among them over the wages *sugya* is manifest from the Vilna Gaon's gloss on bBaba Metzia 87a, as well as from the *Perisha* on *Tur*, HM 331. It appears that Nahmanides on bBaba Metzia ad loc. and the Rashba (as mentioned in *Magid Mishne*, see n. 93 above), hinted that the "they appraise between them" principle applies in other cases, including "when [an item] has been appraised by three" cases (see bAvoda Zara 72a), that is, transactions between a buyer and a seller who have agreed that the price will be set by three assessors. Nahmanides and the Rashba hint that "they appraise between them" applies to cases where such an agreement was made, but the three assessors quoted different values. See also n. 4 above, which points out that the Ritba interpreted the assessors *sugya* as referring to such a transaction.

99 See S. Zamir and R. Beit-Marom, *Introduction to Statistics for the Social Sciences* (Hebrew), (Tel Aviv 1993), 2:88ff.

measure is unimportant. The greater the number of observations that are identical to the measure, the smaller the loss of data as a result of using the measure. The measure that minimizes this function is the mode.

(2) **Maximal deviation**: Checks the distance between the measure and the most distant observation. The measure that minimizes maximal deviation in essence minimizes the greatest contingent 'error' in estimating the data's central tendency. The measure that minimizes this function is the midrange, that is, $mid(\mathbf{x}) = \min_x \max |x_i - x|$.

(3) **The sum of absolute deviations**: Sums the absolute deviations from the measure of all observations. The measure that minimizes the sum of the absolute deviations also minimizes the mean deviation. The measure that minimizes this function is the median, that is, $med(\mathbf{x}) = \min_x \sum_{i=1}^{n} |x_i - x|$.

(4) **The sum of the squared deviations**: Sums the squares of the differences between observations and the measure. The measure that minimizes this function also minimizes the standard deviation. The measure that minimizes this function is the mean, that is, $\bar{x} = \min_x \sum_{i=1}^{n} (x_i - x)^2$.

An additional consideration in the choice of measure of central tendency is the degree of its sensitivity to the distribution characteristics of the data. For example, in a symmetric, bell-shaped distribution, the median, mode, midrange, and mean are identical, and converge on the center of the distribution. In a positive skew distribution, the mode is the smallest measure of those discussed here, the mean is the largest, and the median is located between the mode and the mean. In a negative skew distribution, the mode is the largest measure, followed by the median and the mean (Figure 4). The only measure that is not affected by the shape of the distribution is the midrange. The median is only minimally sensitive to the shape of the distribution, whereas the two other measures, the mean and the mode, are highly sensitive to the shape of the distribution.[100]

100 The degree of sensitivity of the measure of central tendency to the distribution of the data into the different clusters has no halakhic significance, because in the Tanna Kama's opinion, contrary to what R. Eliezer b. Zadok and the others maintain, the aggregated appraisal is not arrived at by cluster analysis.

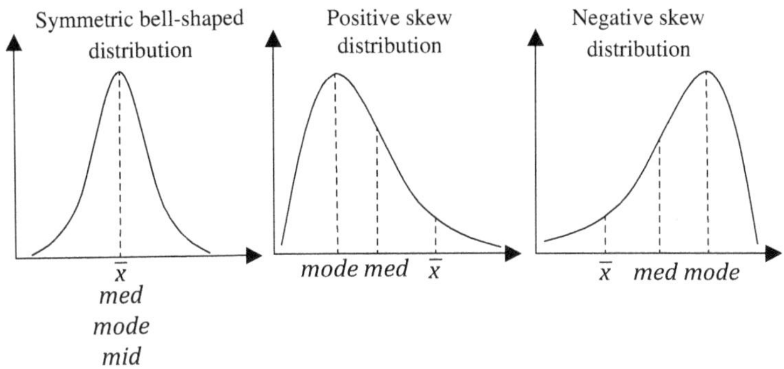

Figure 4

Figure 4 shows that when the distribution is skewed, as in the case regarding asset prices, the median is a better estimate of the measure of a population's central tendency than the mean and the mode. By contrast, the midrange is a highly effective measure for estimating a population's central tendency for small samples if the population's distribution is sufficiently flat (platykurtic). For example, the midrange is highly effective in small samples of uniform distribution, especially when the extremes of the distribution are not known. In this case, the midrange is an unbiased minimal mean variance estimator of the central tendency. But the midrange is not an effective estimator for mesokurtic distributions, such as the normal distribution.

A clear example of a halakhic argument about the effectiveness of the midrange as an estimator of central tendency can be found in mKeilim 17:5-6:

> The pomegranate of which they have spoken refers to one that is neither small nor big but of intermediate size . . . The egg of which they have spoken is neither big nor small but of intermediate size. R. Judah says: The largest of the large and the smallest of the small are brought and put in water, and the displaced water is then divided. R. Jose said: But who can tell me which is the largest and which is the smallest? But rather, it all depends on the observer's opinion.

According to R. Judah, the size of the 'intermediate' item determines the sample's midrange. R. Jose's argument is that the "largest of the large" and the "smallest of the small" mentioned by R. Judah are from the sample itself, and do not necessarily represent the extreme values in reality. In nature, the distribution of the eggs' volume is normal, that is, mesokurtic, and therefore the midrange of the sample is indeed an ineffective estimator. The law is in accordance with R. Jose's view.[101] This elucidates the Rashbam's endorsement of the median in the assessors *sugya*, especially if we assume that the distribution of the assets' prices is positively-skewed. By contrast, though Maimonides upholds R. Jose's view in the *sugya* in Keilim, in the other *sugyot* we examined (the assessors and the wages), he prefers the midrange.

We can explain Maimonides' opinion with regard to the latter *sugyot* by the fact that the samples are small and the distributions uniform. In the case of the assessors, the distribution that interests us is not that of the asset prices, but the distribution of the appraisals around a certain value, which is what we want to estimate. Absent concrete data about each assessor, the working assumption is that their skills are quite similar, if not identical. (Even if in reality, assessors' skills display a normal distribution, 98% of their appraisals are within one standard deviation from the mean.) In the case of the laborer's wages, the nature of the distribution is also of no significance to us, because the objective of the estimate is to interpret the labor agreement, not to estimate the average wage in town.

In choosing the most suitable measure, it is appropriate to take into account its degree of sensitivity to extreme values (which also reflects the degree to which it is strategy-proof). This is an important consideration if we assume that a relatively 'large' deviation reflects an error, or even deliberate manipulation. The measures that are less sensitive to extreme values and strategic manipulation are the mode and the median; the more sensitive measures are the midrange and the mean.

As noted, the commentaries on our *sugyot* do not mention the mean at all.[102] The explanation may lie in the fact that the mean has the disadvantages of the other measures (sensitivity to extreme values, to manipulation, and to skewed distribution), whereas the loss function that it minimizes, the sum of the squared deviations, has no halakhic significance. The two measures that are left (absent the mode) are the median and midrange.[103] Choosing the median is likely to bring the court closer to 'the truth' than choosing the midrange, and will minimize the court's

101 See Maimonides, *Commentary on the Mishnah*, ad loc.; *Code*, Laws concerning Utensils 6:2.

102 Except for the Rashbam's ultimately-rejected initial assumption (*hava amina*), see n. 29 above; and see too n. 82 above and the adjacent text.

103 On the possibility of reaching a decision on the basis of the mode, see below at n. 105.

mean error in its overall adjudication, i.e., adjudication of all the cases it hears. Choosing the midrange is more effective than choosing the median only if the aforementioned conditions obtain (small samples, relatively 'flat' distribution with unknown extremes); what it minimizes, however, is not the court's mean adjudication error, but rather its maximum error. It follows that choosing the median reflects 'daring' in that it takes a risk (namely, the risk of serious error) for the sake of a better prospect (of reaching 'the truth'), whereas choosing the midrange reflects a solid approach and greater aversion to risk.

8. Generalization of the ruling

The *sugya* in bBaba Batra 107a-b involves reaching a decision between three appraisals distributed symmetrically around the median. In this section, we discuss generalization of the decision for cases in which the appraisals are not distributed symmetrically.

8.1 Generalization of the Tanna Kama's method

The Tanna Kama's aggregation method, as it was understood by both the Rashbam (the median) and Maimonides (the midrange), is simple to generalize. Both the Rashbam and Maimonides themselves illustrated their methods for cases in which the distribution of the appraisals is not symmetrical.[104] The Tanna Kama's method, on both understandings, can also be generalized to more than three appraisals, since calculation of the median and midrange is not limited to any specific number of observations.[105]

104 Rashbam, n. 31 above and Maimonides, n. 25 above.

105 When the number of assessors is even, the median quote is the mean of the two median appraisals. A question not raised in this article is how the Tanna Kama would rule in the case of more than three assessors, a minority of whom quote the same value. The question is whether we can apply to each of the assessors who disagree with the minority value, individually, the principle that "the one, being in the minority, is overruled," or an absolute majority is required, in which case it will be necessary to apply a decision rule (either the median or the midrange) in this case as well.

8.2 Generalization of R. Eliezer b. Zadok's method

The generalization of R. Eliezer's method to a general number n of appraisals requires cluster analysis, which merits a separate examination. To generalize R. Eliezer's method to cover asymmetrical cases, we will examine an extreme example. Consider a case with three appraisals (80, 100, 101). The appraisal at 100 can be conjoined with either the appraisal at 80 or at 101. The center of the (100, 101) cluster is $100\frac{1}{2}$, which means that the deviation ascribed to each appraisal in the cluster does not exceed $\frac{1}{2}$. By contrast, the center of the (80, 100) cluster is 90, and the deviation ascribed to each appraisal is 20 times greater than in the (100, 101) cluster. Which is the preferred combination in this case?

The two main possibilities are:

(1) R. Eliezer always prefers to build appraisal clusters in such a way that the majority is based on the lower value (as per the 'adopt the first two' principle).
(2) The Talmud needs an argument to justify R. Eliezer's preference for conjoining the deciding quote to the lower cluster only in a symmetric system. In an asymmetric system, the preferred combination conjoins the median appraisal with the more concentrated cluster, even if this happens to be the higher one, because this combination minimizes the cluster's radius, or in other words, minimizes the mean deviation of each appraisal in the cluster.[106]

Since R. Eliezer's method for determining an appraisal was not accepted as law, there are no commentaries that discuss how it might be generalized, and thus no halakhic sources we can utilize. In this article, we will limit ourselves to exploring this issue in light of the explanations given by the Rashbam and Maimonides.[107]

106 An additional theoretical possibility, which is clearly inconsistent with R. Eliezer's method, is to begin by assembling the clusters on the basis of the principle of minimizing deviations. In our example, we obtain the cluster of (100, 101) vis-à-vis the singleton cluster of 80. At the next stage, the decision will be a weighted average of the centers $100\frac{1}{2}$ and 80, the question being what relative weight to assign to each, and how this relative weight is determined.

107 We hope to investigate various algorithms for performing cluster analysis, in line with R. Eliezer's method, in a future paper. The Ritba's aggregation method calls for a separate investigation; see above at n. 45.

According to the Rashbam, the question is whether the 'if you take hold of too much' principle can prevail over the weight that must be assigned to the fact that the upper cluster is denser. In our opinion, in his comments on the assessors *sugya*, the Rashbam uses two expressions which indicate that recourse to the 'if you take hold of too much' principle is a 'default' decision rule of sorts for cases where we lack a reason to tilt the scale in one direction or the other.[108] One of these is the expression "since it is possible to say this and it is possible to say that" (i.e., both sides are equally reasonable), indicating that the case is symmetrical and evenly-balanced. The Rashbam goes on to say: "They all admit that it is close to a *mane* [100]," that is, the two possible clusters both lead to the conclusion that the 'true' value is equally close to 100 from the right or the left. In asymmetrical cases, the default decision rule turns out to be inferior to other possible decision rules, and therefore the appraisal at 100 should be added to the denser cluster, even if that is the upper cluster.

According to Nahmanides, the question is whether the psychological assumption about the thresholds of the 'orders of magnitude' can prevail over the weight we must assign to the density of the upper cluster. In asymmetrical cases, especially in the extreme case of (80, 100, 101), we can say, on the one hand, that based on Nahmanides' 'orders of magnitude' assumption, the lower cluster is to be preferred, because the two appraisals in it do not cross the 100 threshold. On the other hand, our objective is to determine the true value of the asset with the greatest possible precision. It might well be the case that the assessor who appraised it at 100 wanted – like the assessor who quoted 101 – to quote a little more than 100, but did not dare. Preferring the upper, dense cluster ($100\frac{1}{2}$) would thus express a value that is closer to the truth. The other possibility (90) ascribes greater error to the assessor who appraised the asset at 100.[109]

108 *Rashbam*, bBaba Kama 107a-b s.v. *nekot mihat trei kamai*. On the 'if you take hold of too much' principle, see n. 39 above. According to Rashi, "Wherever you find two alternatives, one that takes hold of a large amount and one that takes hold of a small amount; it is good for you to take hold of the small amount. Because even if you could have taken hold of the large amount, but you took hold of the small amount, your hold is a hold, since the small amount is included in the large amount; but if you took hold of the large amount and [by rights] you should have taken hold of the small amount, you will find that you took hold of it in a manner not in accordance with the law" (*Rashi*, bHagiga 17a s.v. *tafasta merube lo tafasta*).

109 Minimizing error as a guiding principle is emphasized in *Pnei Shlomo*, see above at n. 44.

8.3 Generalization of the others' method

Because the others' method is based on R. Eliezer's method, its generalization for assessors requires a discussion of cluster analysis algorithms, which is outside the scope of the present article. We will limit the discussion to generalization of the others' method, as interpreted by the three proposals presented above, to the case of any three appraisals, not just the Talmud's example (80, 100, 120).

Proposal 1 Given that this proposal is based on weighting the extreme opinions, it can be applied to any collection of three different appraisals. The guiding logic, as in Maimonides' method, is that the median appraisal does not affect the aggregated appraisal. But which end of the range the weights $\left(\frac{1}{3}, \frac{2}{3}\right)$ are assigned to depends on additional considerations.

Proposal 2 On this proposal, the final appraisal is based on a selected cluster, one end of which – under the influence of the third appraisal, which pulls the center of the cluster toward it – is assigned double weight. The question that arises here is which cluster to select in an asymmetrical system, a point over which there seems to be no disagreement between R. Eliezer and the others.[110] If the selected cluster is the upper one (unlike the example discussed in the assessors *sugya*), the lower end is assigned the double weight.

Proposal 3 The generalization of this proposal also depends on the prior choice of the cluster that will be the basis for the aggregated appraisal. Once the cluster is chosen, the calculation is analogous to that described above.

9. Summary and conclusions

The baraita in bBaba Batra 107a-b addresses the aggregation of three appraisals. It presents the opinions of three Tannaim, each of whom suggests a method for calculating the aggregate appraisal in the specific case described in the baraita, which involves symmetrically-distributed appraisals. Although in the course of the talmudic debate over the proposed aggregation methods, R. Huna twice recommends ruling in accordance with the third opinion (that of the others), R. Ashi rejects

110 See the generalization of R. Eliezer b. Zadok's method above.

that recommendation with the argument: "we do not understand the rationale of the others; shall we decide the law in accordance with their view?!" The others' opinion having been rejected as law, the Early Authorities all concur that the law is decided in accordance with the view of the Tanna Kama, but disagree over how to interpret his method.

The others' aggregation method, is, like that of R. Eliezer, based on halakhic considerations that violate the mathematical symmetry and tip the aggregation toward the lower appraisal. In the first part of the article, we tried to work out a compelling analysis of the others' opinion, which we found both interesting and challenging to interpret. We recommended three possible interpretations of the others' method, only one of which appears to be consistent with the unfolding of the *sugya*. The three proposals are based on three different principles: the midrange, cluster analysis, and the measure of mean deviation. We showed that these interpretations disagree as to the meaning of the others' dictum "they appraise between them." Does "between them" refer to the two assessors whose appraisals the Tanna Kama – on Maimonides' interpretation of the *sugya* – uses as the basis for the calculation (namely, the high and the low); to the two assessors whose appraisals are used in R. Eliezer b. Zadok's method (namely, the two lower appraisals), which is presented together with the others' method, or to all three of the assessors whose appraisals are mentioned in the baraita? When R. Ashi says that "We do not understand the rationale of the others," can we assume that he has in mind a specific interpretation of the others' rationale, but rejects it as a basis for deciding the law? The understandings we proposed for the others' aggregation method demonstrate that it is subject to multiple interpretations, all of which yield the same result when applied to the example in the baraita (80, 100, 120), but different results in other cases. This may be why R. Ashi concludes that "we do not understand the rationale of the others; shall we decide the law in accordance with their view?!"

In the second part of the article, we showed that the controversy among the decisors about the "middle course" (*milta metziata*), regardless of whether it refers to the midrange or the median, also occurs in another context involving the aggregation of various values, namely, the *sugya* in bBaba Metzia about the determination of laborers' wages. We concluded that Maimonides consistently upholds the midrange, whereas the schools of Rashi and the Rashbam uphold the median. We showed that each aggregation method has its advantages and disadvantages, and which is deemed preferable depends on which loss function we wish to minimize.

In the last part of the article we raised the question of generalizing the aggregation methods in our *sugya* to cover additional cases, though as noted above, we did not discuss generalization of the ruling to a general number *n* of assessors, because generalizing the methods of R. Eliezer and the others calls for discussion of cluster analysis algorithms, which could not be undertaken here. We noted, however, that the need to generalize the decision rule to a general number *n* of appraisals is rooted in Jewish law itself, which in at least one case, that of appraisal in matters of consecrated land and individuals (*hekdesh*), demands appraisal by a large number of assessors: "And regarding [valuations of land dedicated to the Temple], nine [Israelites] and a priest (*kohen*), and so too regarding [valuations of] people" (mMegila 4:3).[111] The need to make decisions on the basis of an extensive data set arises in many other areas.

In seeking to discuss the generalization of the Tannaitic aggregation methods, two fundamental questions, one a general question about halakhic decision-making which has bearing on the boundaries of the Tannaitic controversy in the baraita, the other about the nature of the ruling in the *sugya*, must be addressed:

(1) Is the principle that "the one, being in the minority, is overruled" valid only in a case of majority vs. minority, or also in cases of a relative rather than an absolute majority, the relative majority being represented by the mode? For example, if we have five appraisals, two of which are identical and the rest of which differ from each other, and an absolute majority is required, the Tannaitic controversy is relevant, since no opinion has an absolute majority. But if the mode, as a measure of relative majority, prevails over each individual opinion, all the halakhic authorities concur that the decision is in accordance with the two identical appraisals, on the basis of the principle that minority opinions are overruled.

(2) Can it be claimed that the ruling in the Tannaitic controversy refers specifically to the case described in the baraita, that is, a case where there are three appraisals? If so, in a case with multiple appraisals, the Tannaim might not disagree as to the aggregation method, and the Tanna Kama might even endorse one of the other

111 See n. 5 above. And see *Arukh Hashulhan*, HM 103:1, which also addresses situations in which there are many assessors.

> methods. If, for instance, hundreds of appraisals are aggregated, it might be the case that the Tanna Kama would prefer a cluster-analysis approach, since the median is not necessarily the most convincing method. Under these circumstances, the ruling that the law is in accordance with the Tanna Kama's view would be valid only in the case of three appraisals, and in cases with a larger number of appraisals, there would be room for the decisors to debate the issue.

As we have not undertaken the generalization of the Tannaitic opinions to a large number of appraisals, which, as noted above, would require a separate investigation, we have not addressed these questions.

Another important question is that of the boundaries of the Tannaitic controversy, and their extension via analogy. In the baraita, the Tannaim address the aggregation of assessors' appraisals. To which additional areas might it be possible to apply the controversy by analogy? For example, the "middle course" (*milta metziata*) decision rule is not applied in political controversies in any democratic country. Over fifty years ago, Arrow raised the question of aggregation of voter preferences and showed that it has no satisfactory answer.[112] The question of drawing analogies from the Tannaitic controversy over the assessors to other contexts was raised with regard to controversy between rabbinical court judges, who do not serve as assessors, but rather hand down rulings after hearing arguments presented by the litigants. How is the court to rule in cases where no single opinion garners a majority? It is reasonable to claim that even Maimonides would admit that in this context, one ought not decide by means of the midrange, if only because, as we saw above, a disadvantage of this decision method is that it can yield a decision that no judge on the panel actually upholds. It stands to reason that a rabbinical court ruling should reflect the opinion of the majority of the judges, and it is not acceptable for the court to issue a ruling that none of the judges supports. The Mahari ibn Lev contends that the Maimonides–Rashbam controversy pertains solely to the case of assessors issuing appraisals. But when three judges disagree about a legal ruling, all the authorities concur that the ruling must be arrived at by the majority principle, as the Rashbam maintains in

112 K.J. Arrow, *Social Choice and Individual Values*, 2nd edn. (New Haven: 1963).

explaining the Tanna Kama's view.[113] Several Later Authorities also make this distinction.[114]

The implications of this *sugya* for other cases involving the aggregation of various values should be pondered carefully. As we argued at the outset of the article, with respect to the *sugya* in bBaba Batra, construing the aggregation as an estimate (*umdena*) is straightforward in light of the assessors' status as expert witnesses, as opposed to judges and witnesses. In other cases, however, it may not be appropriate to view an aggregation as an estimate, and the Tannaitic controversy we have explored in this article may not apply.

113 See *Responsa Mahari Ben Lev*, 2:29.

114 See *Hilkhot Dayanim Im Halakha Psuka* (Jerusalem: 1986), 414 n. 30. A similar argument is made by R. Zechariah Agmati, n. 20 above, who clarifies the issue in the name of R. Joseph Halevi (Ri Migash), and implies that the assessors' appraisals are regarded as testimony before the court ("And it follows that he withdrew [i.e., combined] both testimonies of $93\frac{1}{3}$, and he who said 30 [*sela*], which is actually 120, is one [testimony]. And one testimony is never preferred over two."). See also *Yad Rama*, n. 20 above, which implies that the status of assessors in court is that of witnesses; as we suggested in §3 above, however, they should be regarded as what are today called 'expert witnesses.'

"We Do Not Assess in the Case of the Thief, nor that of the Robber, but [We Assess] in the Case of Damage"

Aaron Orenstein*

* Law School, Safed Academic College

1. Introduction

When damage occurs for which the one who causes the damage (*hamazik*) (henceforth, the injurer) is liable, there are, in principle, several ways to address the problem. The injurer can be held liable to take away the damaged object or what remains of it, and provide the injured party with a replacement, or held liable to pay the injured party monetary compensation for the full value of the damaged object. Another approach is to leave the damaged object in the injured party's possession. Here too there are options. One possibility might be to compensate the injured party and determine the amount of the compensation by applying an assessment rule. Or it might be possible to repair the damaged object and restore its functionality. These various approaches can certainly be combined. If the repair is incomplete or insufficient to return the object to its pre-damage state, monetary compensation can be imposed as an additional remedy.

In this article we will first explore the theoretical question of whether, and under what circumstances, the injurer can be obligated to take away the damaged object and provide the injured party with a replacement. Following this discussion of the general case of one who does damage (the injurer), we will discuss two further cases: that of the thief and that of the robber. More specifically, what is the law when a stolen or robbed object is broken? Can they be obligated to pay the full value of the object, or to return a fully-functioning replacement, or have they fulfilled their obligation by returning the broken pieces and paying some monetary compensation?

Before examining the pertinent halakhic sources, let us first address the issues of justice and legal policy, and ask what the appropriate legal considerations should be when damage is caused.

In the event that substantial damage has occurred, it is, perhaps, appropriate to require the injurer to take possession of the damaged object and to provide the injured party with a replacement object.[1] Prima facie, there is no justification for obligating the injured party to take care of assessing the damage and selling the damaged object, but there is reason to make the injurer responsible for dealing with these nuisances.

By contrast, if only minor damage has occurred, especially if it can be repaired without special effort, there is no need for a transaction transferring ownership of the damaged object to the injurer. It seems that in such a case the preferred solution is to leave the damaged object in the possession of the injured party, using one of the mechanisms mentioned above to compensate him.

With regard to theft and robbery, additional considerations must be taken into account. Theft and robbery are for the most part acts of malice. Moreover, the acts of theft and robbery are carried out by taking the objects out of the owner's domain and concealing them. In many cases, the owner does not know that the object in question has been broken. By contrast, damage to objects often occurs without their being taken out of the owner's domain, making it easier for the owner to discover that the object has been broken. These considerations lead to greater severity in the laws governing the thief and the robber than in those governing the injurer, as we will see below.

2. The plain meaning of the scriptural verses: the injurer takes the damaged object and pays compensation for its full value

2.1 Prefatory remarks

In this context there is a major difference between the plain meaning of the relevant scriptural verses and the Sages' exegeses of them. The difference is not readily apparent, but careful study of the plain meaning of the verses that address civil injury (monetary harm), as opposed to the Sages' exegeses thereof, nonetheless leads to this conclusion. The

1 Achieving such a result would entail a property transaction transferring to the injurer the property rights in the damaged object. This would require an explicit legal source.

question of the relationship between the plain meaning of a scriptural verse (*pshuto shel mikra*) and the law drawn from it, as set down by the Sages, is an old one, and has been much discussed.[2] The phenomenon of disparity between the two is general, and the Torah's tort laws are no exception.[3] In what follows, we will discuss the differences between the law regarding liability for damage to a misappropriated object as set out in the scriptural text, and the law set down by the Sages.

2.2 Pit damages

Regarding what are called "pit damages," damage incurred when someone or something falls into an open pit, Scripture mandates that: "The owner of the pit shall make restitution (*yeshalem*)[4]; he shall pay back [lit., return] the money[5] (*kesef yashiv*) to the owner (*livealav*) [of the

2 R. Neria Guttel has addressed this in several articles, see "The plain meaning of Scripture in the teachings of the Hazon Ish" (Hebrew), *Hama'ayan* 38 (1998), 19-32; "On definitions of 'the plain meaning,' defense of exegesis, and their limitations" (Hebrew), *Tzohar* 13 (2003), 87-96; "The polemic over the plain meaning and exegesis: demarcating the debate" (Hebrew), *Badad* 18 (2007), 5-22.

3 Tort law provides a widely-known example. It is stated in the Torah: "Eye for eye, tooth for tooth, hand for hand, foot for foot" (Exod. 21:24). It is further stated: "If anyone maims his fellow, as he has done so shall it be done to him. . . . The injury he inflicted on another shall be inflicted on him" (Lev. 24:19-20). The Rabbinic interpretation of these verses (bBaba Kama 84a) is familiar: the injurer's eye or tooth is not taken out, but rather, he is obligated to pay the injured party monetary compensation for her lost eye or tooth. In the introduction to his *Commentary on the Mishnah*, Maimonides notes that the interpretation of "eye for eye" as denoting monetary compensation is an interpretation given to Moses at Sinai with which no one has ever disagreed.

4 Also translated "shall make it good."

5 The verse reads: בעל הבור ישלם כסף ישיב לבעליו והמת יהיה לו
(*baal habor yeshalem kesef yashiv livealav vehamet yihye lo*)

It is difficult to discern, in the language of the Pentateuch, rules governing use of the term "shall make restitution" (*yeshalem*) as opposed to "shall pay back [lit., return] the money" (*kesef yashiv*). In the verse under discussion, e.g., both terms are invoked: "The owner of the pit shall make restitution; he shall pay back the money. . ."). See R. A.I. Kook, *Mishpat Cohen*, Inyanei Eretz Yisrael, §132 on the following talmudic statement: "And he shall restore (*veheishiv*) that thing which he took by robbery" (Lev. 5:23). What is the point of the words 'which he took by robbery'? It is to imply that if it is still as it was when he committed the robbery, he shall return (*yahzir*) it, but if not, it is only the value of it that he will have to pay" (bBaba

animal], and the dead [animal] shall be his" (Exod. 21:34). The phrase "the dead [animal] shall be his" calls for clarification. To whom does the word "his" (*lo*) refer? The verse speaks of two individuals, the injurer (the owner of the pit) and the injured party (the owner of the animal). The word "his" could be interpreted as referring to either of them.

From the point of view of syntax, the subject of the verse is "the owner of the pit," and therefore it would seem that the word "his" refers to him. Likewise, from the division, in the second part of the verse, between "the owner" [of the animal] (i.e., the injured party), who receives payment, and "his," referring to the one who gets the dead animal, it would seem that the word "his" refers to the injurer (the owner of the pit).

The Sages interpreted the word "his" as referring to the injured party.[6] This information will help us investigate the extent to which the commentators interpret the verse in accordance with its plain meaning, or alternatively, are constrained by the Sages' understanding of its meaning, their received tradition.

We will begin with the explication of the verse given by Philo Judaeus (Philo of Alexandria): "If an animal should fall and die, its owner shall be compensated in an amount equal to the animal's value while alive, and he shall take the carcass."[7] On this reading, the injured party receives compensation for the animal in the amount of its value while the animal was alive, before the damage occurred, and the injurer takes the carcass.

Turning to the Targums, ancient translations of the Bible into Aramaic, let us examine the difference between Onkelos' translation and

---

Kama 66a). R. Kook suggests that the term 'make restitution' (*yeshalem*) refers to a situation where the original object no longer exists, whereas 'paying back' (*yashiv*) refers to a situation where the original object still exists.

6 The Sages' understanding will be discussed below.

7 Philo Judaeus, *Writings* (Hebrew), edited by Suzanne Daniel-Nataf (Jerusalem: 2000), 3:115. Philo's commentary on the Bible is the earliest that has been found. Cf. the reading in Josephus Flavius' *Antiquities of the Jews*: "Let those that dig a well or a pit be careful to lay planks over them, and so keep them shut up. . . . But if any one's beast fall into such a well or pit thus digged and not shut up, and perish, let the owner pay its price to the owner of the beast" (IV, 8, 37). Although it does not say that the dead animal belongs to the perpetrator of the damage, from the fact that the injurer is required to pay the value of the animal to the injured party, it can be inferred that the carcass is given to the injurer.

the translation attributed to Jonathan b. Uziel. Onkelos translated the verse: "The owner of the pit shall make restitution. He shall pay back [lit., return] money to the owner [of the animal], and the dead [animal] shall be his." What we noted above with respect to the scriptural verse itself is also true of Onkelos' translation: the end of the verse can be interpreted as referring either to the injurer or to the injured party, although as far as the syntax is concerned, and as can be inferred from the separation between "the owner" and "his," it appears that "his" should be interpreted as referring to the injurer.

The translation attributed to Jonathan b. Uziel, however, is different: "The owner of the pit shall make restitution, he shall pay to the owner [of the animals] the **price of his ox and his donkey,** and the carcass will be his." Whereas according to Onkelos, the owner of the pit pays "money," according to this translation, the injurer must pay the value of the ox and the donkey. Since according to the translation attributed to Jonathan b. Uziel, the injurer must pay the entire price of the ox or the donkey, on this reading it is most plausible that the carcass will belong to the injurer.

We now turn to the classic Torah commentators, who are naturally aware of the Sages' received tradition, and of the fact that it is inconsistent with the plain meaning of the scriptural verse. Some of the commentators take pains to emphasize that according to the verse's plain meaning, the word "his" refers to the injurer. The Rashbam (R. Samuel b. Meir), for example, states:

> Since he pays its entire price, the law is that the carcass will belong to the injurer. But the Sages interpreted [the verse as saying] that it goes to the injured party, because the depreciation in the value of the carcass belongs to the injured party.

The Hizkuni (R. Hezekiah b. Manoah) writes: "According to the plain meaning [of the verse], since he pays the entire price, by law the carcass should belong to the injurer."

Rabbenu Abraham son of Maimonides,[8] who points out the disparity between the plain meaning of the verse and the Sages' interpretation, asserts:

> It is conceivable that the verse's import is that the owner of the pit pays the price of the ox or the donkey that fell into the pit to the owner [of the

8 Abraham, son of Maimonides, *Commentary on Genesis and Exodus*, edited by S.D. Sassoon, translated by E. Wiesenberg (London: 1959).

> animal] and takes the carcass, and the term "his" refers to the owner of the pit. However, tradition has explained that it refers to the owner of the carcass.[9] And the import of "he shall pay back money to the owner [of the animal]" (*kesef yashiv livealav*) is – the price of the animal [when it was alive] less the [value of] the carcass.

R. Abraham ibn Ezra writes concisely in his long commentary, and at length in his concise commentary. In his concise commentary, he raises the two interpretive possibilities:

> Some say that he gives the price of the fallen [animal] and takes the carcass. And the Sages[10] said that "the dead [animal] shall be his" refers to the owner of the ox or the donkey. The interpretation is not that he takes the monetary value of his ox and takes the carcass as well, but rather that he deducts the [monetary value of the] carcass from the monetary value of his ox. And similarly, if it [a borrowed item] was broken, he deducts the value of the pieces from the value of the object that was broken, so that he takes part in [paying for] the damage, even though it is a small amount. And this is the correct interpretation.

9 R. Naftali Z. Berlin (Netziv), *Haamek Davar*, Exodus ad loc., discusses the distinction between the plain meaning of the scriptural text and the Sages' tradition as to the scriptural text, arguing that the latter is alluded to in the former: "On the surface, the language means that the carcass will go to the owner of the pit [i.e., the injurer]. But also embedded in the scriptural language is a tradition of the Sages that "he shall pay back [lit., return] money to the owner [of the animal]" is not precise, for were it precise, it would have said, not "shall return money," but rather, 'shall pay money to the owner.' But the verse actually explains the **mode** of payment. "Money": it is necessary to pay money; "he shall pay back [return] to the owner": it must reach the owner's hand, and it does not suffice for it to be placed before him. If it is lost before it reaches the injured party, other payment must be made.' But "and the dead [animal]": the carcass itself; "shall be his": it need not actually reach his [the injured party's] hand, but obviously it belongs to him. And even though it says in Baba Kama . . . that the owner of the pit must extract the carcass from the pit . . . in any event, he [the injurer] does not have to actually bring it to him [i.e., to the owner of the animal] or to his courtyard, but rather, he places it before him, for it is his [the owner of the animal]." The Netziv is addressing the difference between the obligation to pay money to the injured party, and the obligation to return the carcass to him. The former requires that the payment actually reach the owner's hand, whereas with regard to the latter, it suffices to put the carcass someplace where the owner can access it. In any event, according to the Netziv, "and the dead [animal] shall be his" means, shall be the injured party's.

10 The word he uses here is "the translators" (*hamaatikim*, lit., transcribers), a term designating the Sages.

By contrast, in his long commentary ibn Ezra gives only one interpretation, namely, the Sages' traditional interpretation: "he shall pay back [lit., return] money to the owner [of the animal]" – he gives the value of the fallen [animal] when it was alive after deducting from it the value of the carcass."

Rashi, too, puts forward only the Sages' interpretation: "'And the dead [animal] shall be his' – the injured party's, the carcass is assessed and he [the injured party] takes it as [partial] payment and the injurer pays him, in addition to that, [the amount that fills out the] payment for the damage."

Nahmanides continues in the same vein as Rashi, interpreting the verse in line with the Sages' approach:

> "'And the dead [animal] shall be his' – the injured party's, the carcass is assessed and he [the injured party] takes it as [partial] payment and the injurer pays him, in addition to that, [the amount that fills out the] payment for the damage" – this is how Rashi put it. But he did not explain the judgment sufficiently, for there is no need for Scripture to tell us concerning this carcass that the injured party must take it in partial payment [lit., on account of the payment due], when he brings the matter to the court to get restitution for damage; for even if the injurer had other carcasses and carrion (*neveilot vetreifot*) in his possession, he can give it to him in partial payment, for we have already established that [restitution for damages need not be in money], but may "include anything of monetary value [lit., equivalent to money], and even bran" (bBaba Kama 7a).
>
> Rather, the point is to state that the carcass belongs to the injured party and is considered his property; therefore if its value decreased afterwards [i.e., after the damage was caused], or it was stolen, the injurer pays only the loss in value caused by the death. Thus if the ox, when alive, was worth a *mane* [100 *zuz*], and when dead 50 *zuz*, he is obliged [to pay] 50 *zuz*, and he [the other] deals with his carcass and keeps it for himself. And this is the law with respect to all torts, and it is what the Sages call depreciation of the value of the carcass, and it is explained in the Gemara (bBaba Kama 10b).[11]

11 It is easy to see that the talmudic *sugya* (bBaba Kama 10b), which will be adduced below, has been incorporated into Nahmanides' interpretation:

> Rav Kahana said to Rav: The reason [for the ruling] is that the Merciful One wrote: "And the dead [animal] shall be his," and but for this I might have thought that the carcass should remain with the injurer, [yet how can this be]? Now if, when he has with him several carcasses, he may pay him with [lit., give him] them – for the Master stated: "'he

Let me also note that R. Elijah of Vilna, the Vilna Gaon, states that "the plain meaning of the text is that it refers to the injurer, and this is what the commentators have written."[12]

2.3 Ox damages

Regarding an ox that has gored another ox, the Torah writes: "And if one man's ox hurt another's so that it died. . . . Or if it be known that the ox has long been in the habit of goring . . . he shall surely pay ox for ox (*shor tahat shor*) and the dead [animal] shall be his" (Exod. 21:35-36).

There is no doubt that the words "he shall surely pay" (*shalem yeshalem*) refer to the injurer. But it is difficult, with regard to the plain meaning of the text, to take the phrase "and the dead [animal] shall be his" as referring to the injured party, because the injured party is not mentioned in this verse (36), and even in the previous one (35), he is not mentioned explicitly, but only incidentally in the reference to his ox ("another's [ox]").

Moreover, the injurer's obligation is to pay "ox for ox." We must pay close attention to the wording of the verse. The injurer must pay "ox for ox" even if the carcass has some value. Were it written that the injurer must pay "damage for damage," it would be possible to say that the obligation to pay the ox's owner refers only to the difference between the ox's value before the damage and the value of the carcass after the damage. But this is not what the text states. At least at the level of its plain meaning, the words "ox for ox" teach us that the injurer must provide a replacement ox, even if the carcass has some value.

If the injurer pays compensation "for the ox" that was injured, it is clear that he is entitled to receive the carcass. It thus seems that this conclusion about the verse's plain meaning is even stronger, vis-à-vis this verse, than vis-à-vis verse 34, regarding the pit.[13] Accordingly, the word "his" should be interpreted as referring to the injurer.

shall make restitution' (Exod. 21:34) includes anything of monetary value, and even bran" [bBaba Kama 7a] – what question is there about the carcass of his own animal!?

12 *Aderet Eliyahu*, Torah portion 'Mishpatim.'

13 Note that the Sages did not follow the plain meaning of the text with respect to verse 36 either, and interpreted the words "and the dead [animal] shall be his" as referring to the injured party.

Here also, as is the case for verse 34, Philo interprets the word "his" as referring to the injurer:

> If the ox does not gore a person, but rather an animal, the owner of the attacking ox shall take the carcass and pay the value of the animal. And he shall be grateful that a larger fine was not imposed on him, since he is the source of the injury.[14]

Both Onkelos and the Targum attributed to Jonathan b. Uziel translate the Hebrew words "*tahat shor*" as meaning, not "for the ox," but "instead of the ox." From this we can infer that the payment constitutes a replacement for the ox and not only a completion or 'top-up' of the difference between the value of the live ox and that of the carcass. As noted above, if someone pays full compensation, it is only fitting that he take the carcass for himself. Rashi, faithful to his commentary regarding pit damages, and consistent with the Sages' view, asserts: "'And the dead [animal] shall be his' – [shall be] the injured party's, and to it the injurer shall add, until the injured party is compensated for all the damage he incurred." In his concise commentary, R. Abraham ibn Ezra, apparently sensing the interpretive difficulty in the verse, formulates his position thus: "In the opinion of the world's mighty ones,[15] [here the law is] as in the first case."[16]

Nahmanides' commentary on this verse is extremely interesting. As we saw above, Nahmanides interprets verse 34 strictly in line with the Sages' view. In commenting on verse 36, Nahmanides first cites Rashi's interpretation, which upholds the Sages' view, then provides an interpretation according to the plain meaning of the verse, as follows:

> "And the dead [animal] shall be his" – [shall be] the injured party's, and to it the injurer shall add, until the injured party is compensated for all the damage he incurred – this is how Rashi put it, and it is in accordance with the Sages' approach (bBaba Kama 10b). And if so, it is proper that we explain "he shall surely pay ox for ox" [as meaning] with the dead [animal] that will be his [as partial payment]. Similarly, "and Joseph was in Egypt" (Exod. 1:5) [means] with Joseph, who was in Egypt, [included in the count]. So too, "I cannot endure iniquity and the solemn assembly" (Isa. 1:13) [means] with the solemn assembly, as Scripture states, "I hate robbery with a burnt-offering (*beola*)" (Isa. 61:8).

14 Philo, n. 7 above.
15 A term referring to the Sages.
16 I.e., as in verse 34, "his" refers to the injured party.

> And it may [also] be possible to interpret the text in accordance with its plain meaning: "and the dead [animal] shall be his" [means] the injurer's, that is, "he shall surely pay ox for ox and the dead [animal] shall be his" [means] the injurer's, who will pay the amount that fills out the payment due, using it [the carcass] on account of the payment due the injured party. And on both these formulations, the judgment is the same: the owner deals with the carcass, and from the time of the animal's death, [if its value decreases], that is taken into account, as our Rabbis taught (bBaba Kama 10b).

At the beginning of his comments, Nahmanides defends the Sages' tradition and finds support for it in the scriptural text.[17] Nahmanides argues that the conjunction "*vav*" [ו], meaning "and" in the phrase "**and** the dead [animal]" should be interpreted as meaning "with." The injurer's obligation to pay "ox in place of ox" must be fulfilled by taking into consideration the fact that the dead animal is the property of the injured party. Nahmanides then interprets the verse in accordance with its plain meaning. His understanding of the plain meaning, however, does not match the understanding presented above. He maintains that the injurer takes the carcass into account in determining the payment he owes to the injured party, but not that he actually takes the carcass for himself. I would argue, though, that while this interpretation is possible, it is difficult to see it as the plain meaning of the verse. Nahmanides seems to be proposing this interpretation in an attempt to find a basis in the verse, a scriptural anchor, for the Sages' tradition.

2.4 One who causes property damage

Our conclusion with respect to the plain meaning of the scriptural verses is also reflected in two verses in the Torah portion 'Emor' that address the case of one who injures an animal. The first reads: "One who kills [lit., smites] an animal (*make nefesh beheima*) shall make restitution for it (*yeshalmena*): life for life" (Lev. 24:18). Several verses later, another verse states: "And he who kills [lit., smites] an animal (*make beheima*) shall make restitution for it (*yeshalmena*); and he who kills a person shall be put to death" (Lev. 24:21).

17 This so-called 'apologetic' interpretive approach will be discussed below.

Many of the commentators[18] explained that the first verse (*make nefesh beheima*) deals with a case in which the beast dies, whereas the second verse (*make beheima*) deals with a case in which the beast is merely injured. In both cases the law is identical: the injurer is obligated to pay. The injurer's obligation is set out in the phrase "shall make restitution for it," which means that he must pay for the animal. According to the plain meaning, it would seem that this means full payment of what the animal is worth. And indeed, in his commentary on the Torah, R. Saadia Gaon (Rasag) states straightforwardly: "shall make restitution for it – shall pay for one like it."

Furthermore, the fact that the law is identical in the two verses (both saying "shall make restitution") seems to imply that the injurer takes the injured animal, whether alive or dead, for himself, and pays the owner the full value of the animal.

Nahmanides rejects what would seem to be the import of the plain meaning of Leviticus 24:18, and explains the verses in accordance with the Sages' view:

> "Life for life" does not literally mean an animal [for an animal], that he must buy him an animal similar to his animal [as it was prior to being injured], but rather, it means that he is to pay him monetary compensation in the amount of the damage he caused him. And similarly "breach for breach, eye for eye," according to the opinion of our Rabbis.

Nahmanides seeks supporting evidence to reconcile the two parts of verse 18. The second part of the verse, "a life for a life," is similar to verses 19 and 20, which address the case of one who inflicts bodily injury on another: "And if a man maims his neighbor; as he has done, so shall it be done to him; breach for breach, eye for eye, tooth for tooth; as he has maimed a man, so shall it be done to him."

It is a well-known tradition of the Sages that the injurer is not punished by inflicting on him the bodily harm he caused to the injured

18 See *Rasag*, *Rashi*, and *Rashbam* ad loc. Others interpreted these verses differently. R. Hezekiah b. Manoah, e.g., writes as follows: "The scriptural language changes, because at first, it mentions "soul" (*nefesh*), meaning that he struck [the animal] in a dangerous place [i.e., a spot that could be expected to yield a mortal injury], and afterwards, it speaks of anyone who kills, even if he struck him in a place that is not dangerous, and therefore it does not mention "soul" (*Hizkuni* ad loc.). R. Abraham ibn Ezra also adduces this interpretation.

party, but rather, a monetary punishment is imposed on him.[19] Nahmanides invokes this tradition, explaining that just as the perpetrator of bodily harm is not maimed, but rather an assessment is made of the decrease in the value of the injured party as a result of the damage, the same is true with respect to injury to property. The injurer is not required to provide the injured party with a replacement for the damaged object, but rather the damaged object is appraised and the injurer is required to pay for the depreciation in its value.

We see, therefore, that according to the plain meaning of the verses, ownership of the damaged object is transferred to the injurer, and he compensates the injured party for the full value of the object as it was prior to the injury.

3. Damage to property in the Rabbinic literature: the injured party keeps the damaged object

3.1 Tannaitic sources

The Mekhilta de-Rabbi Yishmael contains two exegeses relevant to the subject at hand. The first reads:

> "He shall pay back [lit., return] money to the owner [of the animal]" (Exod. 21:34). I know only that one can pay with money. From where do I know about paying with cattle? You must reason thus: Here it is said, "and the dead [animal] shall be his," and after that it is said, "and the dead [animal] shall be his" (Exod. 21:36). Just as there [Exod. 21:36] one pays with cattle, so too here [Exod. 21:34] one pays with cattle. And just as here one pays with money, so too there one pays with money.[20]

The exegete highlights the difference between verses 34 and 36 of Exodus 21. The first verse, which addresses pit damages, provides that the injurer shall pay money ("he shall pay back the money to the owner"). The second verse, however, which addresses ox damages, requires that the injurer pay with an ox ("ox for an ox"). The exegete tells us that in any case the injurer is required to pay both with an animal and with money. How so? The injurer returns the carcass to the

19 This is discussed at length in bBaba Kama 83b-84a; Maimonides, *Code*, Laws concerning Wounding and Damaging 1:3-6.

20 Mekhilta de-Rabbi Yishmael, Mishpatim, Masekhta de-Nezikin, 11 (Horowitz edition, 289).

injured party and in addition pays monetary compensation to cover the difference between the value of a live animal and that of the carcass.

The second exegesis is as follows:

> "And the dead [animal] shall be his" – you say [that it means], [shall be] the injured party's. Might it not mean, rather, that it [shall be] the injurer's? But you would then reason, if so, why would Scripture need to say "and the dead [animal] shall be his"? Therefore Scripture teaches "[it shall be] the injured party's," but tells us that we appraise the value of the carcass, and deduct it from the amount due him on account of the damage he incurred.[21]

The exegete assumes that if the Torah had intended to teach that the injurer takes the carcass, it would have made do with the words "The owner of the pit shall make restitution; he shall pay back money to the owner [of the animal]," and there would have been no need to add the clause "and the dead [animal] shall be his," since it would be obvious that if the pit-owner, that is, the injurer, paid for all the damage, he is entitled to take the carcass. Since the Torah nevertheless made a point of adding the words "and the dead [animal] shall be his," this is intended to teach us that the carcass remains in the possession of the injured party.

Yet the difficulty presented by the exegete is not intractable. It is certainly possible to interpret the verse as follows. The Torah obligated the injurer to pay the full value of the injured ox; after payment has been made, the Torah completes the transaction from the other direction, as it were, giving the carcass to the injurer. In other words, there is no extraneous language in the verse that requires us to depart from the most natural interpretation of it. Moreover, if, as the exegete says, the Torah intends to inform us that it is the injured party, not the injurer, who takes the carcass, why did the Torah use the nonspecific "his" rather than specify that it was referring to the injured party? I contend, therefore, that the reading in the Mekhilta is forced, and does not follow from the verse as a matter of course.

21 Ibid. s.v. *vehamet yihye lo*. This too is an exegesis of verse 34, and addresses pit damages. In Masekhta de-Nezikin, 12 (Horowitz edition, 291), the Mekhilta discusses verse 36: "'And the dead [animal] shall be his': you say [that it means], [shall be] the injured party's, and so on. But might you not say [that it means] [shall be] the injurer's, and so on, as in the case above [i.e., verse 34]?" But if so, this means that the words "and the dead [animal] shall be his" in both verses can be expounded in the same manner.

In the Mekhilta de-Rashbi, the following interpretation is put forward:

> "And the dead [animal] shall be his" – the injured party's. Could it also refer to the injurer? You say that this is not so? Therefore Scripture teaches: "and the dead [animal] shall be his" [verse 21:34], "the dead [animal] shall be his" [verse 21:36] – to draw an analogy.
>
> Just as [in the case of] "the dead [animal] shall be his" that is stated here [i.e., in verse 21:34] he pays only the value [of the animal], so too [in the case of] "the dead [animal] shall be his" said below [i.e., in verse 21:36], he pays only the value.
>
> So too[22] [in the case of] "the dead [animal] shall be his" said below the owner deals with the carcass, so too [in the case of] "the dead [animal] shall be his" said here the owner deals with the carcass.
>
> Just as [in the case of] "the dead [animal] shall be his" said below, [the verse says] "an ox for an ox" and not 'an ox and a carcass for an ox,' so too [in the case of] "the dead [animal] shall be his" said here, [it means] "an ox for an ox" and not 'an ox and a carcass for an ox.'[23]

This exegesis is complex, being composed of several distinct clauses.[24] In the first of these, the exegete raises a difficulty that was also discussed in the Mekhilta de-Rabbi Yishmael. As in the first exegesis in the Mekhilta de-Rabbi Yishmael, in the introductory part of the exegesis in Mekhilta de-Rashbi, the phrase "and the dead [animal] shall be his," which appears in both verses, is invoked to draw an analogy the details of which are discussed in the continuation of the exegesis. In the first substantive clause, the source is verse 34 (the case of the pit) and the target is verse 36 (the ox case). Just as in verse 34 the injurer pays the value (as we learn from the phrase "he shall pay back money to the owner [of the animal]"), this is so regarding verse 36 as well: despite the fact that it states "he shall surely pay ox for ox," the payment is monetary.[25]

22 The Epstein–Melamed edition suggests replacing "so too" (*veaf*) with the words "just as," and this suggestion makes sense.

23 Mekhilta de-Rabbi Shimon b. Yohai (Rashbi) 21:34 (Epstein-Melamed edition, 186-87).

24 See R. M. Kasher, *Torah Shleima*, Exodus, §639.

25 It seems that the exegete does not seek to disagree with the law "'he shall make restitution' (Exod. 21:34) includes anything of monetary value" (bBaba Kama 7a), which is also derived from the verse, but rather to teach us that the injurer is not required to make restitution with an ox, but can use money or something equivalent to money.

The second substantive clause pertains to the law that "the owner deals with the carcass," that is, the law that it is the duty of the injured party to take the damaged item for himself. The exegesis assumes that it is obvious that in verse 36 the animal's owner takes the carcass, and on the strength of the exegetical rule of *gzeira shava* (analogy on the basis of similar wording), takes the law to apply to pit damages as well. In other words, verse 36 is the source verse and verse 34 the target. But as we saw above, it is actually verse 36, which states that "he shall surely pay ox for ox," that provides the more credible basis for interpreting the plain meaning of the verse as saying that the injurer takes the carcass. This being the case, I maintain that this clause of the exegesis is somewhat forced. In the third substantive clause too, verse 36 is the source and verse 34 is the target. The exegete seeks to teach us that the injured party should not profit from the damage that has occurred. That is, the injured party is entitled to compensation for the damage, but is not entitled to receive more than the value of the damage incurred.

A further Tannaitic source is the Tosefta, which states: "I am liable to make restitution for the damage it caused – this teaches that the owner deals with the carcass."[26] Saul Lieberman explains: "The assessed damage is only the difference between the value of the live animal, and that of the dead one, and nothing else was damaged, and the carcass [stays] in the possession of the injured party."[27]

Elsewhere, the Tosefta explicitly stipulates that the damaged item remains in the possession of the injured party:

> A governing principle has been stated in connection with damages: [If] one killed another's ox, tore his garment, or cut down his plantings, [the injured party] may not say 'take the carcass and give me a cow, take the rags and give me a cloak, take the cut-down plantings and give me [whole] plants." But rather, they make an estimate of their worth before they were damaged and of their worth now that they have been damaged. According to this rule (*lefikhakh*),[28] they pay compensation.[29]

26 tBaba Kama 1:1 (Lieberman edition, 1).
27 *Tosefta Kifshuta* ad loc., p. 2.
28 See the glosses of *Magen Avraham* and *Hasdei David* ad loc., which argue that the Hebrew "*lefikhakh*" should be rendered as two separate words – "*lefi khakh*" (according to this). On this reasoning, the final words are not a logical conclusion, but an endorsement of a method for arriving at the amount of compensation. Lieberman accepts the version of the Tosefta with *lefikhakh* as one word; see *Tosefta Kifshuta*, 29 n. 6.
29 tBaba Kama 3:2 (Lieberman edition, 10).

In this passage, we have an explicit assertion by the Tosefta, illustrated by adducing three examples,[30] that the injured party is not entitled to demand a replacement item. The injured party's right is limited to restitution in the form of monetary compensation.

3.2 Babylonian Talmud

As noted above, the Tannaitic sources state that the damaged item is to remain in the injured party's possession, and that it is the injurer's obligation to **make restitution** to the injured party for the difference between the damaged object's value and its value before the damage occurred.

The talmudic *sugya* in bBaba Kama 10b proves this principle and anchors it by invoking the mishnaic discussion of restitution for damage, as well as exegeses of three biblical verses, from which the principle is derived:

> "I am liable to make restitution for the damage it caused" (*havti betashlumei nizko*) (mBaba Kama 1:2). 'I am liable for [replacing the object that suffered] the damage it caused' is not stated, but rather, "to make restitution for the damage it caused." We have thus learned here that which the Rabbis taught elsewhere: "'To make restitution for the damage' (*tashlumei nezek*) teaches that the owner deals with the carcass" (tBaba Kama 1:1). What is the authority for this ruling?
>
> R. Ami said: Scripture states, "One who kills [lit., smites] an animal (*make nefesh beheima*[31]) shall make restitution for it (*yeshalmena*)"

30 See *Hasdei David*, which argues that the Tosefta changed the examples by way of a "not only is this statement so, but an even stronger one is as well" argument (*lo zu af zu*): "It does not bring only the case of 'killed his ox,' for [though meat from injured animals is not kosher], it is not such a burden to sell the meat to Gentiles, as it is commonplace for many of them to eat it, hence that would certainly be so with respect to the injured party [who could easily sell it]. Moreover, even shredded clothes, which are hard to sell, and even chopped plants, which are just straw, and it is uncommon for anyone to buy them – even in such cases, the injured party takes them."

31 This is the wording in all MSS, with the exception of MS Vatican, which reads: "*make beheima*." Above, we discussed the relationship between Leviticus 24:18 and Leviticus 24:21, noting that most of the commentators take verse 18 to address the case of an animal that is killed, and verse 21 to address that of an animal that is merely injured. In practical terms, the law that "the owner deals with the carcass" applies in both situations, that is, not only in the case of an actual carcass, but also in other cases, where the

(Lev. 24:18): do not read "he shall make restitution for it" (*yeshalmena*), [i.e., pay compensation], but 'he shall make it complete' (*yashlimena*).[32]

R. Kahana said, it is derived from the following: "If it be torn to pieces, let him bring it for witness (*ed*); he shall not make good that which was torn" (Exod. 22:12) – [compensation] up to (*ad*) the value of the carcass, he must pay, but for the carcass itself he does not have to pay.

Hizkiah said, it is derived from the following: "And the dead [animal] shall be his" (Exod. 21:36) – the injured party's. And it has similarly been taught in the school of Hizkiah:[33] "And the dead [animal] shall be his" (Exod. 21:36) – the injured party's. You say 'the injured party's.' But why not the injurer's? You may indeed assert: This is not the case. Why is this not the case? Abbaye said: If you assume that the carcass must remain with the injurer, why did the Merciful One not write "[He shall surely pay] ox for ox" (Exod. 21:36) and stop at that? Why write, "And the dead [animal] shall be his"? We deduce from this that it refers to the injured party.

And all the specific biblical locutions are needed. For if the Merciful One had written [this ruling only in] the verse "One who kills an animal (*make beheima*) shall make restitution for it (*yeshalmena*)"

---

animal is injured but does not die. See also R. Ahai, *Sefer Hasheiltot*, sheilta 111 (Mirsky edition, sheilta 128, p. 249), which cites R. Ami's exegesis. Mirsky renders the text using the verse 21 formulation, but notes variants formulated in accordance with verse 18.

32 *Tosafot*, ad loc. s.v. *yashlimena*, states that this exegesis is possible only vis-à-vis the verses in the Torah portion 'Emor,' where the word "*yeshalmena*" ("shall make restitution for it") appears (Lev. 24:18 and 21). By contrast, the verse in Exodus 21:34, "the owner of the pit shall make restitution (*yeshalem*)" cannot be expounded in this manner. In the words of the *Tosafot*:

> "The owner of the pit shall make restitution (*yeshalem*)" – "make restitution" should not be expounded as 'he shall make it complete' (*yashlim*) [i.e., should not be understood as saying that the injurer should provide a substitute animal, since this conflicts with the law that the owner deals with the carcass]. But "shall make restitution for it" (*yeshalmena*) means, make restitution for it with that very animal, and this is not possible because it is already dead [and depreciating]; therefore it must be expounded as 'he shall complete the restitution' (*yashlimena*) [i.e., give the carcass back in partial payment, and make up the difference between the live animal's value and the carcass's value by paying money].

33 MS Munich reads "and it has similarly been taught in the school of R. Yishmael." This is due to the fact that this interpretation appears in the Mekhilta de-Rabbi Yishmael, as we saw. But see *Dikdukei Sofrim*, which states "and the printed version is preferable."

(Lev. 24:21),[34] it might be thought that the reason for the ruling was that this is not a common occurrence, whereas in the case of an animal torn to pieces [by wild beasts] (*treifa*), which is a common occurrence, the opposite view might have been held [i.e., that no restitution is necessary, see Lev. 22:12]; hence it was necessary to specify this.

If [on the other hand] this ruling had been made known to us only in the case of an animal torn to pieces, it would have been explained by the fact that the injury was inflicted by indirect agency, whereas in the case of one who kills an animal with his own hands, the opposite view might have been held. And had [this ruling] been made known to us regarding both cases, it would have been explained in the one case on account of its being uncommon, and in the other [on] account of the indirect agency, whereas regarding the damage to which "And the dead [animal] shall be his" refers, which is both frequent and direct, the opposite view might have been held.

If [on the other hand] this ruling had been made known to us only in the case referred to by "And the dead [animal] shall be his," it would have been explained by the damage's having been inflicted by injurer's property, whereas in cases where the damage resulted from the injurer's person, the opposite view might have been held. Hence [the cited biblical locutions] are needed.

R. Kahana said to Rav: The rationale [for the ruling] is that the Merciful One wrote: "And the dead [animal] shall be his," and but for this I might have thought that the carcass should remain with the injurer. Now if, when he has with him several carcasses,[35] he may pay him with [lit., give him] them – for the Master stated: "'he shall make restitution' (Exod. 21:34) includes anything of monetary

34 There are two ways of relating to the verse on which R. Ami relies. In every MS, with the exception of MS Florence, the text here reads "*make beheima*" and not "*make nefesh beheima*." It may be, however, that this is not a citation of the verse, but rather a reference to an empirical situation (viz., the situation where someone strikes an animal), hence the Talmud used this abbreviated language.

35 The words "several carcasses" appear in the Soncino printed edition of the Talmud, but do not appear in MSS Munich, Florence, and Vatican. In MS Vatican, instead of the words "when he has with him several carcasses," the reading is: "if the injurer has with him a carcass." In MS Hamburg, the entire clause "Now if, when he has with him several carcasses, he may pay him with them" is absent.

value [lit., equivalent to money], and even bran" [bBaba Kama 7a][36] – what question is there about the carcass of his own animal!?[37]

3.2.1 *The mishnaic formulation*

As it is quoted in the Babylonian Talmud,[38] the wording of the pertinent Mishnah is:

> Regarding everything whose care I am responsible for, I have rendered possible any damage it may cause. When I have rendered possible part of the damage it caused, I am liable to make restitution for the damage it caused (*havti betashlumei nizko*), as I have rendered possible all the damage it caused (*kehekhsher kol nizko*).[39]

The Talmud interprets this as follows: That I am liable for [replacing] the damaged object (*havti benizko*) is not stated, but rather, as was taught elsewhere, [I am liable] "to make restitution for the damage it caused." The Talmud understands that there is a difference between the injurer's being liable for the damage[40] and his being liable to make restitution[41] for the damage. To provide a basis for its conclusion, the Talmud cites a baraita: "We have thus learned here that which the Rabbis taught elsewhere: "To make restitution for damage (*tashlumei nezek*)[42]

36 The words "and even bran" do not appear in MSS Munich, Florence, Hamburg, and Vatican, but are found in the printed Soncino version. In the *Sheiltot*, the text reads "anything he has may be used to repay him."
37 bBaba Kama 10b.
38 bBaba Kama 9b. The wording in the Tosefta, quoted here in the Babylonian Talmud *sugya*, and also quoted above, is "I am liable to make restitution for the damage it caused (*havti betashlumei nizko*)." MSS Kaufmann, Parma, and Paris also have this version of the mishnaic dictum. R. Kafih, too, endorsed this formulation, and noted the variant, cited below, in a footnote.
39 mBaba Kama 1:2.
40 Rashi: "Meaning that he will pay the value of a live healthy ox and will take the carcass."
41 Rashi: "Meaning completion: the injured party will take the carcass and this one [the injurer] will top-up for him the decrease in value as a result of the death."
42 *Masoret Hashas* notes that the baraita in question is the Tosefta quoted above, but the Tosefta derives the law that the owner must deal with the carcass from the phrase "make restitution for the damage" (*tashlumei nezek*) (which appears at the end of mBaba Kama 1:1, "When damage has been caused, the injurer is liable to pay restitution (*leshalem tashlumei nezek*) for the damage with the choicest of his land"), not from the phrase "I am liable

teaches that the owner deals with the carcass" (tBaba Kama 1:1), meaning that the carcass remains in the possession of the injured party and he is compensated by 'completion,' i.e., by being paid the difference between the value of the object before and after infliction of the injury.

Note that there is another version of this mishnaic dictum: "I am liable to make restitution (*havti betashlumin*), as I have rendered possible all the damage it caused (*kehekhsher kol nizko*)."[43] It is doubtful whether the Talmud's interpretation of the mishnaic dictum would apply to this version of it, since it is specifically from the wording "make restitution for the damage it caused" (*betashlumei nizko*) that the Talmud infers that the injurer must pay for the difference between the pre- and post-damage values of the object that was damaged. By contrast, the unqualified locution "make restitution" is broader, and it could hint at restitution along the lines of the plain meaning of the biblical verses in Leviticus 24 (*yeshalmena*), that is, payment for the full value of the object, namely, a replacement object, with the injurer taking the damaged object for himself. In this context, two comments are in order. First, that it is possible that the Talmud preferred to adduce the Mishnah, not by quoting from the original version of the Mishnah directly, but from the version in the Tosefta, in order to provide a basis for the Sages' tradition regarding monetary restitution, as opposed to the law ensuing from the plain meaning of the scriptural text. Second, there is no doubt that the term "restitution for the damage" (*tashlumei nezek*) appears at the end of mBaba Kama 1:1,[44] and thus the Sages' interpretation can certainly be tied to that clause, even if the variant reading of the dictum in mBaba Kama 2:1 is accepted.

3.2.2 *Midrashic exegeses*

It would seem that the exegeses in bBaba Kama 10b are not derived from the plain meaning of the scriptural verses. Let us examine R. Ami's exegesis. The meaning of the locution "shall make restitution for it" (*yeshalmena*) is to pay in exchange for the animal that was injured. The meaning of the locution "he shall make it complete" (*yashlimena*), however, that is, making up the difference between the object's pre- and

to make restitution for the damage it caused" (*havti betashlumei nizko*). See the commentary of Rashash (R. Samuel Strashun) ad loc.

43 This is the wording in the MS of the Mishnah with vocalization (*nikud*) in accordance with the Yemenite tradition (Jerusalem: 1970), and the Rom (Vilna), Albeck, Kehati, and Mishnah Sdura editions.

44 See ad loc. *Nimukei Yosef*, bBaba Kama 4b (Alfasi pagination), and *Hidushei Anshei Shem*, §3.

post-injury value, is different, and it does not follow from the plain meaning of the text. R. Ami uses the "do not read it thus, but rather thus" mode of exegetical inference.[45]

R. Kahana's interpretation seems even weaker. R. Kahana adduces a verse dealing with the laws of bailees.[46] The plain meaning of the verse "If it be torn to pieces [by animals], let him bring it for witness (*ed*)" (Exod. 22:12), is that the bailee is exempt from liability if he had no choice regarding harm to something under his protection [i.e., the damage was due to an unavoidable accident] (*ones*). Moreover, R. Kahana's exegesis is based on the word "up to" (*ad*), whereas the word written in the Torah is "witness" (*ed*).

Hizkiah's exegesis, as cited in the *sugya* in bBaba Kama 10b, was discussed above apropos the Mekhilta De-Rabbi Yishmael.[47] In the

45 See *Talmudic Encyclopedia* (Hebrew), "Do not read it thus," 2:1, which discusses two types of cases in which this mode of exegetical inference is used. The first is when a difficulty in the language of a scriptural verse indicates that it is not to be read in accordance with its plain meaning. The case at hand does not seem to fall within this category because there is no difficulty that would compel us to go beyond the plain meaning. The second type of case is "when what is being taught via the exegesis is a masoretic tradition passed orally from one person to another, and so that it not be forgotten by them or their descendants, they made a sign [i.e., a mnemonic prompt] in the form of a supporting allusion, and said 'do not read. . . .'" This is, in essence, what is known as 'sustaining exegesis' (*midrash mekayem*) – exegesis that anchors a well-known law in a scriptural source. It may also be the case that the "he shall make it complete" interpretation reflects the exegetical principle that "the traditional pronunciation takes primacy" (*yesh em lamikra*) (bSanhedrin 4a). The *Talmudic Encyclopedia* entry goes on to say: "'Do not read' does not take the Scripture beyond its plain meaning, and it was not the Sages' intention to say that the verse really ought to be read differently. Even regarding the manner in which scriptural verses are understood and interpreted, it was not their intention to say that the interpretation departs from the written text, but rather, both are encompassed by Scripture, and their intent is: 'Do not read it only in this manner, but also in this manner.'" These insights direct us to qualify the validity of R. Ami's exegesis. There may be cases where the original law, "he shall make restitution for it" (*yeshalemena*), remains operative.

46 *Tosafot* ad loc. s.v. *lo yeshalem* notes this difficulty and explains that the verse teaches us a general principle, according to which "where he does have to pay, he pays nothing for the carcass itself."

47 David Weiss-Halivni states that the exegeses put forward by R. Ami and R. Kahana are weaker than Hizkiah's exegesis of the verse "and the dead [animal] shall be his" (Exod. 21:36), the source for which is the Mekhiltot

talmudic *sugya*, it is explained by Abbaye, from whom we learn that the exegesis relates to verse 36, which addresses ox damages.

3.3 Jerusalem Talmud

The *sugya* in the Jerusalem Talmud reads as follows:

> R. La said: it needs to be stated for every single case. '[And] the ox' teaches that the owner deals with the carcass. As it is written: "and the dead [animal] shall be his" and as [regarding] the pit it is written: "and the dead [animal] shall be his." R. Yishmael taught: it does not apply to land, which is not movable property; it does not apply to one who does not benefit from the death. . .[48]

The accepted interpretation of this *sugya*[49] is that the words "and the dead [animal] shall be his" written regarding the ox teach a general rule[50] that applies to all of tort law: the owner deals with the carcass, and the words "and the dead [animal] shall be his," written with regard to the pit, are redundant, because the pit also falls under the general law learned from the story of the ox; they therefore teach other laws, which will not be addressed in this article.

In the subsequent *sugya*, the Jerusalem Talmud presents two exegeses that we encountered in the *sugya* in the Babylonian Talmud:

> 'And when he caused damage, the injurer is liable for all of it.' R. Hanina said: "One who kills an animal shall make restitution for it (*yeshalmena*)" (Lev. 24:21) – he shall pay its depreciation.[51] Bar Pedaya said: "If it be torn to pieces, let him bring it for witness" (Exod. 22:12) – he shall not make restitution for that which was torn. R. Nisa said: There is a need for R. Hanina's view and there is a need for Bar Pedaya's view. If you accept R. Hanina's view, and not Bar Pedaya's view, I would say that for rendering possible the damage it caused, he will not pay anything, and for physical damage he

(*Mekorot U'mesorot: Biurim Batalmud, Masekhet Baba Kama* [Jerusalem: 1993], 31). Yet Hizkiah's exegesis is not self-evident either, because as noted, according to the plain meaning of the text, the word "his" refers to the injurer and not to the injured party.

48 jBaba Kama 1:1 (3a).

49 See *Pnei Moshe* ad loc., and *Torah Shleima*, Exodus 21, §643.

50 Cf. *Sefer Mitzvot Gadol* (positive precept 67): "From what the Torah says regarding ox damages and pit damages – "and the dead [animal] shall be his" – the injured party's, we learn [principles] applicable to all torts."

51 The Jerusalem Talmud does not invoke the "do not read" exegetical rule, as R. Ami did in the Babylonian Talmud *sugya*.

> will pay the depreciation. Hence Bar Pedaya's view had to be stated. Or if you accept Bar Pedaya's view, and not R. Hanina's, I would say that for rendering possible the damage it caused he will pay the depreciation, and for the physical damage he will pay for everything. Hence R. Hanina's view had to be stated and Bar Pedaya's view had to be stated.[52]

R. Hanina's exegesis in the Jerusalem Talmud is similar to that of R. Ami in the Babylonian Talmud, whereas Bar Pedaya's exegesis in the Jerusalem Talmud is similar to that of R. Kahana in the Babylonian Talmud. The Jerusalem Talmud's elucidation of the non-redundancy of the biblical verses (*tzrikhuta)* is also similar to that of the Babylonian Talmud, though it adduces only two exegeses, not three.[53]

3.4 Interim summary

The Tannaitic and Amoraic sources cited above anchor and reinforce the rule that "the owner deals with the carcass," even though it is contrary to the plain meaning of the scriptural verses.[54] Note that this rule presumably applies even in cases where the degree of the injurer's responsibility for the damage is high, as in cases of common, predictable damage (which could have been avoided by taking minimal precautions); directly and deliberately caused damage; damage caused by the injurer's body, etc. The law as stated in the scriptural verses is not upheld, even in serious cases of this nature, with regard to which it would have been appropriate, from an ethical perspective, to require that the injurer take the damaged object for himself and provide the injured party with a replacement.

4. Disparity between a verse's plain meaning and the Sages' interpretation of it: 'the Sages have a tradition'

What is the appropriate way to address disparities between the plain meaning of scriptural verses and the Sages' halakhic interpretations of those verses? There are several basic approaches to this question,[55] but examination of this issue is beyond the scope of this article.

52 jBaba Kama 1:1 (3a).
53 See Halivni, n. 47 above.
54 See A. Orenstein, "Means of assessing damage to property in Jewish law" (Hebrew), 9 *Alei Mishpat* (2011), 635.
55 The first is termed the "apologetic approach," which David Henshke characterizes as seeking "to prove that in every place where there is a contradiction between the plain meaning of a scriptural text and the midrashic

As we saw, some commentators claim that the Sages' interpretation follows directly from the plain meaning of the text. I argued, however, that a precise reading of the verses indicates that it is very difficult to take their plain meaning to sustain the Sages' halakhic interpretation. Other commentators recognized the difference between a scriptural text's plain meaning and the Sages' interpretation of it,[56] and, regarding the case at hand, noted that the Sages had a tradition according to which "the owner deals with the carcass," despite the fact that this rule is not consistent with the scriptural text's plain meaning. It seems

---

exegesis of that text, the truth of the matter is that the midrashic interpretation is its plain meaning" (David Henshke, "Scriptural verses do not diverge from their plain meaning" (Hebrew), *Hama'ayan* 17 (1977), 3:7-19, 4:52-69). Among others, R. Jacob Zvi of Kollenberg used this interpretative method in his commentary *Hakhtav Vehakabala*, and the Malbim used it in his commentary *Hatora Vehamitzvot*. Another approach is championed by R. Judah Copperman, who contends that "the plain meaning of Scripture teaches us Torah, but does not necessarily teach us the law. The question, then, is: what is the 'Torah' that the plain meaning teaches, and what is the role of that Torah in the broader framework of the Torah's wholeness and holiness?" (*On the Role of the Plain Meaning in the Torah's Wholeness and Holiness* (Hebrew), [Jerusalem: 2001], 1:1, title page). See also his introduction to *Meshekh Hokhma* (Copperman edition). In other words, the plain meaning does not purport to impart legal rulings, but rather, its function is to impart a Torah message of another kind. Henshke calls this "the functional approach."

Henshke himself proposes a third approach. In his opinion, "in every place where the plain meaning of a scriptural text imparts a law that contradicts the law imparted by the midrashic exegesis of that text, the truth of the matter is that the plain meaning delineates the true boundary of the original law under consideration. The midrashically-derived law is no more than the practical, real-world expression of the law articulated by the plain meaning, seeing that the original law articulated by the plain meaning does not exist in practice because of various circumstances that are incidental to the substance of the original law" (3:15). Henshke brings examples which show that despite the primacy of the Sages' interpretation, the law imparted by the plain meaning is manifested in certain cases, and below, we will consider applying his approach to the case of tort damage.

56 The Vilna Gaon (Gra), e.g., writes: "And also from the greatness of our Oral Law, which is law given to Moses at Sinai, yet it transposes itself like sealing wax. . . . Hence one needs to know the plain meaning of the Torah in order to know the seal" (*Aderet Eliyahu*, beginning of Torah portion 'Mishpatim'). The Gra compares the relationship between the Written Law and the Oral Law to that between a seal and the stamp it imprints on sealing wax: the seal's letters are reversed so that imprinted letters read in the right direction.

that we cannot escape the conclusion that the Sages attached the law to the verses through the mechanism of 'sustaining exegesis' (*midrash mekayem*).[57] The exegeses discussed above are sustaining exegeses that derive the law, already known by way of tradition, from the scriptural verses.[58]

57 Menachem Elon terms what I will call "creative exegesis" (*midrash yotzer*) "explanatory-creative interpretation," and what I called "sustaining exegesis" (*midrash mekayem*) "integrative interpretation." He describes them as follows:

> There are two types of interpretation in Jewish law: one whose purpose is to explain and clarify what is stated in the Torah, or to create new laws, and the other, whose purpose is to support concededly preexisting law by integrating it with the Torah.
>
> There is a corollary to this proposition: explanatory-creative interpretation and integrative interpretation differ in both form and style. When the interpreter seeks to explain the Torah or to create new law out of the Torah, his approach must be constrained by logic and by the text; for it is the Scriptural verse that the interpreter seeks to explain, and it is the Scriptural verse that is the source for the new law. However, the interpreter who merely integrates an already existing law with a verse has wide latitude to expand beyond the confines of the verse, and to take liberties in the course of his interpretation. . . . Explanatory-creative interpretation observes the principles and keeps within the bounds of legal logic and genuine interpretation; it is the preponderant type of interpretation in Jewish law. But interpretation that aims solely to connect an existing law to some Scripturally supportive text seizes upon the verse, its letters, and even the crownlets of its letters, with full awareness that it is not extracting the true meaning of the verse. This type of interpretation is justified because its only purpose is to create a bridge between the Oral Law and the Written Law, and use of such an extravagant literary device for such a purpose was accepted and understood in the entire civilized world in the Talmudic period. (Menachem Elon, *Jewish Law: History, Sources and Principles*, trans. B. Auerbach and M.J. Sykes [Philadelphia: 1994], 305-307)

On the relationship between sustaining exegesis (*midrash mekayem*) and creative exegesis (*midrash yotzer*), see M. Halbertal, *Interpretative Revolutions in the Making* (Hebrew), (Jerusalem: 1997), 13ff.

58 See, e.g., the comment made by R. Abraham, son of Maimonides, n. 8 above: "tradition has explained." See too *Haamek Davar*, Exodus 21:34: "On the surface, the language means that the carcass will go to the owner of the pit [i.e., the injurer]. But also embedded in the scriptural language is a tradition of the Sages." It seems plausible to apply the functional approach here. We can say that the plain meaning of the scriptural verse expresses the **ideal** law, according to which in every case where the damage inflicted

5. The halakhic boundaries of the rule "the owner deals with the carcass"

We have seen that the damaged object is to remain in the possession of the injured party. The Later Authorities addressed the question of

---

is significant, and involves the burden of selling the damaged object and buying a replacement, or repairing the damage, it is wrong to burden the injured party with the task of retrieving the damaged object and acquiring a replacement. On the contrary, these tasks should be the obligation of the injurer, whose improper conduct caused the damage. The existing law, as we said, is – from the perspective of the injurer – more flexible, but the scriptural verse presents the ideal law, for the purpose of imparting an educational message.

The "eye for eye" rule is similar in this respect. R. Abraham ibn Ezra, commenting on Exodus 21:24 ("eye for eye, tooth for tooth, hand for hand, foot for foot"), asserts: "And the interpretation of 'eye for eye' is, his eye for his eye would be fitting if he does not make reparation." In the same vein, Maimonides states: "What is said in the Torah, 'As he has maimed someone, so shall it be done to him' (Lev. 24:20) does not mean to injure him the same way he injured his fellow, but rather, that it would be fitting to take away one of his organs or to injure him as he has done, and therefore, he pays for the damage he caused" (*Code*, Laws concerning Wounding and Damaging 1:3). Clearly, the practical ramifications of carrying out the "eye for eye" law and implementing bodily punishments as per the plain meaning of the scriptural text are far more serious than those ensuing from implementing the "and the dead [animal] shall be his" law as per the plain meaning, but the principle – that the ideal law must be distinguished from the actual law – is similar.

Returning to exegesis of Exodus 21:34, it may also be that the Sages were disturbed by the injustice that would be caused by imposing the obligation to carry out a property transaction in cases where the damage was relatively minor. At the same time, implementing the law according to the plain meaning of the scriptural text only in cases where the damage was serious, and hence a property transaction was justified, would require making a determination in each separate case as to whether a property transaction was warranted. It may be that the Sages preferred to have a uniform law for all cases. See also A. Enker, "Foundations of Jewish criminal law" (Hebrew), *Mishpatim* 24 (1994), 198-99, which explains in similar fashion the tension between the severity of the punishments specified in the Torah and the many formal conditions that must be met before such punishments can be imposed.

Henshke's approach can also be applied in this context. On his approach, the law to be applied in practice would indeed be the law as interpreted by the Sages, but there would still be some cases where the law applied would be the law according to its plain scriptural meaning, as we will see below.

the halakhic boundaries of this determination. R. Y.M. Rabinowitz also expressed concerns about this:

> And it should be examined: If what is being said, namely, that the carcass goes to the injured party, as part of the restitution [due him], is indeed the case, then it is truly the obligation of the injurer to pay him the full value of the ox that was injured. But if Scripture had not revealed to us that the owner deals with the carcass, we would have thought that the injurer must pay him all that his ox was worth, and take the carcass for himself, for the value of the carcass is also included in the overall [accounting of the] damage that he must pay him according to the "ox for ox" law. . . . Or is it the case that what Scripture informed us, namely, that the owner deals with the carcass, is saying that the carcass is not included in the overall [accounting of the] damage? Because the main damage was only the depreciation [in the animal's value] caused by the death, and the carcass belongs to the injured party as it did from the outset, and should not be taken as part of the restitution.[59]

This question was also considered by R. Moses Mordechai Epstein[60] in a responsum,[61] and by other Later Authorities.[62]

R. Moses Mordechai Epstein sides with the first approach, according to which the carcass is transferred to the injurer's possession but is returned to the injured party as part of the restitution. By contrast, *Afikei Yam* sides with the second approach, according to which the

59 *Afikei Yam* (Vilna, 1905), §21.

60 R. Moses Mordechai Epstein, a decisor at the Slobodka Yeshiva.

61 *Responsa Levush Mordekhai*, #8.

62 See *Responsa Sridei Esh*, HM #158. R. Jekutiel Judah Halberstam, the Admor of Klausenberg (1904-1995), examines the three exegeses in the *sugya* in bBaba Kama 10b and tries to categorize them in terms of the points discussed above:

> And perhaps it may be said that it depends on the inference drawn there. If it is from "One who kills an animal (*make nefesh beheima*) shall make restitution for it (*yeshalmena*)" (Lev. 24:18) – this means payments. And if it is from "If it be torn to pieces, let him bring it for witness; he shall not make good that which was torn" (Exod. 22:12) that means that there are no payments at all, because it is still in the possession of the injured party. Regarding what Hizkiya inferred from "And the dead [animal] shall be his" (Exod. 21:36): since the verse did not say 'and the dead [animal] **is** his,' it means that it must be given to the injured party as part of the payment. (*Responsa Divrei Yatziv*, #74).

It seems that, with regard to the second and third exegeses, there is room for further discussion of this categorization.

carcass remains with the injured party from the outset and throughout the interaction. I believe that the second option is simpler. It appears that the Sages, in formulating the rule as "**the owner** deals with the carcass," emphasized that the injured party was and remains the owner of the damaged object. The Sages could have said "**the injured party** deals with the carcass," which would be more natural in a tort case. The word "owner" emphasizes that the tortious event does not generate a property transaction.

This point can have various halakhic ramifications. It is agreed that if the carcass rots between the time the damage occurred and the time of the legal action for redress, the ensuing depreciation is at the injured party's expense. This situation is termed 'carcass depreciation.' But is the 'carcass depreciation' at the expense of the injured party even if he does not know that damage was incurred? If, at the time of the injury and subsequently, the carcass is owned by and in the possession of the injured party, it could be argued that the carcass's depreciation is at his expense even if he does not know that the damage was incurred. On the other hand, if the carcass goes to the injurer, and is then returned to the injured party as partial payment, it would not be possible to make the payment without the injured party's knowledge, and therefore, until he has been made aware of the damage, the depreciation is borne – so it could be argued – by the injurer.[63]

Rabbenu Meir Hakohen of Saragossa[64] maintained, with respect to pit damage, that in the opposite case, that is, if the carcass appreciated in value when it was still in the pit before the injurer removed it and gave it to the injured party, the injurer is entitled to this appreciation. This opinion is more plausible if we uphold the view that the carcass goes to the injurer but is returned to the injured party as part of the restitution.

Additional ramifications are possible not only with regard to changes in the value of the carcass, but also with regard to legal actions conducted between the time the damage occurred and the time the carcass is returned to the injured party. Some went so far as to argue that the injurer, and not the injured party, has full ownership of the carcass before it is removed from the pit, and therefore, during this

63 See *Responsa Sridei Esh*, ibid.
64 Cited in *Shita Mekubetzet*, bBaba Kama 11a.

intermediate period, only the injurer can dedicate it to the Sanctuary, whereas the injured party is not entitled to do so.[65]

6. Assessment in the case of damage and assessment in the case of theft and robbery

6.1 The plain meaning of the scriptural verses and their exegesis

With respect to torts, we were able to arrive at relatively clear conclusions on the basis of the plain meaning of the scriptural verses, but with regard to theft and robbery it is difficult to reach an unequivocal conclusion. Regarding the payments applicable to a thief, the Torah states: "If the theft be at all found in his hand alive (*hayim*), whether it be ox, or ass or sheep; he shall pay double (*shnayim yeshalem*)" (Exod. 22:3). Does this verse suggest something with respect to the questions we are grappling with? The words "if the theft be at all found" (*himatzei timatzei*) and "alive" contrast with what is written at the end of the previous chapter of Exodus (Exod. 21:37), according to which, in the case of a thief who steals an animal and then slaughters or sells it, the law of fourfold and fivefold payment applies. The situation referred to by "be at all found" is contrasted to sale, and "alive" to slaughter.[66] In these cases, the thief is obligated to make double payment ("he shall pay double") instead of four- and fivefold payment. According to the vocalization marks used for Torah cantillation, the word "alive" is connected to the first part of the verse, and not to the words "he shall pay double." If so, this verse does not contribute in any way to clarifying the questions we are concerned with vis-à-vis the status of the dead animal/broken object.

In the Mekhilta de-Rabbi Yishmael,[67] however, there is an exegesis that connects the word "alive" to the second part of the verse: "alive:

65 See R. J.B. Soloveitchik, *Reshimot Shiurim*, Baba Kama, 1:92 and n. 151. Note that the said ramifications render Henshke's approach applicable here. We have seen that there are cases in which, on some interpretations, the carcass is deemed to belong to the injurer. Hence the aptness of Henshke's thesis that the plain meaning of the verse, namely, that "his" = the injurer's, has not been eclipsed, since there are intermediate stages during which the carcass indeed belongs to the injurer.

66 See *Rasag* ad loc.

67 Mekhilta de-Rabbi Yishmael, Mishpatim, Masekhta de-Nezikin, 13 s.v. *mishor*. This exegesis is cited in the Jerusalem Talmud *sugya* discussed below.

he shall pay with two that are alive, and not dead."[68] Regarding the return of stolen objects, the Torah commands: "and he shall restore that thing which he took by robbery" (Lev. 5:23).[69] This verse, in the context in which it is found in Leviticus, deals with the case where someone committed robbery (or denied that he owed money), swore a false oath, then repented and wished to atone for his misdeeds. The Sages derived from this case several general laws regarding robbery.

In terms of the plain meaning of the verse, the provision that he must restore "that [robbed] thing which he took by robbery" does not give an unequivocal answer to the question of whether or not the robber may return the object after it has been broken. In the Talmud,[70] the differences of opinion as to whether 'change confers ownership'[71] exemplify the extent to which the verse's provisions are not unequivocal.

> Rav Hisda said in the name of R. Jonathan: How do we know that change confers ownership? Because Scripture states: "and he shall restore that [robbed] thing which he robbed" (Lev. 5:23) What do the words "which he robbed" teach us? **If it is as it was when he committed the robbery – he returns it, and if not – he only has to pay the monetary equivalent.** But is not "which he robbed" needed to exclude robbery carried out by his father, since he does not pay an additional fifth for a robbery carried out by his father?! But if so, the Merciful One would have written 'and he shall restore the robbed object.' What is the point in writing "which he robbed"? We can deduce from it two things. And some say that Rav Hisda said in the name of R. Jonathan: How do we know that change does not confer ownership? Because Scripture states: "and he shall restore that [robbed] thing" – **in every case**. And that which is written: "which he robbed"? This is needed to inform us that he adds a fifth to [the value of] an object he robbed, and does not add a fifth to [the value of] an object his father robbed.[72]

We can see from this that contrary inferences can be derived from the same words.

68 See *Rashi*, Exodus 21:37, where this interpretation is developed: "and he shall not pay him with dead ones, but rather live ones, or the monetary equivalent of live ones."
69 Lit., that robbed thing which he robbed.
70 bBaba Kama 66a-67a.
71 See below for further discussion of the question of whether change 'confers ownership' or 'leaves the object's status unaffected.'
72 bBaba Kama 67a, emphasis added.

6.2 The *sugya* in the Babylonian Talmud

In an adjacent *sugya*, bBaba Kama 11a, the Talmud addresses the differences between the injurer, the thief, the robber, and the borrower with respect to assessment of damage to an appropriated object. It is significant that this *sugya* is found near the *sugya* on "the owner deals with the carcass"; the interpretive import of this juxtaposition will be addressed below. In between, the Talmud addresses "carcass depreciation," i.e., the depreciation in the carcass's value between the time the damage occurred and the time of the legal action seeking redress; it rules that such depreciation is at the injured party's expense. Also discussed between these *sugyot* is "the nuisance of dealing with the carcass." Some Tannaitic authorities contend that the injurer must remove the carcass from the pit, whereas others disagree and argue that this obligation falls on the injured party as part of his general obligation to deal with the carcass.

After addressing carcass depreciation and nuisance, the Talmud proceeds to the thief, the robber, and the borrower:

> Samuel said: We do not assess in the case of the thief, nor that of the robber, but in the case of damage (לנזקין),[73] and I say: also in the case of the borrower, and Abba agrees with me.[74] They asked him: did he say, We also assess in the case of the borrower, and Abba agrees with me, or did he perhaps say, And I say: we also do not assess in the case of the borrower, and Abba agrees with me? Come and hear: A certain man borrowed an axe from his friend, and broke it, and came before Rav. He said to him: Go and recompense him with a good axe. From this we deduce: we do not assess. On the contrary, R. Kahana and R. Asi asked Rav, is the law thus? and he remained silent. From this we deduce: we assess. It was said: Ula said in the name of R. Eleazar: we assess in the case of the thief and the robber; R. Papi said: we do not assess. And the law is: we do not assess in the case of the thief, nor that of the robber, but in the case of the borrower we do assess, according to R. Kahana and R. Asi.[75]

Samuel's dictum raises several difficulties. It explicitly mentions three sorts of perpetrators who bear liability for damage: the thief, the

73 On the identity of the author of this dictum, see *Sefer Hasheiltot*, sheilta 111 (Mirsky edition, sheilta 128); see *Tosafot* s.v. *basheiltot*; *Tosafot Rabbenu Peretz* on bBaba Kama 11a. And see nn 105, 109 below.

74 The Jerusalem Talmud, which will be discussed below, raises two possibilities as to Abba's identity, but endorses Rav Hisda's determination that it refers to the Amora Rav.

75 bBaba Kama 11a.

robber, and the borrower. A fourth category is mentioned in the dictum, but is not completely clear: 'in torts' (לנזקין) (*lenezikin*). Alfasi,[76] citing these words of the Talmud as law, reads this term as *lenizakin*, with a *yud* between the *nun* and the *zayin* (i.e., the pl. of *nizak*), meaning "in the case of injured parties." Accordingly, there are those who point the word "לנזקין" in the Talmud with a *hirik* under the *nun* and a *kamatz* under the *zayin*,[77] in which case the reference is to the one who incurred the damage. The question that arises in this case is why the term would be formulated in the plural, whereas with respect to the thief, the robber, and the borrower, the singular is used.

The accepted, and more plausible reading, is "לנזקין" (*lenezikin*), with no *yud* between the *nun* and the *zayin*,[78] in which case the reference is to torts in general, or more precisely, to the compensation paid for the various types of torts.[79] Some[80] thus point the word with a *shva* under the *nun* and a *hirik* under the *zayin*.[81]

This raises a further question. What is the meaning of the verb "assess" in this context? In answering this question, it is helpful to adduce another *sugya* on the laws of borrowing, bBaba Metzia 96b-97a, which discusses the "a certain man borrowed an axe from his friend" case that was referred to in the 'we assess in the case of damage' *sugya* (bBaba Kama 11a) we just discussed. The *sugya* in bBaba Metzia 96b-97a rules, regarding a borrower whose borrowed vessel breaks while in

76 *Rif*, bBaba Kama 4b (Alfasi pagination); the Nissan Zaks edition of the Rif gives this reading too.

77 E.g., the Steinsaltz edition and the Talmud vocalized in accordance with the Yemenite tradition.

78 As in the printed Vilna edition. *Dikdukei Sofrim* does not cite any MS variants. The *sugya* is quoted in the *Sheiltot*, sheilta 111 (Mirsky edition, sheilta 128). Mirsky adopted the "*lenezikin*" reading, but notes "*lenizakin*" as one of the variants. The Frankel edition of Maimonides' *Code* (Laws concerning Damage by Chattels 7:8) gives the "*lenezikin*" reading, without citing any variants in the appended critical apparatus that lists variant readings, and so does the Kafih edition.

79 mBaba Kama 1:1 lists four "basic categories" (lit., fathers) of torts. In bBaba Kama 4b, R. Osheia gives 13 basic categories, and R. Hiya, 24. And see *Rosh*, Baba Kama 1:11: "and this is so with regard to all 24 basic categories."

80 E.g., the Schottenstein edition.

81 It might have been expected that there would be an additional *yud* between the *zayin* and the *kuf*, i.e., נזיקין, but examination of other *sugyot* shows that in several of them, the spelling is נזקין without the *yud* though it is clear that the reference is to payment of damages. See, e.g., bBaba Kama 7b, where the spelling "נזקין" appears five times in the printed Vilna edition.

his care: "he returns the broken pieces to him and makes up the vessel's full value." This ruling helps us understand the term "assess." The unanimous view of the commentators is that the reference is to estimating the value of the broken pieces of the original object.[82] The Tur [83] interprets the words "שמין לנזקין" (we assess in the case of damage) by adding "the broken pieces": "in the case of damage, we assess the broken pieces" (*shamin hashvarim benezikin*).

The Amoraim were divided on the question of whether or not an assessment is made in cases of theft and robbery. Samuel and Rav Papi maintain that there is no assessment in the case of the thief or the robber, whereas Ula, in the name of R. Eleazar, maintains that there is.[84] The Talmud does not explain these opposed views, but rules that there is no assessment in the case of the thief or the robber. Samuel's dictum is mentioned in the Babylonian Talmud *sugya* about whether a change 'confers ownership' or 'leaves the object's status unaffected.' Before continuing, it is important to clarify the connection between the laws of acquisition and the laws of theft and robbery. This connection arises in two separate contexts. An act of theft is carried out **at the outset** in a manner of acquisition. mBaba Kama 7:6 asserts:

> If he [a thief] pulls on [the animal] and it goes out and dies while [still] on the owner's premises – [he is] exempt. If he lifts it up, or takes it out of the owners' premises and it dies – [he is] liable.

This Mishnah addresses the case of a thief who steals an animal from the owner's premises, and the animal dies from something other than the act of theft itself. It states that if the thief 'pulled'[85] on the

82 There is a dispute between the Geonim and the Early Authorities over the interpretation of the "we do not assess" rule; this controversy will be adduced below. As we will see, some argue that there is no assessment at all, others argue that an assessment is made in the case of theft and robbery, but the 'carcass depreciation' rule applies from the time the damage is incurred until the time payment is made.

83 HM 403. A similar stance is taken in *SA*, ad loc. In some printed editions the word appears as "שוורים" – oxen, although it is clear that this is a misprint and the correct word is "שברים" – broken pieces (the words are homonyms in Hebrew).

84 Cf. the Jerusalem Talmud *sugya*, quoted below, where it is stated in the name of R. Leizer that there is no assessment in the case of the thief or the robber.

85 'Pulling' on an object (i.e., drawing it near to one) and 'lifting' it up are symbolic acts of acquisition carried out to effect transfer of ownership.

animal, he is liable only if the pulling was done outside the owner's premises, whereas if the thief 'lifted up' the animal, he is liable even if he raised it up on the owner's premises.[86] The distinction stems from the laws of acquisition. 'Pulling' is not effective as a mode of acquisition when it takes place on someone else's premises, whereas 'lifting up' is effective everywhere.

The initial act of theft or robbery does not constitute a complete acquisition, but only a partial one, from which is derived, among other things, the thief's liability for any damage caused to the stolen object. As the Talmud puts it: "The Merciful One placed it under the thief's control only with respect to unavoidable circumstances [that cause breakage] (*onsin*); but as to ownership, it remains in the possession of the owner, just as in the case of a borrower."[87]

The next stage in an acquisition by a thief/robber is a change in the stolen/robbed object. If 'change confers ownership' (*shinui kone*) this means that after there has been a change in the stolen/robbed object, the thief/robber has acquired it, in the sense that he is not obligated to return the object, as it was, to its owner. If, on the other hand, 'change leaves the object's status unaffected' (*shinui bimkomo omed*), the change does not exempt the thief/robber from returning the object, as it was, to the owner. Maimonides explains the relevance of this question:

86 The standard version of *Rashi* ad loc. states that in the absence of an act of acquisition, the thief is entirely exempt: "exempt from [paying] anything" (*patur miklum*). In *Masoret Hashas*, however, a different version of Rashi's comment appears: "exempt from double payment" (*patur mikefel*). The phrase "exempt from double payment" also appears in the commentary referred to as *Rashi* printed around the pages of the *Rif*, bBaba Kama 29a (Alfasi pagination).

Maimonides too (*Code*, Laws concerning Theft 2:16) writes that the act of acquisition is required in order to impose double payment on him, and it follows from his ruling that the thief is obligated to pay the principal (*keren*, i.e., the value of the stolen object) even if the act of acquisition does not meet all the halakhic conditions. "One who steals from the owner's premises, is – since the stolen object is still in [the owner's] possession – exempt from double [payment] (*min hakefel*). And so too, if he slaughtered [the stolen animal] and sold it, there on the owner's premises, he is exempt. And if he lifted up the stolen object he is liable for stealing even if he has not yet removed it from the owner's premises." It seems that in MS, Rashi's comment was written using a contraction (מכ'), which was later transcribed in two different ways, namely, as "from [paying] anything" (*miklum*) and "from double [payment]" (*mikefel*).

87 bSanhedrin 72a.

"A robbed item that has not been changed but remains as it was . . . itself returns to its owner. And if it was changed by the robber . . . he acquired it by this change and he pays its value as it was at the time of the robbery."[88]

A vessel that was damaged and is not whole is a vessel that has undergone a change, and through that change the robber has acquired it, in the sense that he does not return the vessel, but rather its value.[89]

Having familiarized ourselves with these fundamental principles regarding the connection between the laws of acquisition and the laws of theft and robbery,[90] let us now examine a statement by Abbaye, according to which several Tannaim, including R. Shimon b. Eleazar, "were all of the opinion that change leaves the object's status unaffected."[91] The Talmud quotes R. Shimon b. Eleazar's view as follows:

> What is R. Shimon b. Eleazar's [opinion]? For it was taught: R. Shimon b. Eleazar stated this rule: any improvement that the robber made gives him the upper hand: if he wishes, he can take his improvement, if he wishes, he can say [to the owner], here, your object is in front of you. What is the import of what he said? Rav Sheshet said, he said thus: as to the improvement, he takes his improvement, [in the case of] deterioration, he says [to the owner], here, your object is in front of you, because change leaves the object's status unaffected. If so, why should this not also be the case if he improved it? They said: it is because of the "enactment [in support of] the penitent" (*takanat hashavim*).[92]

According to Rav Sheshet's explanation of R. Shimon b. Eleazar's statement, the robber can say to the robbed party, 'here, your object is in front of you,' despite the change (namely, deterioration) that occurred in the course of the robbery, and therefore, "change leaves the object's status unaffected."

Later in the *sugya*, a statement made by Samuel that supports R. Shimon b. Eleazar's view is adduced, and the Talmud discusses whether

88 *Code*, Laws concerning Robbery and Lost Property 2:1.

89 But see §6.8 below: according to Maimonides, if the person from whom the vessel was stolen demands the broken pieces, despite the change that the vessel has undergone by being broken, he is entitled to them.

90 On the status of thefts and robberies as acts of acquisition, see also I. Warhaftig, "Fees for use of misappropriated property" (Hebrew), *Tehumin* 6 (1985), 235; A. Weinroth, *Theft and Plunder, Fundamental Chapters* (Hebrew), (Jerusalem: 2002), chs. 1-4.

91 bBaba Kama 93b.

92 bBaba Kama 94a. And see below at nn 135-36.

Samuel's opinion that we assess in the case of damage and we do not assess in the case of the thief and the robber can be viewed as consistent with the opinion that "change leaves the object's status unaffected."

> Rav Judah said in the name of Samuel: The law is in accordance with the view of R. Shimon b. Eleazar. But did Samuel really say so? Didn't Samuel say: We do not assess in the case of the thief, nor that of the robber, but [we assess] in the case of damage? This makes sense according to the view of Rava, who said: R. Shimon b. Eleazar said that it pertained to cases of reversible deterioration, and there is thus no difficulty, since he [Samuel] said: the law is in accordance with the view of R. Shimon b. Eleazar because "change leaves the object's status unaffected" applies to reversible deterioration, and what Samuel said there [bBaba Kama 11a] – "We do not assess in the case of the thief, nor that of the robber, but in the case of damage" – applies to irreversible deterioration.
>
> But according to Abbaye, who said: what R. Shimon b. Eleazar said applies to irreversible deterioration, what is there to say? [i.e., how can we resolve this contradiction?] Abbaye taught thus: Rav Judah said in the name of Samuel: They stated that the law is in accordance with the view of R. Shimon b. Eleazar, but he [Samuel] does not think so.[93]

The Talmud succeeds in reconciling Samuel's view that "we do not assess in the case of the thief, nor that of the robber, but [we assess] in the case of damage" with the view that "change leaves the object's status unaffected," only by restricting R. Shimon's view to reversible deterioration. Deterioration that is not irreversible enables the robber to say "here, your object is in front of you," which does not contradict Samuel's statement that we assess in the case of damage. In other words, the rule that we do not assess in the case of the thief or the robber applies in the case of irreversible deterioration, when the damage caused to the misappropriated object cannot be reversed.

We learn from this *sugya* that the rule "we do not assess in the case of the thief, nor that of the robber" arises from considerations pertaining to acquisition relations. The acquisitional action carried out by the thief/robber vis-à-vis the misappropriated object has legal consequences regarding assessment of damage, and it is because of the acquisition that "we do not assess," but rather require the thief/robber to give back a replacement object worth the full value of the original object, or the monetary equivalent.

93 bBaba Kama 94b-95a.

6.3 The *sugya* in the Jerusalem Talmud

The Jerusalem Talmud discusses the question of restitution for the misappropriated object in tractate Kidushin:

> Rav Judah sent to ask R. Eleazar [about] the coercive misappropriator, the robber, and the thief. He answered: There is a presumption that the owner does not deal with the carcass. And whence do we know that the owner does not deal with the carcass? R. Ba b. Memel said: "Alive he shall pay double" (Exod. 22:3) – and not for the dead. This is the rule regarding theft; but what about robbery? R. Abun said: "And he shall return the robbery that he robbed" (Lev. 5: 23). As it was.[94]

In tractate Kidushin, the Jerusalem Talmud does not mention "assessment," but only discusses the question of whether the owner (the one coerced into giving something up, robbed, or stolen from) deals with the carcass. Assessing damage is discussed in jBaba Kama:

> Rav Judah said in the name of Samuel: We do not assess in the case of the thief, nor that of the robber, nor that of the borrower, but [we assess] in the case of damage. And I say: In the case of the borrower, too, we do {not}[95] assess. And Abba agrees with me. And who is Abba – Rav, or Abba b. Abuha? Rav Hisda said: The main thing has become secondary.[96] Rav Judah said in the name of Samuel: We do not assess in the case of the thief, nor that of the robber, nor that of the borrower, but [we assess] in the case of damage. And bailees[97] are akin to the case of damage.
>
> Rav Judah sent to ask R. Eleazar: What do we do regarding assessment in the case of the coercive misappropriator, and that of the robber, and that of the thief? He said to him: We do not assess in the case of the

94 jKidushin 1:4 (60c).

95 The meaning of the curly brackets around "do not" (*ein*) is that the word is redundant, a redundancy introduced somehow in the transmission of the text; this means that the word should be disregarded. The printed edition of the Jerusalem Talmud also reads: "In the case of the borrower, too, we {do not} assess." The "do not" is problematic here, since the view attributed to Samuel is that we do not assess in the case of the borrower, and if so, what is Rav Judah adding? Indeed, *Pnei Moshe* and *Mare Hapanim* ad loc. note that the correct reading is "In the case of the borrower, too, we assess."

96 *Pnei Moshe* explains that Rav Hisda sought to decide between the two possibilities concerning Abba's identity: "It is clear that he means Rav, because if he meant Abba, his father, would it be appropriate to turn the main issue into a secondary issue and to say 'and my father agrees with me'; for this is not honorable conduct, and he should have stated the rule in his father's name!"

97 The other three bailees, but not the borrower; see *Pnei Moshe* ad loc.

> thief, nor that of the robber. And whence do we know that we do not assess in these cases? R. Abba b. Memel said: "Alive he shall pay double" (Exod. 22:3) – alive, and not dead: this is the rule regarding theft. Regarding robbery, whence [do we know it]? R. Abin said: "And he shall restore that thing [in the same condition as that[98]] which he took by robbery" (Lev. 5:23).[99]

According to the plain meaning of the texts, the two *sugyot* complement one another.[100] The thief and the robber must deal with the broken object (as we learn from the *sugya* in Kidushin) and compensate the owner by either paying him the object's monetary value or providing him with an undamaged replacement.

Comparing the Babylonian Talmud *sugya* with its Jerusalem Talmud counterpart reveals two differences. Firstly, in the Babylonian Talmud, the law is a matter of controversy, whereas in the Jerusalem Talmud there is agreement that no assessment is made in the case of the thief or the robber. Granted, the Babylonian *sugya* does conclude that there is no assessment in the case of the thief or the robber, and there is assessment in the case of damage, but as I said, there is a controversy about this. Second, whereas in the Babylonian Talmud it is difficult to pinpoint the basis for the rule (because in the main *sugya* no reason is given for the rule, and in the *sugya* that considers whether "change confers ownership," the reason is not stated explicitly, but just implied), the ruling in the Jerusalem Talmud is based on exegesis of scriptural verses. R. Abba b. Memel adduces the exegesis that appears in the Mekhilta de-Rabbi Yishmael: "alive . . . he shall pay double: [he shall pay with two that are] alive, and not dead."[101] This exegesis is laconic, and gives no detail as to the meaning of the phrase "alive, and not dead." R. Abba b. Memel, we saw, endows it with content, interpreting it as pertaining to the obligation of the thief and the robber to return, not the broken object, but rather an undamaged object or money.

98 The exegesis inserts the preposition "like" (כ) before the words "which he took by robbery" (אשר גזל) rendering it כאשר גזל.

99 jBaba Kama 1:1 (3a). A similar exegesis of "Alive he shall pay double" appears in jKidushin as well, where it is invoked to justify the rule that "the owner does not deal with the carcass" in the case of the coercive misappropriator, the robber, and the thief.

100 But see *Bah*, HM 355:5, which takes a different view.

101 Mekhilta de-Rabbi Yishmael, Mishpatim, Masekhta de-Nezikin, 13.

6.4 First interpretation of the *sugya*: the thief and robber are not entitled to return broken pieces

Adducing the "we assess in the case of damage" *sugya*, R. Shimon Kaiara (Babylonia, 8th c.), author of *Halakhot Gedolot*,[102] compares the injurer to the borrower and applies the aforementioned rule from Baba Metzia to both cases, asserting: "and they assess what it was originally worth, and he makes up its full value."[103]

Accordingly, most of the Early Authorities and decisors[104] interpreted the *sugya* as meaning that the thief and the robber, unlike the injurer, are not entitled to return the stolen/robbed object to the party from whom it was stolen/robbed if it is not whole, but rather they must return a whole and functioning object; or, if the misappropriated object is broken, they must pay money. By contrast, as was explained in detail above, in the case of damage, the party who suffered the damage takes the broken object, and the injurer adds to it the difference between the broken object's value and the value of the object before it was damaged.

This interpretation fits well with the *sugya* in bBaba Kama 10b, which establishes that "the owner deals with the carcass." The law that "the owner deals with the carcass" and the law that "we assess in the case of damage" are two sides of the same coin. In bBaba Kama 10b, the owner is required to take the carcass for himself, and in 94a-95b, the injurer is required to pay the difference between the damaged object's value and the object's value prior to being damaged. The innovative aspect of Samuel's statement is not his ruling vis-à-vis tort damage, but rather, vis-à-vis the case of the thief/robber, where he rules that no assessment is made,[105]

102 Baba Kama ad loc. (Makhon Yerushalayim–Makhon Or Hamizrah edition, 150).

103 *Halakhot Gedolot* mentions this rule again in the context of the laws of interest (ibid. 495), where the case of the borrower is also compared to that of damage.

104 *Rabbenu Hananel*, Baba Kama, ad loc.; *Rashi*, Baba Kama 11a and 94a, and bBaba Metzia 97a s.v. *dina hakhi*; *Tosafot*, bBaba Kama 11a s.v. *ein shamin*; *Rosh*, Baba Kama 1:11; *Rashba*; *Meiri* in the name of "the great authors," etc. See also *Yam Shel Shlomo*, 1: 29. The dissenting views will be discussed below.

105 *Dikdukei Sofrim* adduces the formulation of the dictum in the Venice edition of the Jerusalem Talmud: "Samuel said, It has been taught that we do not assess," which presents Samuel as reporting a Tannaitic dictum, but notes that this formulation was rejected by the Maharshal (first printed

because the ruling vis-à-vis damage (namely, "the owner deals with the carcass") had already been affirmed in the Tannaitic period, as explained above.[106]

6.5 Second interpretation of the *sugya*: 'carcass depreciation' is borne by the thief and the robber

We have explained the views of R. Shimon Kaiara (author of *Halakhot Gedolot*), Rashi, the Tosafists, and additional Early Authorities on the question of redress for damage to objects.[107] We now turn to another view, which appears for the first time in R. Ahai's *Sefer Hasheiltot.*

> This was only written regarding carcass depreciation, [namely,] if it depreciated between the time it was damaged and the time it was sold, it **remains in the owner's possession . . .**
>
> But it is necessary [to address the case of] the thief and the robber, where the stolen object or animal died in [the thief's] possession, and he pays the owner. If the object was broken and he pays for its depreciation, is it in the possession of the owner or in the possession of the robber? Do we say that it is analogous to the case of damage, or perhaps it is not analogous, for in the case of damage, it remains in the owner's possession, and [the injurer] pays for the damage he caused, but in case of a thief and a robber, it **was in their possession, and therefore the depreciation too is in their possession** [i.e., falls on them]? Should you say that it was in the possession of the thief and the robber, what about the borrower? Since [the object] remains in the possession of its owner, is it analogous to the case of damage, or is it, perhaps, because one is liable for [damage caused by] unavoidable circumstances (*onsin*), like the case of the thief and the robber?
>
> Come and hear: For Samuel said in the name of Abba: we do not assess in the case of the thief, nor that of the robber, but in the case of damage, and I say: also in the case of the borrower, and Abba agrees with me. They asked him: and Abba agrees with me that we assess, or that we do not assess? Come and hear: A certain man borrowed an axe from his friend, and it was broken. He came before Rav. He said to him: Go and recompense him with a good axe. From this we deduce that we do not assess. On the contrary, R. Kahana and R. Asi asked Rav, is the law indeed thus? and he

edition), who relies on *Rashi* and *Tosafot* on bBaba Kama 11a. See also Rabbenu Hananel's interpretation, in *Otzar Hageonim*, Baba Kama, p. 11 n. 3, which surveys the different variants of the dictum to ascertain the source of Samuel's statement.

106 In discussing the "we assess in the case of damage" *sugya*, Rabbenu Hananel does not even mention the injured party, and addresses only the case of the thief/robber.

107 Maimonides' view will be discussed below; see too *Rosh*, Baba Kama 1:11.

> remained silent. From this we deduce: we assess. It was said: Ula said in the name of R. Eleazar: we assess in the case of the thief and the robber, and R. Papa said: we do not assess. And the law is: we do not assess [in the case of the thief, nor that of the robber], but we do assess in the case of the borrower, according to R. Kahana and R. Asi.[108]

Sefer Hasheiltot explains that after being damaged, the damaged object remains in the hands of the injured party, and this is the source of his liability for 'carcass depreciation.' By contrast, in the case of theft/robbery, the owner cannot be held liable for 'carcass depreciation' because the object was damaged when it was not in the owner's domain, but had been taken away by the thief/robber.

The Rashbam's approach is similar to that of *Sefer Hasheiltot*, but for a different reason.[109] According to the Rashbam, the thief and the robber can use the broken pieces to pay the owner. The Rashbam relies, among other things, on a baraita that lists the thief and the robber among the 24 categories of damage.[110] The Talmud asserts that the categories of torts are "like categories of things restitution for which must be made with the choicest goods." Since the Talmud also states that, "Everything is considered to be the choicest, for if it does not sell here, it will sell elsewhere, except for land, regarding which he must give him the choicest, so that a prospective purchaser will be eager to acquire it,"[111] the Rashbam contends that there is no difference between the thief/robber and the injurer with respect to the manner of making payment, and the

108 *Sheilta* 111 (128 in the Mirsky edition), using Mirsky's rendering of the text.

109 His view is quoted in *Tosafot*, bBaba Metzia 96b s.v. *zil shlim* and in other sources from the period of the Early Authorities, see *Otzar Mefarshei Hatalmud*, bBaba Kama 11a n. 62. Note that the Rashbam does not cite the *Sheiltot* or invoke it in support of his view. *Tosafot*, bBaba Kama 11a s.v. *basheiltot*, comments on the source of Samuel's dictum, from which it is clear that the Tosafists were familiar with the *Sheiltot*'s position. Yet immediately following this comment, s.v. *ein shamin*, the *Tosafot* takes issue with the view of R. Ahai and the Rashbam, though without mentioning them by name: "even though we have already established that he may make restitution [with anything], including anything of monetary value, it is like money, and even bran [bBaba Kama 7a] – the case of the thief and robber is different."

110 bBaba Kama 4b-5a.

111 bBaba Kama 7b.

thief and robber can also pay by means of the broken pieces, which are considered to be 'choicest goods,' according to talmudic law.[112]

Hence according to the *Sheiltot* and the Rashbam, the difference between the case of the thief and robber, and that of the injurer, involves the damaged object's depreciation between the date the damage occurred and the date of the legal proceeding seeking redress. Regarding the injurer, the rule is that 'carcass depreciation' is borne by the injured party, whereas the thief and the robber bear the cost of the depreciation until restitution is made.[113] Those who endorse this inter-

112 Would the aforementioned commentators be receptive to the Rashbam's stance? Rabbenu Jonathan of Lunel ad loc. (Friedman edition, p. 20) addresses this explicitly: "Regarding the thief and the robber, it is unlikely that they will in every case "pay back" (Exod. 21:34) even the monetary equivalent, except in cases where there was no intent to harm." Other perspectives on this also come to mind. If we take the exegeses in the Jerusalem Talmud to be complete exegeses, or what is often called 'creative exegesis' (*midrash yotzer*) (as seems to follow from *Tosafot*, s.v. *ein shamin*, cited in n. 109 above), it could be argued that their purpose is to exclude the thief and the robber, with respect to the mode of restitution, from the 24 categories of torts. By contrast, if these exegeses are not 'creative,' it would follow that according to the law itself, the thief and the robber may pay with broken pieces, but over time a different custom developed, prohibiting them from doing so, and the Sages found support for this custom in scriptural verses. This may be the import of Rashi's term "a custom of the judges" (*minhag dayanim*); see n. 134 below. Note that vis-à-vis the robber, Rashi commented: "The Merciful One was not particular about his payments, as it is written: "shall make restitution" (Exod. 21:34) – includes anything of monetary value, and even bran" (bPesahim 32a s.v. *ibeaya lehu*). Here he refers to the original law, but as I said, a different judicial custom developed.

113 Those who uphold the first interpretation also agree that the thief and the robber bear the depreciation between the time of the theft and the time restitution is made. This position can be defended in various ways. It can be argued that the 'carcass depreciation is borne by the injured party' rule pertains to torts in the strict sense of the word and not to the thief and the robber, because the exegeses adduced to support the rule that 'the owner deals with the carcass' are derived from scriptural verses about tort law in the narrow sense (except for the verse, "If it be torn to pieces, let him bring it for witness; he shall not make good that which was torn" (Exod. 22:12), which pertains to the laws of bailees, as we saw). If, as suggested above, the exegeses are 'sustaining exegesis' (*midrash mekayem*), providing a basis for a tradition already known to the Sages, we can adduce an ethical rationale for the difference between the case of the injurer and that of the thief and robber. Generally, the injurer does not act intentionally,

pretation emphasize the proximity of the "we do not assess in the case of the thief, nor that of the robber" *sugya* to the 'carcass depreciation' *sugya* that precedes it. In other words, in torts, depreciation is borne by the injured party, whereas in cases of theft/robbery, the depreciation is borne by the thief/robber and not by the owner.

Note that this interpretation does not fit well with the wording of the assertion "we do not assess in the case of the thief, nor that of the robber," since the broken pieces need to be assessed in the case of theft or robbery no less than that of damage.[114] By contrast, on the previous interpretation, in the case of theft or robbery there is no need for an assessment, which fits the "we do not assess" rubric much better.

Another question is how to interpret the phrase "good axe." On the *Sheiltot*–Rashbam interpretation, the reference is to the full value of the axe at the time it was damaged, without depreciation. Whereas with regard to the carcass, rotting makes the depreciation evident, the value of a broken axe would not decrease simply due to the passage of time. Yet another question is how the *Sheiltot* and Rashbam would handle the *sugya* in Baba Metzia, which states: "he returns the broken pieces to him and makes up the vessel's full value." This seems to be consistent with the interpretation put forward in *Halakhot Gedolot*, according to which neither the lender nor the injured party has the right to demand a replacement object, but must accept the broken pieces plus compensation. Both these approaches interpret the statement in a manner that departs from its plain meaning. *Tosafot* formulates the matter thus: "The borrower returns the broken pieces to the lender and we assess for him the value of the pieces at the time of the breakage, and he pays him the vessel's full value and the depreciation, for a lender is like an injured

---

whereas the thief and robber do, hence it is appropriate to make them bear the depreciation. The depreciation rule's applicability to the robber also follows from a rule in the mBaba Kama 9:1: "All robbers must make restitution according to the [object's] value at the time of the robbery." The next Mishnah illustrates this rule in the context of assets whose value has depreciated: "If he robs an animal and it has aged . . . he pays according to the value at the time of the robbery. . . . [if he robs] a coin and it cracks, fruits and they rotted, wine and it soured, he pays according to the value at the time of the robbery" (9:2)

114 The Maharshal makes this point in *Yam Shel Shlomo*, Baba Kama, 1:29: "And it does not, as some commentators insist, refer only to carcass depreciation, whereas the broken pieces can always be given back in their current state. Because the expression "we do not assess" is to be understood completely in accordance with its plain meaning."

party [in the case of damage]."[115] The words "at the time of the breakage" would include the Rashbam's rule, according to which the depreciation (the decrease in value after the breakage) is borne by the lender (and by the injured party).[116]

On the *Sheiltot*–Rashbam interpretation, the difference between the case of the injurer, and that of the thief and robber, stems from the divergent character of the acts in question. The injurer does not intend to negate the injured party's possession and ownership of the object that is damaged. The injured party retains ownership, and thus he is the one who must make the effort to prevent further depreciation. By contrast, the thief and the robber take the object, removing it from the owner's domain and possession. When the object is broken while in the thief or robber's hands, the depreciation cannot accrue to the owner, because in most cases he is unaware of the damage and in any event can do nothing to prevent a decline in the object's value, since it is not in his possession. Moreover, the breakage constitutes a change and "change confers ownership," hence the liability for depreciation is borne by the thief or the robber.[117]

The Rashbam[118] rejects the *Tosafot*'s interpretation of the *sugya* in the Jerusalem Talmud, and interprets it in line with his own approach:

> And as to what the Jerusalem Talmud said, "Whence do we know that we do not assess in the case of the thief, nor that of the robber? R. Abba b. Memel said: "Alive he shall pay double" (Exod. 22:3) – and not dead" : this

115 bBaba Metzia, 96b-97a. Cf. *Rosh*, Baba Metzia 8:5: "'He returns the broken pieces to him' means, what they were worth at the time of the breakage, and pays him on top of that [the amount needed to cover] the cost of an axe."

116 We noted above that this interpretation is inconsistent with the plain meaning of the *sugya*, as was already pointed out in *Tosafot Talmid Rabeinu Tam Verabeinu Eliezer* (Baba Kama, p. 54): "And what it says, 'He returns the broken pieces to him,' means, this teaches us that he can give him broken pieces, but it does not mention depreciation."

117 This is how *Tosafot Rabeinu Peretz* and the *Mordekhai* ad loc. (Makhon Yerushalayim edition, 20-21) explain the Rashbam's approach. Above, I quoted *Tosafot*, bBaba Kama 11a s.v. *ein shamin* on the difference between an injurer and a thief or a robber vis-à-vis acquisition, this difference being the basis for the different laws in the two cases. *Kehilot Yaakov* (Baba Kama, §11) claims that acquisitional status accounts for the Rashbam's approach and "it may be that there is a defect in the text of the *Tosafot*: reference to the Rashbam's approach is missing."

118 *Tosafot*, bBaba Metzia 97a.

> is the rule regarding theft. Regarding robbery, whence [do we know it]? R. Bun said: "And he shall restore that thing which he took by robbery" (Lev. 5:23). This does not mean that he pays him another animal that is actually alive, and not bran, but rather, as he said: "Alive he shall pay double," that is to say, if they are alive but devalued, he returns them as they are, but if they have been devalued because they are dead, he must pay the depreciation. Another interpretation: "alive" [means,] he must pay for the full value without depreciation, as per [the ruling that] "the principal must be restored [lit., revived] in accordance with its value at the time of the theft" (*ahaye lakeren keein sheganav*), (bBaba Kama 65a), and this is the meaning in the Jerusalem Talmud. For there in Kidushin, it is stated, "Whence do we know that the owner does not deal with the carcass? R. Abba b. Memel said: "Alive he shall pay double" (Exod. 22:3) – and not dead," meaning that it refers to carcass depreciation.

As suggested above, the exegeses in the Jerusalem Talmud are general, and can be construed in line with the Rashbam's interpretation.[119]

6.6 Third interpretation of the *sugya*: combining the two previous interpretations

Rabbenu Jonathan of Lunel combines the two interpretations (*Halakhot Gedolot* and *Sheiltot*–Rashbam) as follows:

119 The Ribam (R. Isaac b. Meir), quoted in the *Tosafot*, accepts the Rashbam's approach in principle, but adds a detail:

> And this is the Ribam's interpretation, but he added the comment that there is disagreement even if there is no depreciation, because usually, when a vessel is broken while in the possession of a borrower, he has the option of [recompensing the lender by] paying the price of a good axe, and is not instructed to pay with the broken pieces, but in any event if he wants to pay by taking the pieces into account, he can do so. But according to R. Kahana and R. Asi, he is instructed to pay with the pieces because they are in the possession of the lender" (*Tosafot*, ibid.)

Assuming that this comment applies to the thief and the robber, not just the borrower, it appears that the difference between the case of the thief/robber and that of damage is that in the latter case, the court suggests to the injurer that he return the broken pieces to the injured party, but in the former case, the court does not make that proposal. But should the thief/robber insist on returning the pieces, together with an amount that makes up the difference between the pieces' value and the value of the object prior to the theft/robbery, he can do so, just as he can in the case of damage. See *Otzar Mefarshei Hatalmud* ad loc. n. 65.

> Although the Torah shows compassion to the injurer, in that if the carcass depreciates from the time the animal fell until the legal proceeding, he does not have to pay, [the Torah] does not have compassion for the thief and the robber, and all depreciation of the stolen or robbed object, from the time of the robbery until the legal proceeding, is depreciation he brought upon himself, and he recompenses him according to what it would have been worth at the time of the legal proceeding.[120] And he pays him the entire value of the robbed property as it was, a good animal or vessel; and the [dead] animal or broken pieces, the thief or robber keeps for himself.[121] For since he did the damage with his own hands, we are strict with him, and the owner does not have to deal with the misappropriated object. But in the case of damage, if his animal or his pit caused the damage, we are lenient, and the owner [of the damaged animal or object] deals with the carcass, and the depreciation that has been incurred is borne by the injured party and not the injurer.[122]

We can see that according to Rabbenu Jonathan, the "we do not assess in the case of the thief, nor that of the robber" law has two halakhic implications.

6.7 Rationales for distinguishing the injurer from the thief and the robber

Having explored both the talmudic *sugya* and commentaries on it by the Early Authorities, we now consider the rationales for the "we do not assess in the case of the thief, nor that of the robber" law. Three rationales have been suggested.

6.7.1 *The acquisitional rationale*

As we saw, the Talmud, in adducing Samuel's remarks on whether "change confers ownership," and contrasting them to Tannaitic views that "change leaves the object's status unaffected," indicates that the acquisitional element to the acts of the thief and the robber is the reason

120 Up to this point, Rabbenu Jonathan adopts the *Sheiltot*–Rashbam interpretation, on which depreciation is borne by the thief and the robber, not the object's owner.

121 Here, Rabbenu Jonathan accepts the view of Rashi and the Tosafists that the thief and the robber must return an intact object, and are not entitled to return the broken pieces.

122 Rabbenu Jonathan Hakohen of Lunel, *Commentary on the Rif*, Baba Kama (Friedman edition, p. 20).

they cannot return the broken object, but are required to make restitution with an intact replacement.[123]

The *Tosafot* explains that the controversy between Samuel and R. Eleazar regarding the question of whether we assess in the case of the thief and robber stems from the controversy as to whether "change confers ownership."[124] Moreover, in explaining the "we do not assess" rule, the *Tosafot* asserts: "and the reason is that the thief and the robber acquired it immediately[125] upon moving it out of the owner's domain, but the injurer is not obligated except to the extent that he caused damage."[126] There is thus a significant difference between the thief and robber, who acquire the object, and hence are not entitled to return a broken object, and the injurer, who does not acquire the object (the damaged object remaining in the injured party's possession), and hence is obligated to compensate the injured party for the damage by supplementing the value of the damaged object to make up the full value of the intact object.[127]

123 See *Rashi*, bBaba Kama 94a s.v. *ein shamin*: "but in the case of the thief/robber who took an animal, which [then] died or deteriorated, we do not assess the carcass, but rather it shall belong to them, and they will make restitution with a good animal, hence it constitutes a change that confers ownership."

124 bBaba Metzia 96b s.v. *zil shlim*.

125 The Later Authorities noted that the acquisition ensues from the change in the object, in this case, the fact that it was broken. The *Tosafot*, in writing "immediately," intends to make the thief/robber obligated with respect to unavoidable circumstances [that cause breakage] (*onsin*), but a change is still required in order to apply the "we do not assess" rule. See *Otzar Mefarshei Hatalmud*, Baba Kama, 1:398.

126 *Tosafot*, bBaba Kama 11a s.v. *ein shamin*. The *Tosafot* cites the *sugya* in the Jerusalem Talmud, which adduces the scriptural verses, then discusses the acquisitional rationale. Regarding the need for two rationales, *Shita Mekubetzet* states that the exegesis is the chief consideration, and it is the scriptural verses that anchor the acquisitional rationale. By contrast, *Tosafot Rabeinu Peretz* ad loc. has reservations about deriving the law from the verses, and observes: "there are those who reject the account in the Jerusalem Talmud." See *Shita Mekubetzet* ad loc.

127 See mBaba Kama 9:4, where R. Meir and R. Judah disagree as to whether a damaged item, with respect to which a craftsman breached his obligation, remains in the possession of the craftsman or is returned to its owner (the injured party). In this Mishnah, the relationship between the parties is contractual, and does not ensue from the damage caused to the object, but in this contractual case too, the Talmud explains that the Tannaitic disagreement stems from divergent stands on the question of whether

6.7.2 *The exegetical rationale*

The exegeses in the Mekhilta de-Rabbi Yishmael and in the Jerusalem Talmud, which address the context of theft and robbery, mandate the return of intact vessels, but we do not find similar exegeses in the context of assessing damage. Quite the opposite, the Sages emphasize and attempt to reinforce the rule that "the owner deals with the carcass," which is contrary to the plain meaning of the scriptural text, which obliges the injurer to take the damaged object, as described in detail above.

As we saw, R. Abba b. Memel's interpretation of the Mekhilta's exegesis of the verse "alive he shall pay double," is not the principal meaning of the biblical verse, understood in accordance with its plain meaning, nor is it derived from the verse's traditional cantillation marks. The full verse is: "If the theft be at all found in his hand alive (*hayim*), whether it be ox, or ass or sheep; he shall pay double (*shnayim yeshalem*) (Exod. 22:3)." As there is an *etnahta* cantillation mark under the word "alive," this word is connected to the first part of the verse. And indeed,

---

change confers ownership: "One who brings wool to be dyed . . . to dye it red and he dyed it black, black and he dyed it red: R. Meir says: He gives him [the owner] what the wool costs. R. Judah says: If it has appreciated [in value] beyond the [dyer's] expenditure, he gives him [the dyer] what he spent; if the expenditure is greater than the appreciation, he [the owner] gives him the value of the appreciation." Both R. Meir and R. Judah use the term "gives **him**." But on R. Meir's approach, the item remains in the craftsman's possession, and the craftsman pays the **wool's owner** the cost of the wool. By contrast, R. Judah contends that the wool is returned to the owner, who pays **the craftsman** a reduced price for the job, determined by the amount of the appreciation in the wool's value, or the craftsman's outlay, whichever is lower. The Talmud (bBaba Kama 95a) explains R. Meir's view as reflecting the idea that change confers ownership (see also *Rashi*, bBaba Kama 100b, and cf. bBaba Metzia 78b and *Rashi* ad loc.). In other words, the dyer's work constitutes a change that has a legal consequence: the wool has been acquired by the dyer. The law was decided in accordance with R. Judah's view; see Maimonides, *Code*, Laws concerning Hiring 10:4. After so ruling, Maimonides adds: "If the owner of the item says, I do not want this improvement, but rather, give me what the wool costs or what the wood costs, we do not listen to him. And similarly, if the craftsman says, here is what the wool costs or what the wood costs, now go away, we do not listen to him. Because the artisan does not acquire an item he has worked on through its appreciating." That is, the parties cannot unilaterally deviate from the established law, according to which the wool is returned to its owner and does not remain in the craftsman's possession. See also *Hasagot Haraavad* and the *Magid Mishne* ad loc.

the Talmud focuses on the word "alive," which is connected to the first part of the verse, taking it as the basis for the Amora Rav's rule that payment of the principal for the stolen object or animal is "based on its value at the time of the theft, whereas the double, four-fold, and five-fold payments are based on its value at the time the case is brought before the court."[128] As the Talmud puts it: "What is Rav's reason? Scripture says: "theft" and "alive." Why did Scripture [lit., the Merciful One] say "alive" with regard to the theft? [To teach that] the principal should be restored [lit., revived] as per what it was like when it was stolen."

This exegesis assumes that the word "alive" is connected only to the first part of the verse, because were we to deem it applicable to the second part as well, we would arrive at the opposite conclusion, according to which the double payments, which we deduce from the words "he shall pay double," are also to be based on the object's value at the time the case is brought before the court, and not at the time of the theft. The discrepancy between the exegeses in the Mekhilta and that of R. Abba b. Memel, on the one hand, and the verse's punctuation according to the cantillation marks, on the other, gives rise to a discussion among the Later Authorities[129] about whether the said exegeses are 'complete' exegesis or are invoked as mere supportive allusions to bolster the Sages' understanding of the law.

6.7.3 *The ethical rationale*

Rabbenu Jonathan of Lunel asserts:

> For since [the thief or robber] did the damage with his own hands, we are strict with him, and the owner does not have to deal with the misappropriated object. But in the case of damage, if his animal or his pit caused the damage,[130] we are lenient, and the owner [of the damaged animal or object]

128 bBaba Kama 65a.

129 See *Torah Shleima*, Exodus, ad loc., and see too the Netziv's comments in *Harhev Davar* ad loc.

130 According to this reasoning, we would apparently be required to assert that the law applicable to one who causes damage with his own hands and intentionally (as opposed to indirectly via his animal or pit) is that which applies to the thief/robber. But the law as set down is general, and applies to less common situations in which the damage is caused maliciously. This point is addressed by R. Yehiel Mikhel Epstein, who offers another rationale:

> Although according to the logic of that reasoning we should compare [one who causes injury maliciously] to the thief and the robber, in any

deals with the carcass, and the depreciation that has been incurred is borne by the injured party and not the injurer.[131]

Rashi too, like Rabbenu Jonathan, upholds the moral rationale. In explaining the rule that "we do not assess in the case of the thief, nor that of the robber," Rashi writes that "this is a custom of the judges (*minhag dayanim*)."[132] This expression is unique to Rashi and is not mentioned in the Talmud or in other sources.[133] Rashi may have been referring to a custom that emerged among the judges, out of recognition of the moral difference between a injurer, on the one hand, and a thief or robber, on the other.[134]

The relation between the severity of this treatment of the thief and the robber, and the enactment that "robbers . . . who [seek to] return [that which they robbed] – it is not to be accepted from them, and [as to] one who accepts it from them – the spirit of the Sages is not pleased with him,"[135] merits examination. Some argue that this regulation applies

---

> event, **since he derived no benefit**, he should be treated as one whose assets caused damage, and we assess [the value of] the broken pieces [and deem it partial payment] to the injured party. Therefore, if he killed an animal or broke vessels belonging to his fellow, **even maliciously** . . . the carcass is given to the injured party, and the injurer, from his own pocket, makes up [the difference between the carcass's value and] the animal's worth when alive. (*Arukh Hashulhan*, HM 387:1)

This argument invokes an additional difference between the injurer and the thief/robber. An injurer, in most cases, derives no benefit from the damage he causes, whereas the thief and the robber act in order to derive benefit, hence there is reason to treat them severely. R. Epstein adds: "the robbed party should not have to be burdened twice, [once] with selling [what he receives as] equal in value [to the misappropriated object] and [once] with buying, with the money he receives, a replacement for the misappropriated object" (HM 403).

131 Rabbenu Jonathan, n. 122 above.

132 bBaba Kama 11a s.v. *amar shmuel*.

133 Cf. *Tosafot Talmid Rabeinu Tam Verabeinu Eliezer* ad loc., which asserts, "the judges do not customarily assess in the case of the thief and the robber."

134 *Tosafot*, ad loc. s.v. *basheiltot*, expresses reservations about Rashi's interpretation of "a custom of the judges" (*minhag dayanim*). The Tosafists' reservation is understandable in view of their approach to the *sugya*, which emphasizes the acquisitional rationale, and the exegesis in the Jerusalem Talmud.

135 bBaba Kama 94b. On this rule, known as the "enactment [in support of] the penitent" (*takanat hashavim*), see N. Rakover, *The Rehabilitation of Criminals* (Hebrew), (Jerusalem: 2007), 120-31.

only to the robber who repented.[136] If this is indeed the case, there is no difficulty in reconciling the two dictums, and the *sugyot* where they are voiced (bBaba Kama 11a and bBaba Kama 94b): nothing at all is accepted from a robber who has repented and seeks, of his own volition, to make restitution, whereas the unrepentant thief or robber who is caught at his misdeed is required to make restitution, and "we do not assess" in cases of theft and robbery.

A further restriction on the rule "robbers . . . who [seek to] return [that which they robbed] – it is not to be accepted from them" limits its validity to a situation in which the misappropriated object no longer exists (*ein gzeila kayemet*).[137] For if the item exists, there is no difficulty in returning it, and therefore the robber is required to return it. But if the robbed item does not exist, "it is not to be accepted from them," due to the difficulty involved in determining the monetary value to be repaid, and so that the robber's repentance will not be impeded. Yet how can the rule that "we do not assess in the case of the thief, nor that of the robber," but rather, we require him to return an undamaged vessel or to pay an amount equivalent to the value of the undamaged vessel, be reconciled with the rule that restitution is not to be accepted from the robber when the item no longer exists? After all, is not a broken vessel nonetheless a vessel that exists?

The answer is that the concept of the misappropriated object's 'existing' was interpreted broadly by the Early Authorities. According to the Rabad, for instance: "And it seems to me, that what R. Nahman stated – "in a situation in which the misappropriated object no longer exists" – [means] he has neither the misappropriated object nor a replacement."[138] And the Meiri adds: "The law is [that it is deemed to still exist] if he possesses something arising from the robbery, or the robbery gave rise to something that is still generating a benefit, even though he does not possess the misappropriated object itself."[139] It should be noted that the robber's having the broken pieces in his possession constitutes a situation where the misappropriated object exists. The robber can derive benefit from the object, whether by using the broken object (if this is possible) or parts thereof, or by using the parts as raw material, which has monetary value.

136 Ibid., 123-27.
137 bBaba Kama 94b, in the name of R. Nahman.
138 *Hidushei Haraavad* ad loc. (Atlas edition, 230).
139 *Beit Habehira* ad loc. (Schlesinger edition, 275).

6.8 Maimonides' approach: victims of theft and robbery may demand return of the broken pieces

In interpreting the "we do not assess in the case of the thief, nor that of the robber" rule, Maimonides adopts the approach taken by Rashi and the *Tosafot*. We will compare three of his rulings, presenting them in the order in which they appear in the *Code*'s Book of Torts.

Maimonides' decision regarding infliction of damage is as follows:

> We assess in the case of damage. How? Suppose he broke his fellow's vessel, whether he did it [himself], or his animal: we do not say to the injurer, you take the broken vessel and pay him the price of his vessel, but rather we assess how much the vessel depreciated from its value [when intact], and he gives him the full depreciation if the injurer was prone to do damage (*muad*), or half of the depreciation if he was innocuous (*tam*) [i.e., a first-time offender], as it was said, "and the dead will be his" – the injured party's.[140]

Regarding the injurer, Maimonides rules:

> We assess in the case of one who causes damage by his own hand, the same way we assess in the case of his causing damage by means of his assets. How so? Suppose he killed his fellow's animal or broke his vessels. We assess how much it was worth when it was alive, and how much the carcass is worth, and how much the vessel was worth when it was whole, and how much it is worth now, and he pays the depreciation to the injured party with the carcass or the broken vessel, as we explained in the case where his ox did damage. It is the same rule as in the case where he trod on his fellow's grapes: we assess the damage he caused, and so on.[141]

As opposed to this, regarding the thief, Maimonides rules:

> One who stole a vessel and broke it or caused it to depreciate, or [the vessel] broke or depreciated by itself: we do not assess the depreciation in this case, but we see how much the vessel was worth, and he pays the owners twice its value, and the broken vessel will belong to the thief. And so on. And if the owners wish to take the broken vessel, and have him pay them [the amount of] its depreciation, and the double payment [mandated in the case of theft], their wish is heeded.[142]

140 *Code*, Laws concerning Damage by Chattels 7:8.
141 *Code*, Laws concerning Wounding and Damaging 7:15.
142 *Code*, Laws concerning Theft 1:15.

And he rules similarly regarding the robber:

> One who robbed a vessel and broke it: we do not assess the depreciation in his case, but he pays the vessel's value, and the broken vessel belongs to the robber. And if the owners wish to take the broken vessel, they take it, and he pays the depreciation. For this is a remedy for the owners, and if they do not wish [to avail themselves of it], it is their prerogative. And so on.[143]

We can see that Maimonides rules in accordance with the first interpretation adduced above.[144]

In his rulings on the thief and the robber, Maimonides adds that one who was robbed or stolen from may demand to receive the broken pieces, in which case the robber and the thief are required to return them to the owner. This law is not mentioned in either the Babylonian

143 *Code*, Laws concerning Robbery and Lost Property 2:15.

144 Cf. Maimonides' ruling regarding the borrower: "One who borrowed a vessel from his fellow and it broke: we assess in this case the same way we assess in the case where damage was caused. We estimate how much the vessel was worth when it was whole, and how much it is worth now, and he returns to him [the owner] the broken vessel or injured animal, and pays the depreciation; and if the animal died, he returns the carcass and pays the depreciation" (*Code*, Laws concerning Borrowing and Depositing 1:3). The *Magid Mishne* comments: "And if the value of the broken pieces decreases between the time of the breakage and the time the case comes before the court, the depreciation is borne by the lender, just as the 'carcass depreciation' is borne by the injured party, as explained in ch. 7 of *Code*, Laws concerning Damage by Chattels."

The *Magid Mishne*'s comment seems unwarranted. Maimonides interprets the term "we assess" as signifying that the return of the broken pieces is permitted (as per the first interpretation cited above), and not as imposing the depreciation costs on the injured party. Indeed, the 'carcass depreciation' is borne by the injured party, but it seems that in saying "we assess in this case the same way we assess in the case where damage was caused," Maimonides did not refer to the borrower's bearing the depreciation, but only referred to the borrower's right to return the broken pieces. Note that according to the individuation of the laws in the Frankel edition, 'carcass depreciation' is not part of law 8, which begins with "we assess in the case of damage" (as in the printed editions), but part of the next law. In the Frankel edition of *Magid Mishne*, the clause "carcass depreciation is borne by the injured party" is also placed, not in law 8 (as in the printed editions), but at the beginning of law 9.

Talmud or the Jerusalem Talmud, and it is generally considered to be a Maimonidean innovation.[145]

In the Laws concerning Theft, Maimonides laconically states: "And if the owners wish to take the broken vessel, and have him pay them [the amount of] its depreciation, and the double payment [mandated in the case of theft], their wish is heeded." In the Laws concerning Robbery and Lost Property, he expands slightly on this point: "And if the owners wish to take the broken vessel, they take it, and he pays the depreciation. For this is a remedy for the owners, and if they do not wish [to avail themselves of it], it is their prerogative."

Above, we put forward three rationales for distinguishing the case of the injurer from that of the thief/robber. To what extent do Maimonides' rulings reflect these rationales?

They seem to be quite consistent with the exegetical rationale. Although the Sages' scriptural exegeses entitle one who has been stolen from or robbed to demand a replacement object or monetary compensation, and not the broken object, this is consistent with Maimonides' ruling that the owner may waive this right and demand to receive the broken pieces.

This is also the case vis-à-vis the ethical rationale. Ordinarily, in light of their moral responsibility for the damage, and the reprehensibility of their actions, the thief and the robber would be obligated to provide the owner with a replacement object, but if the owner is interested in receiving the broken pieces, she ought not be prevented from receiving them.

The problem arises with respect to the acquisitional rationale. On this rationale, the thief and the robber have acquired the broken object, because the breakage constitutes a change, and change confers ownership. If so, why can the owner, at this late stage in the theft/robbery saga – namely, the stage when restitution is made for the misappropriated object – compel the thief/robber to give him the broken pieces? Both the Early and the Later Authorities emphasized that the robber's 'acquisition' is weak, and it is this weakness that enables the owner to

145 *Beit Yosef*, HM 354, cites Maimonides' statement and asserts: "And the rationale is that it stands to reason that they only said 'we do not assess' to provide a remedy for the owner [of the broken object], and if they do not want [to use] this remedy, their wish is heeded."

demand that the pieces be returned to him, even if the robber objects to this.[146]

146 The *Magid Mishne* finds this point problematic (*Code*, Laws concerning Robbery and Lost Property 2:15 s.v. *veim ratzu*). It argues that the robber does not acquire the object immediately upon taking it, but the breakage is considered a 'change by way of an action' (*shinui maase*) that confers ownership of the stolen object on the robber: "It seems that the Rabbi, of blessed memory, seeks to claim that the broken pieces are taken from the robber against his will, because if it is of his own free will [that they are returned to the one who was robbed], it would be a simple case, since [both sides] would be satisfied. And why the robber did not acquire the object as a result of the 'change by way of an action' requires further study."

The Maharshal (*Yam Shel Shlomo*, Baba Kama 1:29) does not accept the *Magid Mishne*'s reasoning. He proves, on the basis of bBaba Kama 94a, that breakage, which is considered to be irreversible deterioration (*kehash delo hadar*) (כחש דלא הדר), constitutes a change that confers ownership of the object on the robber. This is so because the Talmud concluded that Samuel's view that "we do not assess in the case of the thief, nor that of the robber," can be reconciled with the view that change leaves the object's status unaffected only on the opinion that reversible deterioration (*kehash dehadar*) does not change the status of the object, whereas irreversible deterioration is indeed a change that confers ownership. The Talmud adds that the "we do not assess in the case of the thief, nor that of the robber" rule contradicts the opinion that reversible deterioration constitutes change that affects the object's status. The upshot of this discussion is that an object that was broken (which is irreversible deterioration) has undergone a change that confers ownership of the object on the robber.

The comments in *Shiltei Giborim*, bBaba Kama 5a (Alfasi pagination) reflect a slightly different approach to the nature of the robber's possession of the robbed object: "But since [the robber] did not fully acquire the object, the robbed party can say that he wants the broken pieces that are being held by the robber, and the robber cannot prevent [their return]."

We can conclude from these statements that the robber's acquisition of the robbed object is not absolute. If the owner is interested in the broken pieces, the owner can force the robber to return them.

R. Joshua Falk argues that the ruling is limited to one specific situation (*ukimta*), namely, "when the robber has no coins and comes seeking to compensate the robbed party with chattels." In such a case, the robbed party can say "since you came to pay me with chattels, which is not in accordance with law. . . at least give me the broken pieces of my object" (*Sefer Meirat Einayim, SA,* HM 362:23). But R. Elijah of Vilna rejected this explanation, characterizing it as being "like vinegar to the teeth" (*Biur Hagra, SA,* HM 362:13).

7. Conclusion

Having examined the scriptural verses that address damage caused by property (pit damages), animals (ox damages), and people (damage to property), we have seen that in all these situations, according to the plain meaning of the biblical text, the injurer takes the damaged object for himself, and is required to provide the injured party with a replacement object, or to pay him monetary compensation that enables him to buy a replacement object.

The Sages, however, did not interpret the verses in accordance with their plain meaning, but according to a tradition they had received: "the

---

Commenting on mBaba Kama 7:1, the *Hazon Ish* raises an additional difficulty regarding the *Magid Mishne*'s explanation. If the object can still be referred to by its name, the robber may return it to the owner and say, 'here, your object is in front of you.' The law that "we do not assess in the case of the robber" applies when the object, after having been broken, has changed and lost its identity, so to speak (see Maimonides, *Code*, Laws concerning Robbery and Lost Property 2:1). The *Hazon Ish* states that when the owner is interested in the broken pieces, their return constitutes fulfilment of the precept, "And he shall restore that thing which he took by robbery" (Lev. 5:23). He asserts:

> It seems that the reason that he takes the broken pieces is that it is a way of collecting [compensation for the robbed object]. Because the Torah diligently sought to appease him and facilitate restitution of his loss, he [the robber] cannot remit payment with chattels [that are] worth money, but rather must do so with coins, so that it is convenient for him [the robbed party] to buy the object he was robbed of. Or [the robber] can compensate him with an object similar to the one he robbed him of, which is preferable to compensating him with coins, since if paid in coins he will then have to go buy such an object [with the coins anyway]. Therefore if the owner likes his animal or vessel, even though they have been damaged, and prefers them to money, the robber must compensate him [as he wishes], for . . . were it possible to give him back the very same vessel [that was robbed and broken], we would certainly compel him [to do so], but because it was broken, necessarily it is impossible to compel the robber to pay anything except money. But if the owner likes the broken pieces, we invoke the words "which he took by robbery" (Lev. 5:23), and he [the robber] must pay with his broken pieces.

The *Hazon Ish* interprets Maimonides' ruling pragmatically. The robbed party's preference for receiving the broken pieces, taken together with the biblical precept that robbed objects must be returned, prevails over the laws of acquisition.

owner deals with the carcass," i.e., the damaged object remains in the possession of the injured party, and the injurer provides the injured party with compensation that makes up the difference between the object's value before and after being damaged. We analyzed various Rabbinic exegeses, according to which the damaged object is to remain in the injured party's possession, discussed problems arising from these exegeses, and suggested that they be seen as 'sustaining exegesis' (*midrash mekayem*), which seeks to anchor known Rabbinic laws in scriptural verses.

We saw that the verses of the Torah that address theft and robbery do not, in themselves, provide an unequivocal answer to the question of whether the thief and the robber are entitled to return a broken object to the injured party as partial restitution.

We discussed the contrast, set forth in the Talmud, between the role of assessment in the case where someone damaged an object (what we have called the case of the injurer), and in the cases of theft and robbery during which damage was done to the misappropriated objects. We explored the *sugyot* in the Babylonian and Jerusalem Talmuds which state that "We do not assess in the case of the thief, nor that of the robber." The Geonim and the Early Authorities concur that the *sugya*'s import is that the thief and the robber deserve harsher treatment than the injurer. On one approach, the thief and the robber are not entitled to make (partial) restitution by returning a broken object, but rather obligated to return a replacement object or to pay an amount sufficient for purchase of a replacement. On another approach, the thief and the robber are entitled to return the broken pieces and make up the remainder of the compensation due the owner, but whereas in the case of damage, the object's depreciation ('carcass depreciation') is borne by the injured party, in cases of theft and robbery, the depreciation is borne, in its entirety, by the thief or robber. A third approach combines elements from each of the first two approaches, applying to the thief and the robber both stringencies: [1] the thief and the robber are not entitled to make (partial) restitution by returning a broken object; [2] in cases of theft/robbery, the depreciation is borne entirely by the thief/robber.

We have addressed various rationales for the law's differential treatment of the case of the injurer, and those of the thief and robber. The first rationale pertains to acquisition. Whereas the injurer does not carry out an act that confers on him ownership of the damaged object, the thief and the robber negate the injured party's possession and ownership of the object, thereby rendering acquisition applicable to them.

The second rationale is exegetical. The Rabbinic exegeses of scriptural verses pertaining to damaging, which, I have argued, constitute 'sustaining exegesis' (*midrash mekayem*), teach that the carcass belongs to the injured party. By contrast, the exegeses pertaining to the thief and the robber teach that in these cases, we do not assess the value of the carcass or damaged object. As explained above, however, the Geonim and Early Authorities did not agree as to how the locution "we do not assess" is to be understood.

The third reason is ethical. In most cases damage is caused unintentionally. By contrast, acts of theft and robbery, by their very nature, are intentional, and therefore with respect to restitution for stolen or robbed items, stringencies that do not apply in the case of damage are imposed.

BOOK REVIEW

Yitzhak Cohen, *The 'Or Sameah' – Halakhah and Jewish Law: R. Meir Simcha Hakohen's Writings on Maimonides' Code* (Hebrew), Jerusalem: Ben Gurion University Press and Bialik Institute, 2012, 408 pp.

Ilan Fuchs*

The late Isadore Twersky lamented the fact that post-talmudic rabbinical literature does not get the academic attention it deserves.[1] The breadth of rabbinical literature, he felt, had much to offer scholars in the liberal arts and social sciences. Over the past decade, we have been witness to a renewed academic interest in this body of work, and young scholars are mining this rich repository to further our knowledge in multiple and diverse areas. A growing number of works on post-talmudic halakhic literature are now available, works that reflect a range of perspectives and methodologies.

Research into talmudic literature often focuses on philology. By scrutinizing and comparing different versions and manuscripts, scholars attempt to arrive at the original text as it emerged from its author's hands, though some question the feasibility of this goal.[2] That research into early rabbinical literature focuses on philology is not surprising: after all, it is difficult – some would say, impossible – to write biographies of figures from antiquity. With respect to the study of antiquity, the paucity of primary sources shapes research methodologies far more decisively than is the case vis-à-vis the study of later periods. The questions with which the burgeoning scholarship on the post-talmudic halakhic literature is engaged thus differ significantly from those that engage scholars who study the Rabbinic period. Given the accessibility of knowledge about historical, economic, and sociocultural conditions in the early modern and modern periods, scholars can explore the

* Ilan Fuchs is a visiting scholar at Michigan University's Frankel Institute.

1 I. Twersky, "R. Joseph Caro, author of the *Shulhan Arukh*" (Hebrew), *Asufot* 3 (1989), 245.

2 See Peter Schafer, "Current views on the editing of Rabbinic texts of late antiquity: reflections on a debate after twenty years," in Martin Goodman and Philip Alexander (eds.), *Rabbinic Texts and the History of Late-Roman Palestine* (Oxford: 2010), 79-82).

influence of such conditions on halakhic thinking and practice, subjects that must remain, to a great extent, closed to scholars of antiquity.

Yitzhak Cohen's book is a good example of the new wave of research monographs. It offers a jurisprudential analysis of *Or Sameiah*, the key halakhic work by R. Meir Simha Hakohen of Dvinsk. R. Meir Simha was a prominent leader of Eastern European Orthodoxy, and his *Or Sameiah*, on Maimonides' *Mishne Torah* (*Code*), and *Meshekh Hokhma*, a commentary on the Pentateuch, are considered to be among the most original and thought-provoking rabbinical works of the twentieth century.

Cohen's book focuses on jurisprudence, and does not address other aspects of *Or Sameiah*. Among the specific questions addressed are R. Meir Simha's perceptions of authority and hierarchy in the rabbinical literature, philology in Rabbinic texts, meta-halakha, and invocation of the Jerusalem Talmud and the Tosefta.

The book begins by addressing the mix of genres found in *Or Sameiah*. On the one hand, it exemplifies the novellae genre – so popular in the context of commentaries on the *Code* – but as Cohen demonstrates, it also reflects R. Meir Simha's goal of developing Maimonides' *Code* to serve as a practical tool. Cohen describes the different ways in which R. Meir Simha utilized the *Code* to adjudicate actual cases. He shows, for instance, how, by introducing dilemmas constructed on the basis of Maimonides' adjudication, but not directly dealt with in the Maimonidean text, or by changing various details in the halachic scenarios discussed there, *Or Sameiah* fosters evolution of Maimonides' *Code* with a view to its further development as a viable resource for contemporary halakhic adjudication.

Although *Or Sameiah* is a commentary on Maimonides' *Code*, R. Meir Simha does not, Cohen claims, give preference to Maimonides' legal opinions in formulating his own rulings. Cohen contends that *Or Sameiah* does not have a specific policy of 'protecting' the Maimonidean position. Rather, R. Meir Simha maintained a certain distance, and retained his independence, adjudicating on a case-by-case basis without making deference to the views of any specific Early Authority his default position. Cohen argues that the goal of *Or Sameiah* was not merely to further develop Maimonides' *Code*, but to do so with independence and self-awareness. This independent outlook puts R. Meir Simha in a category of his own among the contemporary decisors. Cohen brings a number of examples to show how other decisors perceived R. Meir Simha's works. Though not all agreed with his independent and novel stances, he was accepted as an authority who could legitimately take such bold positions (175-206).

R. Meir Simha's originality comes to the fore, in particular, in Cohen's discussion of the innovative manner in which the *Or Sameiah* adduces the Jerusalem Talmud. His careful analysis of *Or Sameiah* reveals that R. Meir Simha refers to the Jerusalem Talmud to the same extent as the Babylonian Talmud. He also refrains from reinterpreting the Jerusalem Talmud in light of the Babylonian Talmud. The fact that R. Meir Simha does not evince any systematic adherence to a specific tradition of adjudication, and hardly quotes opinions from the Later Authorities, can be seen as attesting to his approach to the rabbinical literature in general. He prefers a deductive approach to the sources, as opposed to an inductive approach, favoring essence over form (133-70).

Cohen brings several examples of what he sees as R. Meir Simha's unifying approach to the sources. For example, in the case of the biblical law of the pursuer (*rodef*), the wording of Maimonides' ruling permits a pursuer to be killed only in cases of direct causation: "If anyone intends to strike his fellow a death-blow, the pursued party should be saved at the cost of the pursuer's hand. And if this is impossible [i.e., if they cannot target a blow precisely], he is saved even by [taking] the pursuer's life, for Scripture says, "[you shall cut off her hand,] show her no pity' (Deut. 25:12)."[3]

R. Meir Simha, however, seeks to interpret Maimonides' ruling on the scriptural law of the pursuer, which permits pre-emptive killing of the pursuer, purposively, as also covering cases in which by Torah law the pursuer would – theoretically – be exempt from the death penalty. He takes it to apply, for example, when the pursuer will release a venomous snake, an action that is considered indirect causation (*gerama*). That is, he takes it to apply to cases where the link between the impending action (release of the snake) and the outcome that will be pre-empted by killing the pursuer (the snake's poisoning someone) is weaker than direct causation. In such a case, though the pursuer would be exempt from the punishment of death imposed by the court, R. Meir Simha rules that the pursuee (i.e., the intended victim) may kill him (249-50).

This essentialist/substantive approach can also be seen in cases in which there are procedural difficulties, such as the case of one who collected money by presenting a bogus promissory note. Ex post facto, it was established that there had been an outstanding loan, i.e., that the money was indeed owed. R. Meir Simha rules that the money need not be returned even though it was collected on the strength of a bogus document (251-52). Cohen concludes from these examples that

3 *Code*, Laws concerning Murder and the Preservation of Life 1:8.

R. Meir Simha had a very clear view of his jurisprudential role: it was that of an adjudicator. When looking at halakhic questions and texts, he was guided by a sense of practicality. In other words, his characteristic approach is to focus on the facts, a sense of justice, and objectivity, rather than on formal/theoretical constraints.

R. Meir Simha's uniqueness among the decisors of the period is highlighted in Cohen's discussion of *Meshekh Hokhma*. Cohen's analysis reveals that in *Meshekh Hokhma* there are a number of examples of recourse to midrashic exegesis of scriptural verses, a phenomenon that is virtually unheard of in the writings of contemporary rabbinical authorities. Cohen argues that these examples are not merely theoretical discussions, but have practical ramifications (212-32). R. Meir Simha's use of this unusual method of deducing legal rulings points both to a belief in the essential unity and continuity of the halakhic sources, and to a self-perception that does not downplay his own worth qua decisor vis-à-vis earlier generations.

Another example of this holistic perception of the halakhic literature is evidenced, Cohen argues, by R. Meir Simha's willingness to emend the talmudic text, not always on the basis of philological evidence. In *Or Sameiah*, he sometimes does so simply to resolve a contradiction by changing the text, where no support for the emendation can be adduced from manuscripts or variant readings quoted in the works of Early Authorities. This practice is unusual to say the least; it is often mentioned apropos R. Elijah of Vilna, who undeniably had the stature and authority to undertake such bold actions.

Cohen's book creates a foundation for future research on R. Meir Simha, and further research into contemporary rabbinical jurisprudence in general. Along with the book, Cohen set up a website with data from his research on *Or Sameiah*.[4] The tabulated data details the frequency with which, and the purpose for which, R. Meir Simha adduces the Babylonian and Jerusalem Talmuds, the Tosefta, and specific Early and Later Authorities, among other things.

In light of this book, and several others that can be classed as falling into the same genre, a genre I would characterize as 'intellectual biographies of rabbinical authorities' (these works include Amir Mashiach's book on R. Solomon Zalman Auerbach,[5] Benjamin Brown's book on the

4 http://web2.ono.ac.il/docs/table_summary6.xls

5 *Rabbi Shlomo Zalman Auerbach's Halakhic Philosophy in a Dynamic Era of Socio-technological Transformation* (Hebrew), (Ramat-Gan: 2013).

Hazon Ish,[6] and Harel Gordin's dissertation on R. Moses Feinstein[7]), an important question must be addressed. The question is that of the genre's underlying methodological principles: the principles governing linkage of historical and sociocultural conditions to a given thinker's views. In the case of decisors, intellectual biography presents a special challenge, since jurisprudence is a discipline that perceives and presents itself as objective, and perceives the jurist as arriving at decisions by means of a rigorous, formulaic, and almost scientific process. Unlike other intellectuals, jurists tend to lack awareness of the context in which they operate, and halakhists are no exception.

Critical analysis of halakhic authorities can therefore focus on two different trajectories. The first of these would examine the specific legal mechanisms used by a given decisor, and the mode of their employment, with a view to identifying individual patterns and thus unique decision-making profiles. The second would focus on the context within which a given decisor was active. This enterprise would require the use of historical tools and primary source materials from outside the halakhic literature. Such scholarship would not, obviously, disregard the said decisor's legal writings and their internal coherence and logic, but must also go beyond it to address historical conditions not part of the legal discourse.

The two trajectories differ considerably, and tackling both might be challenging for a scholar who lacked training in both spheres. But there is no reason such monographs cannot be more targeted in their scope, covering a very specific angle and leaving room for additional research by others.

There is certainly room for additional research on R. Meir Simha, which will likely draw on Cohen's work. Suggested topics for research along the second trajectory include historical questions about the role of the rabbinical leadership in Eastern Europe; the relationship between hasidic and non-hasidic halakhic authorities (an issue of special relevance given that R. Meir Simha was a neighbor of the influential hasidic figure R. Joseph Rosin, known as 'the Rogatchover'); and the Lithuanian rabbis' attitude to Zionism. It seems, then, that Twersky's lament did not fall on deaf ears.

6 *The Hazon Ish: Halakhist, Believer and Leader of the Haredi Revolution* (Hebrew), (Jerusalem: 2011).

7 *Halacha* and *Halachic* Decisions in a Changing World: an Interdisciplinary Approach to Examining the *Halachic* Decisions of Rabbi Moshe Feinstein (Hebrew), (PhD dissertation, Tel Aviv University, 2007).

STYLE SHEET

STYLE SHEET

In preparing your manuscript, please conform to the following guidelines. Manuscripts not so prepared will be edited by JLA staff or returned for revision.

1 Please provide a line or two of information about yourself, such as an institutional affiliation, before the first footnote.
2 Manuscripts should be submitted electronically, in WORD 2010 or lower, and should be double-spaced (text and footnotes).
3 The file should not contain any tracked changes, comments, electronically linked cross-references, highlighting, underlining, different font colors, or other markings. 12 pt. font, preferably Times New Roman, should be used throughout, including the notes.
4 All references must conform to the *Jewish Law Annual* house style specified below.
5 All references containing titles originally in Hebrew should provide both the original title of the work in transliteration, and the official title in English if it is given in the book or appears in an English table of contents (often found at the end of the volume). If no English title is given, please suggest a translation, indicating that it is your own.
6 Authorized Version abbreviations for books of the Bible, listed in dictionaries and style guides such as *The Chicago Manual of Style*, should be used. In referring to the Talmud, tractate names should not be abbreviated. m, b, j, or t should be prefixed to the tractate name to indicate whether the Mishnah, the Babylonian Talmud, Jerusalem Talmud or Tosefta is being referred to.

CITATION STYLE

Halakhic literature

Beit Yosef, *Tur*, HM 362:57
Kli Hemda, Torah portion 'Pinhas'
Maimonides, *Code*, Laws concerning Robbery and Lost Property 11:1
R. Jacob Castro (Maharikash), *Erekh Lehem*, EH 143
Perisha, HM 201:1 (at the end)
Rashi, bBaba Kama 27a s.v. *lemikah umimkar*
Responsa Beit Shlomo, OH #57

Responsa Igrot Moshe, YD 2:174
Responsa Mabit, #37
Responsa Tzitz Eliezer, 9:28:3
Sefer Hasidim, §723
Sefer Mitzvot Katan, #265 (Rosenberg edition, 2:371)
Shulhan Shlomo, 2:14-16

Books

W.C. Kaiser, *Toward Old Testament Ethics* (Grand Rapids MI: 1978), 99
E. Urbach, *The Sages: Their Concepts and Beliefs*, trans. I. Abrahams (Jerusalem: 1987), 1:343

Journal articles

R. Kleinman, "Early interpretations of the Bible and Talmud as a reflection of medieval legal realia," 16 *Jewish Law Annual* (2006), 25-50
Joseph Raz, "Legal principles and the limits of law," 81 *Yale L.J.*, 823, 828-30 (1972)
A. Shaffer, "Cuneiform tablets from Palestine I: the letter from Shechem" (Hebrew), *Beer-Sheva* 3 (1988), 163-69

Articles in edited volumes

B.S. Jackson, "Legalism and spirituality," in E.B. Firmage, B.G. Weiss and J.W. Welch (eds.), *Religion and Laws: Biblical, Judaic and Islamic Perspectives* (Winona Lake IN: 1990), 243-61
D. Sinclair, "Defending the lives of the mortally ill, the embryo, and the non-Jew" (Hebrew), in G. Frishtick (ed.), *Human Rights in Judaism* (Hebrew), (Jerusalem: 1992), 37 n. 19

Cross-references in notes

22 S. Assaf, *The Courts and Their Procedures after the Finalization of the Talmud* (Hebrew), (Jerusalem: 1924), 38-41.
23 D. Sperber, *Material Culture in Eretz-Israel during the Talmudic Period* (Hebrew), vol. 1 (Jerusalem: 1993), vol. 2 (Jerusalem: 2006).
24 See Assaf 1924, n. 22 above, 67.
25 Ibid., 121.
26 Sperber, n. 23 above, 2:126-33.

TRANSLITERATION

Wherever possible, essential Hebrew is to be transliterated into English rather than word-processed in Hebrew characters, as follows:

alef	a	lamed	l
bet	b	mem	m
vet	v	nun	n
gimel	g	samekh	s
dalet	d	ayin	a
hei (pronounced)	h	pei	p
vav	v	fei	f
zayin	z	tzadi	tz
het	h	kuf	k
tet	t	reish	r
yud	y	shin	sh
kaf	k	sin	s
khaf	kh	tav	t

patah; kamatz	a
hirik	i
shva (pronounced)	e
segol	e
shuruk; kubutz	u
holam	o
tzeirei (long)	ei
tzeirei (short)	e

No diacriticals, apostrophes, hyphens, doubling of consonants or capitalization should be used as elements of the transliteration or to indicate prefixes and the definite article.

These transliteration guidelines are not intended to apply to papers addressing linguistic or philological issues.

For Product Safety Concerns and Information please contact our EU representative GPSR@taylorandfrancis.com
Taylor & Francis Verlag GmbH, Kaufingerstraße 24, 80331 München, Germany

www.ingramcontent.com/pod-product-compliance
Ingram Content Group UK Ltd.
Pitfield, Milton Keynes, MK11 3LW, UK
UKHW011002180926
475701UK00004B/523

* 9 7 8 0 3 6 7 5 9 7 3 0 6 *